MORGAN

HAYNES CLASSIC MAKES SERIES

MORGAN

PERFORMANCE PLUS TRADITION

JONATHAN WOOD

First published in October 2004

A catalogue record for this book is available from the British Library

ISBN 1 85960 881 7

Library of Congress control no 2004106163

Published by Haynes Publishing, Sparkford, Yeovil, Somerset BA22 7JJ, UK.
Tel: 01963 442030 Fax: 01963 440001
Int.tel: +44 1963 442030 Int.fax: +44 1963 440001
E-mail: sales@haynes.co.uk
Website: www.haynes.co.uk

Haynes North America Inc., 861 Lawrence Drive, Newbury Park, California 91320, USA.

Edited by Jon Pressnell
Designed and typeset by Chris Fayers
Printed and bound in Britain by J. H. Haynes & Co. Ltd., Sparkford

Acknowledgements
First and foremost my thanks must go to many members of the Morgan Motor Company's helpful workforce, who readily answered my questions regarding how Morgan sports cars are built today. This information was supplemented by sales manager Mark Ledington while parts manager Paul Trussler explained the extraordinary and unique service the factory undertakes to help keep its past products on the road.

Thanks are also due to three-wheeler enthusiast Chris Booth, whose Kent-based motor museum (see page 28) contains an impressive collection of trikes, for his advice on the labyrinthine intracies of the species – although I need hardly add that I am alone responsible for the finished product.

I am particularly indebted to Morgan 4/4 specialist George Proudfoot of TG Proudfoot Coachbuilding and Trimming (134 Kiln Road, Fareham, Hants PO16 7UW), who kindly shared his extensive knowledge of the marque with me. The information he supplied appears in the Buying Hints sections of this book and I have complemented this with my own knowledge garnered from a wide variety of sources over the years.

Others whose help and advice has been appreciated include Bill Noble and Tony Oliver of the Morgan Sports Car Club, John Worrall of Heart of England Morgans, Mervyn Rutter of Mervyn Rutter Ltd, and Phil Benfield of Allon White and Son.

The majority of the illustrations are from LAT Photographic (0208 251 3000) and are principally drawn from the archives of (The) Autocar and Classic & Sports Car magazines. Other photos are mainly from the author's own collection, with additional material kindly supplied by Cheffins auctioneers, Transmission Public Relations, and the Morgan Sports Car Club's Roger Tatton.

contents

Introduction 6

1 The Three-Wheelers 8

2 The First Four-Wheelers 34

3 The Plus 4 50

4 Return of the 4/4 74

5 The Plus 4 Plus 86

6 The Plus 8 94

7 The Aero 8 120

8 Maintaining the Morgan Tradition 128

9 Morgan in Competition 138

10 Engines 153

Bibliography 165

Index 166

Introduction

Morgan – performance plus tradition

Of the dwindling number of car companies that today constitute the British-owned motor industry, the Morgan, still built in Malvern Link, reassuringly remains a model of consistency and tradition.

For this is a marque that has been in the ownership of the same family since 1910. Tradition is also underlined by the fact that these sports cars are still built by hand in the factory which has been Morgan's home since the early 1920s.

Inevitably, the first of the line, the three-wheeled Runabout, bears no relationship to the current flagship, the Aero 8, apart from the fact that its name once graced one of HFS Morgan's light, lively trikes. At the heart of the appeal of these three-wheelers was an ingenious sliding-pillar independent front suspension system, a concept which survives on two Morgan models to this very day.

Even before the Runabout entered production, 'HFS' ran his prototype three-wheeler in a sporting event, and competition has remained at the very heart of the Morgan's appeal from that time onwards.

Another all-important aspect of the Runabout was that it was powered by a proprietary engine. Wisely Morgan has never succumbed to the lure of producing a bespoke power unit. 'HFS' and his successors have left the cost of designing, manufacturing and developing an engine to outside

suppliers, whereas many long-forgotten contemporaries embarked on a contradictory route to their cost.

It can therefore be seen that Morgan is still very much in business today because of the engineering abilities and financial sagacity of its founding father. The three-wheeler, born in those days before the First World War when motoring was in its infancy, was destined to survive, in essence, until 1952.

But it says much for the pragmatism of 'HFS' that with the dawning of the 1930s he recognised that the trike's

appeal was dwindling, and in 1936 introduced the four-wheeler 4-4 derivative. As a concept it is visually and mechanically perpetuated in the current Morgan four-cylinder and Roadster lines.

In the years after the Second World War, son Peter took over the running of the company, and oversaw the introduction of the uprated Plus 4 which replaced the 4/4, as it was by

The marque's fortunes were built on the success of HFS Morgan's three-wheelers. This is a Family Sports model of 1933 vintage. (LAT)

Launched in 2000, the Aero embraces visual elements of Morgan's heritage which are combined with 21st-century mechanicals in the shape of a BMW V8 engine and aluminium chassis. (LAT)

The Malvern Link factory still produces its cars in a manner that would have been recognisable to HFS Morgan. Current build quality is better than ever. (LAT)

then rendered, in 1950. The latter model was revived in 1955 and has benefited from successive Ford engines ever since.

Peter Morgan carefully nurtured a business which was widely regarded as manufacturing outdated products, at a time when demand from America was crucial in maintaining production. Fortunately there was a dramatic turnabout in the 1960s. It was then that customers, both in Britain and Europe, began to respond to a car with its appearance and manufacturing methods so clearly rooted in pre-war days. Before long there was a waiting list, numbered in years rather than months, for the Malvern-built Morgan – a wait that has only abated, on the company's initiative, in recent years.

In addition Peter Morgan successfully saw the Plus 8 into production in 1968. Powered by Rover's versatile Buick-based V8, it was destined to be the most enduring four-wheeled model in the company's history, and survived for a total of 36 years.

Today the Morgan Motor Company is flourishing under the direction of Peter's son, Charles, the architect of the Aero 8, a model which reflects Morgan's carefully nurtured traditions while embracing the automotive technology of the 21st century. Launched in 2000, its specifications have now been tailored for the all-important American market which it entered in 2004.

Currently manufacturing a three model line, Morgan has succeeded in surviving in the highly competitive world of motor industry for close on a century. Long may it continue to flourish!

The Three-
Wheelers

'HFS' at the controls of his first three-wheeler, an 8hp Eagle forecar which could carry one rather exposed passenger! He is outside the Stoke Lacy rectory. (Morgan)

It is the great survivor. Of the 950 or so car companies that once constituted the British motor industry, a mere handful endure. Of these Morgan is unique in still being owned by its founding family and in building sports cars with their styling and construction firmly rooted in the 1930s.

Ironically, this is a business that came late to four wheels: the 4-4 from which the current line sprang did not reach the public until 1936, when the company had been established for 26 years. Its fortunes were based on its three-wheeler 'runabout' of 1910, but HFS Morgan was not only an accomplished engineer, he also possessed an impressive grasp of finance, a desirable but all too rare combination. It was on these firm foundations that the house of Morgan was built, which goes some way to explaining why this still-buoyant business has survived into the 21st century.

Henry Frederick Stanley Morgan – 'HFS' as he was invariably known, or Harry to his intimates – was Henry and Florence Morgan's eldest child, and was born at Moreton Jeffries, Herefordshire, on 11 August 1881. He had the good fortune to grow up in the comfortable environment of a rambling country rectory, his father, the Rev Prebendary Henry George – 'HG' – Morgan having in 1886 become rector of Stoke Lacy, a village nestling in a fold of the hills, some ten miles to the north-east of the county town of Hereford.

The Rev Morgan was a multi-faceted character, financially shrewd, a keen photographer and an accomplished artist. A lack of money worries meant that he could indulge his passion for mechanical matters, and 'HG' became a pioneer motorist. He joined the Hereford Automobile Club, was soon appointed its vice-president, and was also a member of its Midlands equivalent. In 1907 he enthusiastically reported that since December 1902 he had driven 12,000 miles in his air-cooled 10hp Lanchester. Its output was subsequently increased to 12hp, at which point water-cooling had been introduced.

Unlike many heavy-handed Victorian fathers, Henry Morgan did not choose to inflict a chosen career on his son but was determined that the boy should pursue his own interests. 'HFS' for his part inherited many of his father's qualities although he was a quieter, more introverted character. He went to prep school at Stone House, Broadstairs, Kent, and then to Marlborough College public school in Wiltshire. By this time he had decided that he wanted to pursue an

engineering career and so he received a technical education at the Crystal Palace Engineering College located in one of the towers of the Crystal Palace at Sydenham in South London.

In 1899, as an 18-year-old, and through the good offices of his father, he became a pupil of William Dean, locomotive superintendent of the prestigious Great Western Railway, at the GWR's Swindon workshops. Destined to spend seven years as a draughtsman with the GWR, his commitment to steam did not prevent him from pursuing his other passion, that of the motor car.

In Germany Gottlieb Daimler and Karl Benz, each working independently of the other, had in 1886 produced automobiles, inventions that provided the impetus for the birth of a global motor industry. France had quickly seized the initiative and was soon dominating the European market. British car production did not begin, albeit tentatively, until 1896.

We know of HFS Morgan's first encounters with the internal combustion engine because in 1950 he shared highlights of his career with readers of *The Light Car* magazine, a publication with which he had been closely associated since its foundation in 1912. It is therefore possible to highlight, in his own words, some of the events that shaped his remarkable life, beginning in 1899.

The church of St Peter and St Paul, Stoke Lacy, Herefordshire, where the Rev Prebendary Henry Morgan, father of 'HFS', was rector. (Author)

That year, he recalled, 'I rode a Minerva motorcycle; a little later a 3½hp Benz ran away with me on a steep hill . . . and cost my father £28 for repairs'. Both machines had been hired from Arthur Marriott, who was probably Hereford's first motor trader. Morgan had to wait until 1901, when

The Morgan family plot in the churchyard at Stoke Lacy. In the background is the rectory where 'HFS' grew up. (Author)

Independent front suspension

When HFS Morgan introduced his three-wheeler in 1910, practically all cars were fitted with front axles suspended by leaf springs, a concept inherited from the horse-drawn carriage. Independent front suspension (ifs), which is now a universal fitment, was very much the exception. The system that Morgan applied to his 'runabout' is effectively still in use on the current Morgan range, the Aero 8 excepted.

With the then conventional cart-sprung axle, the rise of one wheel on an uneven road surface caused its opposite number to tilt through an angle. On steered wheels, that is to say those at the front of a car, this caused wheel wobble or shimmy, in other words a vibration of the wheel and stub axle. When ifs was fitted, this wobble was eliminated; despite this, independent front suspension did not become a popular fitment until the 1930s, if even then. So HFS Morgan was well ahead of his time.

The Morgan was not however the first British car to feature the arrangement, which had been in use on the continent from the late 19th century. Indeed, 'HFS' was following well-established French practice, for probably the first production car to feature ifs was the two-cylinder 3½hp tubular-framed Decauville of 1898. A crude machine, it featured an unsprung rear axle. By way of making up for this deficiency it was fitted with ifs in which each wheel moved up and down on its own sliding pillar, with a transverse leaf spring supplying the suspension medium. Ironically the arrangement did not excite much comment at the time.

Across the Channel in Britain, a similar installation featured on the short-lived Critchley-Daimler of 1899, although this was not the first British-designed car to feature ifs. That accolade should probably be

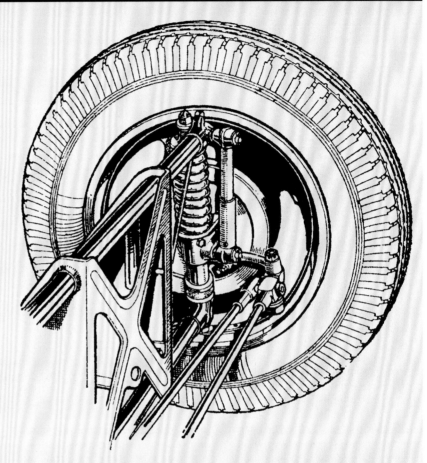

Morgan's sliding-pillar independent front suspension, introduced in 1910 and still going strong over 90 years later. The illustration shows the version used in the 4-4 of the 1930s. (LAT)

accorded to the Stephens of 1898, which featured independently-sprung front wheels, each located within its own bicycle-style fork.

However, the make most closely associated with ifs was the French Sizaire-Naudin of 1905 which perpetuated the by-then familiar transverse-spring and sliding-pillar layout. When in 1910 *The Motor Cycle* reported on Morgan's first trike it noted that 'the principle was somewhat suggestive of the Sizaire-Naudin car'.

In truth this only referred to the pillars, there being no transverse spring on the Morgan Runabout: instead coils were used, there being a main spring above the (imaginary) axle centre-line and a shorter rebound spring below. The result was

a hard, unyielding ride to which was coupled excellent handling, a combination that was as true then as it is today.

HFS Morgan had the good sense in 1909 to patent his design. His agent was Stanley, Popplewell and Co, of Chancery Lane, London, and in later years he recalled that the patent drawings were executed by 'a bright youth' named John Black. This was the Black who in his later years, from 1934 until 1953, ran the Standard Motor Company and would supply Morgan with many of its engines.

Some of the components for HFS Morgan's Runabout were produced in the workshops of Malvern College; over 90 years on, a number of its pupils contemplate the Morgan Aero 8, introduced in 2000. (LAT)

he was 21, before he had 'collected a little cash' and was able to buy his first 'horseless carriage', an 8hp Eagle forecar. Interestingly, in the light of future events, this vehicle, which hailed from Altrincham, Cheshire, and used a De Dion Bouton engine, was a three-wheeler with two wheels at the front and a single chain-driven rear wheel.

It was, he remembered, 'fast, but not too reliable, and gave me considerable experience during the 18 months I owned it. I then bought a 7hp two-cylinder car called 'The Little Star', which, with modifications, gave good service for many years'.

Morgan had been bitten by the motoring bug. In 1905, at the age of 23, he left the GWR to join the motor trade, having purchased a house, Chestnut Villa, on Worcester Road at Malvern Link just to the north of the spa town of Great Malvern. There, about ten miles from his home and in

the shadow of the Malvern Hills, he built a garage on an adjoining plot of land, flanked to the south by Howsell Road. It marked an association with the community that endures to this day. Morgan opened for business in May 1905, having secured agencies for three popular makes: the Wolseley and the Siddeley, together with the Darracq from France.

The creation of the Morgan three-wheeler came about almost by accident and stemmed, in part, from a dislike of motorbikes. 'I had purchased a 7hp 'twin' Peugeot engine, intending to build up a motorcycle. Although I had been a keen cyclist, I never cared for motorcycles', he recalled in the magazine article. 'I therefore decided to fit this engine into a light three-wheeled chassis I had designed, and as I had little facilities for machine work this was mostly done for me'.

Morgan had been able to draw on the workshops of nearby Malvern

College. There a friend, the engineering master, William Stephenson-Peach – the grandson, no less, of railway pioneer George Stephenson of Rocket fame – helped 'HFS' to turn his dream into reality. Further work was also undertaken at Repton school, where Stephenson-Peach had previously taught.

'I drove the machine, which I called the Morgan 'runabout', in 1909', he told *The Light Car*. 'It was most successful, due to its rigid frame, independent front-wheel suspension and light weight; the power-weight ratio was about 90hp per ton and it was therefore more than capable of holding its own with any car on the road at that time'.

The prototype Morgan three-wheeler with 'HFS' at the tiller; it was completed in 1909, but not registered for the road until June 1910. Chassis tubes came from Repton School, Derby, and the frame may have been made in the city by J Smith and Co. Power was provided by an air-cooled 7hp Peugeot V-twin motorcycle unit, although Morgan used JAP engines for the production version. (Morgan)

The site of Morgan's original Worcester Road works, in 2003. Located on the corner of Howsell Road, retirement apartments now occupy the ground where the Morgan Runabout was once made. (Author)

As with the Eagle, this first vehicle had two wheels at the front and one at the rear, but there the resemblance ended. Whereas that forecar had its engine mounted amidships, Morgan's design was more innovative and was clearly the product of a highly inventive mind, underpinned by a sound engineering training.

While the Peugeot engine would have been mounted longitudinally within a motor cycle frame, Morgan repositioned it transversely, ahead of the front axle line. As he was using an air-cooled engine, 'HFS' so located it to benefit from uninterrupted air flow. It made the little vehicle nose-heavy

but this location also made a positive contribution to the trike's roadholding. Such a layout did not begin to appear on conventional European cars until the mid-1930s.

The other radical feature of the design was the sliding-pillar and coil-spring independent front suspension: Morgan's 'runabout' was the first significant British motor vehicle to feature such an arrangement. As the accompanying notes indicate, the practice and indeed the essentials of the design had first appeared on the French Decauville of 1898. At the rear the runabout's single wheel was suspended on a pair of stubby quarter-elliptic springs. The front suspension was mounted on a pair of transverse crossmembers to which the engine was also secured. There was a simple metal-to-metal clutch, and the propeller shaft ran inside the tubular backbone to a bevel box. Final drive was by two chains, each running either side of the single rear wheel, and being alternately engaged by dog clutches operated by a side-mounted lever. This two-speed system did not allow for the provision of a reverse gear. On the prototype, tubes ran from either side of this bevel box to the extremities of the lower front crossmember. Once production began these doubled as pipes for the exhausts of the sidevalve-engined models.

The rider's position, as *The Motor Cycle* put it, was 'half reclining'. To the right was the tiller, with the gearchange on the left, and there was a lever throttle. The petrol tank sat above the engine and there was absolutely no protection from the weather. With practically no bodywork in the accepted sense, and aided by the use of the light, rigid motorcycle-style tubular frame, the vehicle weighed a claimed 2cwt and performance was accordingly impressive for the day. Whilst the concept would evolve over the years, this chassis would always be retained as the basis of the Morgan three-wheeler. The company would build nothing else until 1936, and the trike was destined to survive, in essence, until 1952.

Tax matters

When HFS Morgan introduced his three-wheeler in 1910 it was able to benefit from a considerable tax advantage, when compared with its four-wheeled contemporaries. For the Morgan was in the class defined as motor vehicles with 'less than four wheels', this including 'motor bicycles, tandems and tricycles'. The cost? A flat-rate charge of £1 per annum, a fee which, unlike with motor cars, was not dependent on the size of the vehicle's engine. Four-wheelers were then taxed on the RAC rating of their power unit, which was based on the diameter of the bore and number of cylinders.

Subsequently, in 1921, Morgan owners were subjected to a quadrupling of the duty to £4 per annum, but it was still levied at a flat rate, a tax advantage which the company regularly highlighted in its advertising material. This figure remained in force until 1940 when it was increased to £5 and it applied to the Morgan three-wheeler, as 'a tricycle of under 10cwt', until production ceased in 1952. This was despite the fact that on 1 January 1948 all new motor cars were the subject of a flat-rate tax of £10.

Back in 1921 car owners had been charged a new annual rate of £1 per RAC horsepower, a protectionist

move that was intended to halt the flood of big-bored American imports into Britain. For this reason motor manufacturers stressed the RAC rating of their engines. For example, the owner of an 11.9hp Bullnose Morris paid an annual rate of £12, while his next-door neighbour with a Model T Ford in his garage was faced with the sum of £22, the US-designed car being rated at 22.4hp.

When the Morgan 4-4 arrived in 1936 it benefited from a reduction in the tax rate in 1934 to 15s (75p) per hp. With its Coventry Climax engine

Morgan was to claim in the 1920s that its three-wheelers were 'Fast, Economical and Reliable and the tax is only £4'. (LAT)

having a bore of 63mm, it was rated at 9.8hp. Accordingly it was classed as a 'Ten' and the owner paid £7.10s (£7.50p) per year to tax it. The Standard Special engine, which replaced the Climax F-head 'four' in 1939, had a bore of 63.5mm, so the same amount of tax was due. The model was so evaluated until 1948 when the flat rate of tax was introduced.

When charting the evolution of the Morgan three-wheeler, it is important for the reader to be aware that customers could, and sometimes did, request a non-standard combination of engine, chassis and body. This accounts for the fact that while the year of manufacture of some surviving trikes is not in dispute, they do not always conform to the expected specifications. Furthermore, modifications were also introduced at unexpected dates, and occasionally some vehicles do not even match the factory records.

On a broader canvas, HFS Morgan

had constructed what was then called a cyclecar, in other words a stepping stone between a motorcycle and a car. He can thus be seen as a British pioneer of the movement that boomed in the years between 1910 and the outbreak in 1914 of the First World War.

With this trend in mind, in November 1910 the Cycle and Motor Cycle and Manufacturers Traders Union staged its first show at Olympia. The event marked the debut of the Morgan 'runabout', as 'HFS' had two machines on display. By this time he had dispensed with the Peugeot

engine and replaced it with a choice of British-made JAP power units – a single-cylinder 4hp engine, which never attained production status, and an 8hp V-twin. Both were air-cooled sidevalve units. The year 1910 thus marked the beginning of an association between Morgan and John Prestwich's JAP company that was destined to endure until the early 1930s.

Wisely, 'HFS' had decided to remain a buyer of proprietary engines and did not attempt to manufacture a bespoke power unit with all the demands of time and money that this would have entailed. Although problems

The starkness and simplicity of the original Morgan, a Runabout of 1913 which sold for £85 Guineas. The absence of doors and the chain drive are readily apparent. (LAT)

A 1913 Runabout. Morgan was to claim it as the 'Car of Economy' and said it was able to cover '60 miles per hour' at '60 miles per gallon' . . . (LAT)

The 1913 Runabout from the rear, displaying the unconventional position of the starting handle. It was so located until a three-speed gearbox was introduced to the range in 1932. Thereafter it was positioned at the front of the vehicle. (LAT)

The same Runabout's sidevalve air-cooled 964cc JAP engine. (LAT)

occasioned by a lack of engines regularly punctuate the Morgan story, it is a creed that endures to this day. Only once did Morgan succumb to the temptation but – as recounted in Chapter Ten – the project never progressed beyond the paper stage.

Morgan's three-wheeler was commended by *The Motor Cycle* as 'a very cleverly designed 'runabout' for the single rider'. In the course of the article in *The Light Car*, 'HFS' remembered that these first machines 'caused quite a stir'. However, they were, he said, too novel to attract more than about 30 orders – 'but I found there would be a very much larger demand for a two-seater model'.

He therefore created the definitive Morgan three-wheeler by adding a second seat – although the original single-seater continued to be offered for a time. The two-seat conversion was completed by August 1911 and the Runabout, now elevated to a model name, also acquired wheel steering with a motorcycle-style accelerator now firmly attached to the wheel's right-hand spoke; at this point the gearlever was transferred to the right. Rudimentary bodywork was introduced, along with a coalscuttle bonnet with a heart-shaped aperture.

'HFS', who had no doubt inherited his excellent artistic sensibilities from

The competition

HFS Morgan's 'runabout' of 1910 with its two wheels at the front and single one at the rear followed the configuration of the Edwardian tri-car. It proved to be by far and away the most popular British three-wheeler of the inter-war years, but there were competitors.

Santler, a near-neighbour of Morgan at Malvern Link, who had produced a pioneering British motor car in 1889 or thereabouts, built the Rushabout in about 1920, this being clearly inspired by Morgan's Runabout. It was powered by 10hp MAG water-cooled or air-cooled engines and there was independent front suspension, although of a different pattern from that of the Morgan.

In 1919 Coventry Victor had launched a motorcycle powered by a 688cc water-cooled flat-twin engine and in 1926 this power unit was fitted to a three-wheeler with chain drive to the single back wheel. Priced at £99, by 1929 no fewer than four models were being produced from the firm's premises in Cox Street, Coventry. The two more expensive Sports versions used an enlarged 749cc engine. Although motorcycle production ceased in 1930, the three-wheeler continued to be available until 1938.

Of far greater significance, in 1929 the BSA combine announced a three-wheeler which resembled a car rather than a motorcycle. Daringly having front-wheel-drive, with independent transverse springing, it was powered by the 1021cc V-twin air-cooled Hotchkiss engine, enhanced with overhead valves, that had been used in the BSA Ten of 1922–25. It sold in two-seater form for £120 and there was a family model with rudimentary rear seats. Capable of a respectable 60mph, the BSA was improved from 1933 by the availability at extra cost of a 1075cc four-cylinder engine – although this pushed the price up to £125. Both versions survived until

A 1935 BSA *with car-style radiator and front-wheel drive: it challenged the Morgan in a declining three-wheeler market from 1930.* (LAT)

1936 and about 5200 examples of the 'twin' were built, with the 'four' accounting for a further 1700 or so. Although the BSA was to many eyes an inferior product to the Morgan, it was more modern in appearance and in a contracting market took sales from the Malvern car.

By contrast, the Raleigh for 1933 had clear motorcycle antecedents, as the driver sat on a saddle and steered the single front wheel with handlebars. Produced by the bicycle manufacturer of the same name, it was based on the company's delivery van and powered by a 598cc single-cylinder engine. The saloon version sold for £89 and the tourer cost less, but few were built.

More successful was the Raleigh

Safety Seven of 1933, still with a similar three-wheel layout but with more car-like looks. Powered by a 742cc V-twin with shaft drive, the price was £110. Some 3000 had been built by the time the name disappeared in 1936; meanwhile, in 1935, rights to the Raleigh van, a bizarre device with a girder-fork motorcycle front end, had been sold to its creator, Tom Lawrence Williams, who since 1930 had run Raleigh's motor department. The vehicle re-emerged as the Reliant van, a car only arriving in 1952 with the launch of the glassfibre Regal.

Destined for a similarly brief existence, the JMB was produced between 1933 and 1935 and hailed from Ringwood, Hampshire. It thus has the distinction of being the only car to have been produced in the New Forest. A Morgan-like three-wheeler, perversely the 497cc single-cylinder JAP unit was mounted *behind* the two seats, from where it drove the single rear wheel by chain. The frame was of ash, the body in fabric, and the price £75. A noisy 50mph was possible, or a little more from the Mustang sports version with overhead valves which cost £91. About 100 JMBs were sold before Messrs Jones, Mason and Barrow decided to call it day.

The JMB Mustang had an ohv JAP engine developing 21bhp; note the kick starter. With a weight of 6cwt, maximum speed was a claimed 68–70mph. (Jon Pressnell collection)

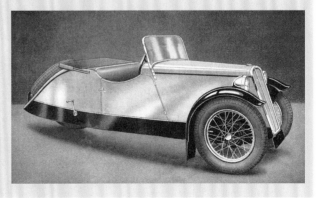

This 1913 JAP-engined Runabout belongs to Chris Booth and it can be seen at his Morgan motor museum at Rolvenden, Kent. (LAT)

his father, in addition to being responsible for his Runabout's mechanicals also designed its bodywork. Once production was underway he would sketch his next design with a stick of chalk on a black-painted wall at the factory, a process that would be watched by Mr Firth, his pattern-maker, and other workmen. They were expected to interpret it immediately and build a prototype body which Morgan would then view. His team would make further alterations to the body, changes being purely dictated by its creator's eye, with measurements confirmed by a piece of string or a stretched-out handkerchief, until he was fully satisfied with the results.

The improved Runabouts made their appearance at the 1911 Motor Cycle Show, with the cyclecar boom gathering momentum. 'They attracted a good deal of attention, and with trade support, I obtained far more orders than I thought I could meet', recalled Morgan. 'I approached several large manufacturers and (luckily) they turned the proposition down, so, partly with the aid of deposits on orders, I bought machine tools, built some new workshops and, giving up my garage business, did my best to satisfy the demand'.

Power for the Runabout was provided by a 964cc JAP engine and initially there were additional 'De Luxe' and 'Sporting' bodies listed alongside the 'Standard' model, together with a van version capable of carrying loads of up to 1.75cwt. Despite an increase in weight over the very earliest cars, the Edwardian Morgan was capable of over 60mph. This was at a time when William Morris's famous Bullnose Oxford light car could comfortably attain only a rather more sedate 40mph.

The importance of competition as a spur to sales became apparent in March 1912 with a Morgan victory by motorcyclist Harry Martin in the inaugural International Cyclecar Race

A De Luxe model of 1918 with its short scuttle, high body line and passenger's door. The wire mesh in front of the radiator replaced louvres – but these were reintroduced in the following year. (LAT)

The Morgan company's connections with Malvern Link date back to 1905, an association which is recognised by the local authority whose road signs greet motorists as they enter the district. (Author)

at Brooklands, this producing a flurry of demand. Over a hundred orders were placed on that very day and led directly to an expansion of the Worcester Road works. As recounted in Chapter Nine, activities on road and track were henceforth to make a pivotal contribution to Morgan affairs.

The enterprise was now on a firmer footing and this led, on 1 April 1912, to the formation of the Morgan Motor Company. Although this possessed a nominal capital of £100,000, the Rev Henry Morgan contributed £3000, the equivalent of some £140,000 by today's values. He was chairman and

therefore ran the business while 'HFS', as managing director, was responsible for building the cars.

Production began later in 1912. On a personal level, in June of that year 'HFS' married Hilda Ruth Day, the daughter of the vicar of St Matthias, Malvern Link. She would regularly accompany Morgan on trials and rallies, and their honeymoon was spent touring in Wales in a white-painted three-wheeler. They returned to live in Chestnut Villa and were to have five children of whom four were daughters. Their only son, Peter, (1919–2003) would eventually succeed his father.

In 1913, as 'HFS' later put it, 'I produced some racing cars with a lower chassis, low seats and ohv JAP engines'. One of these was bought by Oxford graduate Gordon McMinnies, founder editor of The Cyclecar (later The Light Car), a magazine established in the previous year. McMinnies went on to win the cyclecar prelude to the 1913 French Grand Prix held at the Amiens circuit in July. For Morgan this was 'a wonderful performance, as he had to change the inner tube to one of the front tyres during the event'. But

Under the bonnet of the 1918 De Luxe, with the radiator clearly visible. The engine is a 980cc sidevalve water-cooled JAP unit. Behind it is the petrol tank and beyond that the filler for the total-loss oil system. (LAT)

despite the tenacity of McMinnies, the organisers disqualified the three wheeler for being a 'sidecar'.

No matter. The company immediately proclaimed that it could supply 'exactly similar machines' for £115, with other models starting at 85 guineas. For 1914, indeed, there were no fewer than three versions of the Grand Prix offered: a sidevalve model with either a narrow or a wide body, and a more expensive car with an ohv water-cooled JAP engine. From 1915 there was only one body style, with a choice of engines; this sportiest of Morgans continued to be listed until the end of 1926, when it was effectively replaced by the Aero model introduced in 1923.

Up until 1913 all production trikes were powered by air-cooled JAP engines. But overheating was a problem and 'HFS' thereafter looked to other suppliers who offered water-cooled alternatives. Such three-wheelers are easily identifiable by the presence of a radiator – although because of the forward location of the engine this was mounted *behind* the power unit rather than in front of it. Most notably, in 1916 the Swiss-made water-cooled 10hp MAG unit became available as an option, having already appeared in the car of Morgan's sister Dorothy in 1914.

The outbreak of the First World War in August 1914 initially had little impact on the company; 'HFS' was, in any event, a pacifist. Meanwhile, in 1911 he had started work on an experimental four-wheeled car (see page 36) that was completed in 1912 but which did not enter production. It was to be another 24 years before such a Morgan became a reality.

By 1915 the Standard model had been deleted, and the range consisted of the Sporting, Grand Prix and De Luxe. That same year 'HFS' built a four-seater model 'for myself and my family to get about in', based on a

model which he had designed in 1912. It proved to be a valued stepping-stone, when marketed for the 1920 season as the Family Runabout, fulfilling a long-felt want and selling in substantial numbers.

A contemporary bird's-eye view of one of the first Family models built in 1920. It is identifiable by its absence of doors – later cars have them – and by its long running boards. (LAT)

Morgan's French cousins

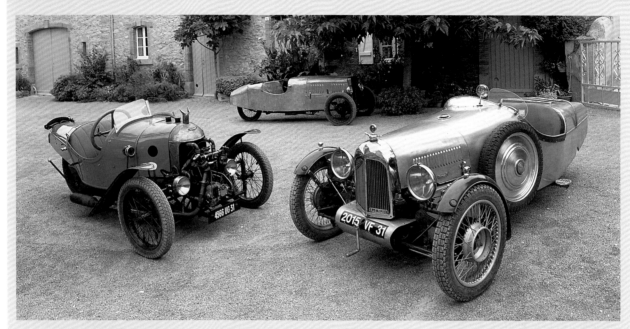

1. The Darmont (1920–39)

The Darmont from France was closely related to the Morgan, as it began life in 1919 when 'HFS' granted a manufacturing licence to his French agent, Robert Darmont of Courbevoie, Seine. By being produced in France, Morgan's cars avoided import duty and sales were spurred by Paul Houel's success in the Circuit de l'Eure event of August 1919.

Entering production in 1920, the Parisian-built Morgans closely resembled the Malvern Link cars and were produced by the hundred each year; after an interim period when they were called Darmont-Morgans, the cars latterly became known simply as Darmonts. This move reflected the fact that Robert Darmont – by all acounts a bit of a dodgy customer – had broken with Morgan, and ceased paying his licence fee. JAP and Blackburne V-twins were used at first, in air-cooled and water-cooled forms, with later Darmonts being powered by French-built copies of these engines. Top of the range was a 100mph supercharged version of the sports

Darmont Spécial model. In 1934 a modernised Darmont called the Aéroluxe appeared. This had a cowled dummy radiator, an air-cooled 1087cc V-twin (either sidevalve or ohv), and an orthodox three-speed gearbox, as first seen on the Darmont Spécial a year earlier. Darmont introduced a four-wheeler in 1935, but only a handful of the toy-like V Junior were made. Manufacture of Darmonts ceased in 1939.

2. The Sandford (1923–39)

Similar in concept, the Sandford was produced in Paris by the Birmingham-born Malcolm Stuart Sandford. He had begun importing the Morgan trike but was outsold by the locally-produced Damont. The Sandford appeared in 1923, and was powered by the Ruby proprietary engine in sidevalve and ohv forms; it was a quality product which sold for about the twice the price of its rival, doubtless reflecting the fortnight it took 12 men to produce one car. Sandford tended to be ahead of Malvern Link in his specifications, front-wheel brakes and three speeds arriving in 1924.

Malvern Link's French spin-offs. A Morgan by Robert Darmont (left) which began life as a 'Morgan, Type Darmont Spécial' and ended as a plain Darmont when the licensee ceased royalty payments! Right, the Sandford with Bugatti-style body but 950cc Ruby engine under its bonnet. In the background is a D'Yrsan, also Ruby-engined, and one of only three known survivors. (LAT)

In 1927 there were three models on offer, the Tourisme, Sport and Super Sport, the latter powered by a 50bhp ohv Ruby 1088cc engine that was also available in supercharged form. Bodywork, usually in polished aluminium with a pointed tail, was purchased from Lecanut. Manufacture ceased in 1936, with the last trikes additionally being available, from 1934, with an air-cooled 950cc sidevalve flat-twin. A four-speed gearbox was used from 1933.

Sandford went on to assemble Morgan three-wheelers and 4-4s under licence, with French-sourced bodies, and in 1939 he fitted a Ruby engine to one of his 4-4s, in an attempt to produce a more gallicised car. Distinguished by a different radiator, only the one car was built before the Second World War intervened. As a British subject, Stuart Sandford was imprisoned in France during hostilities.

3. The D'Yrsan (1923–30)

The Paris-built D'Yrsan was introduced in 1923 and was priced between the Darmont and the Sandford that were clearly its inspiration. Its creator was motorcycle racer and engineer Raymond Siran, Marquis de Cavannac, who decided to set up on his own after an attempt to join forces with Sandford had failed to get off the ground.

The layout of the D'Yrsan superficially resembled that of the Morgan in that it had a tubular chassis with independent front suspension, in this instance by twin transverse leaf springs. There was, however, no projecting motorcycle unit at the front, a Ruby 'four' (initially a 904cc sidevalve) instead being tucked under the conventional bonnet. There was an orthodox three-speed gearbox, and final drive was by chain. The car's identity was proclaimed by a large letter 'Y' on the radiator.

In 1926 came the supplementary Type BS which used an overhead-valve 972cc Ruby engine, while the most potent version was the DS, with a 1097cc power unit that developed 35bhp; available in touring and sports guises, the latter could exceed 80mph. The trikes were joined in 1927 by a four-wheeler, although a mere 54 had been completed by the time that all D'Yrsan production ceased in 1930. This compared with 533 three-wheelers, of which almost all were the BS model.

Luggage is relegated to a rack on the Sandford, dubbed 'The Aeroplane of the Road' by its manufacturer. (LAT)

Although the Darmont was originally powered by JAP or Blackburne engines, it soon went its own way and produced locally-built variations on the same themes. This, however, is a Swiss-built MAG unit. (LAT)

In the foreground is Stuart Harper's 1922 Ware replica, named after the three-wheeler Brooklands racer created by Edward Bradford Ware, JAP's experimental engineer. Perversely, the engine is an overhead-inlet/side-exhaust MAG unit, complete with twin magnetos; a more appropriate JAP 'twin' has now been fitted. Behind it is a 1922 Family model, also MAG-powered. (LAT)

Demand for the trike had shown no signs of abating in the immediate pre-war years and had begun to outstrip the confines of the Worcester Road works. So in 1913 Morgan acquired some land on the Madresfield estate in Pickersleigh Road, about half a mile away, and a factory was built there, details of which are set down in Chapter Eight. It has been Morgan's

home ever since, although up until 1919 only the bodies were completed at the new works.

In November of that year the first post-war Motor Cycle Show opened at Olympia. Morgan chose the occasion to introduce two new models for the 1920 season. These were the Family four-seater, which sprang from his 1915 experiment, and the Aero, which was powered by a 976cc sidevalve JAP engine and was distinguished by its twin Auster screens in place of a windscreen and by its stylish pointed tail; later versions had an elegant rounded two-piece screen. In the interests of practicality, access to the rear wheel was improved on the Aero by the introduction of a hinged panel at the back of the body. Initially only used for competition, Aero production proper did not get under way until 1923.

For the 1921 season Morgan introduced some refinement. In particular there were modified fork ends which permitted the rear wheel to be detached more easily, and the lengths of the two driving chains were standardised. A year later came the reintroduction of the basic model, now named the Standard Popular. Power came from an air-cooled 8hp JAP engine which provided a top speed of 50mph and a respectable return of 60mpg. This was but one element of a six-model line. The basic Standard air-cooled model sold for £150, followed by the De Luxe in air-cooled guise at £170 and water-cooled at £186. Going up a notch, the Grand Prix cost £180, as did the air-cooled Family model. Finally at the top of the range came the £191 water-cooled version of the Family.

The important news for 1922 was that owners could now specify a Sports engine for their cars, this being a new air-cooled 980cc JAP sidevalve, the KTC, initiated by chief designer Val Page. With this, top speed was in excess of 60mph and acceleration was improved. By 1921 the performance of the V-twin had already been enhanced by the replacement of its cast-iron pistons with aluminium ones, while roller-bearings took the place of the plain variety. For the KT, Page

Driving a Darmont Morgan

In essence an early Darmont is scarcely different from a Morgan of the same year – with the *caveat* that with so many variations on the Morgan theme being possible, no two trikes will ever drive in exactly the same manner. Anyway, the car in question is the 1923 car illustrated on these pages, and the writer confesses that the driving experience remains etched in his consciousness.

The MAG water-cooled V-twin – as used in some Morgans – delivers a raucous tap-tap-tap that the howl from the transmission does its best to drown. Performance is brisk, of that there's no doubt, and the engine has impressive torque. The two-speed gearbox is seductively easy, too. Operating in conjunction with a minimal-travel leather-cone clutch, it

is simplicity itself: you push forward for first and pull back to second.

No, the main effort consists of trying to pilot the Darmont in a straight line. The direct-acting steering feels almost rigid, and attempting to keep on line is a real challenge, not least as the kidney-bashing suspension has the car thrown about on all but the best surfaces. Brakes? Working on the rear wheels only, they are spongy and don't feel as if they're doing much.

All-in-all, the experience of driving the Darmont, at least for a novice, is frankly terrifying. Much the same can be said of being a passenger when an experienced *Morganiste* is showing you the machine's capabilities…

Jon Pressnell, series editor

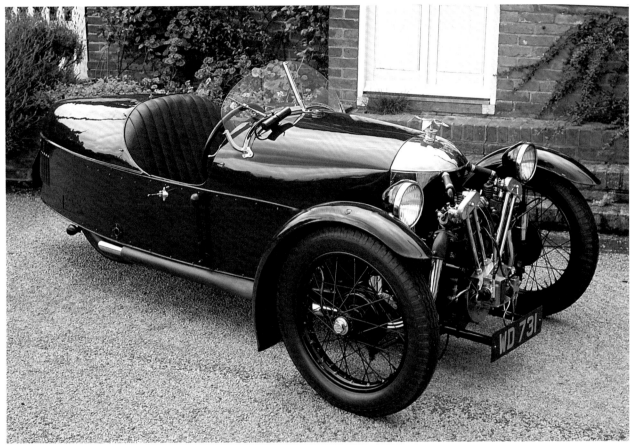

increased the size of the valves: revs experimentally soared to 8000rpm and even touched 10,000rpm. Further development work followed, and the KTC line, instantly identifiable by its 'fir-cone' valve-cap coolers, continued in production throughout the decade.

The trikes in their various guises were well suited to the years following the First World War. A boom, fuelled by the pent-up emotions of the conflict and a heady optimism, endured until the end of 1920. But 1921 produced some of the bleakest trading conditions in living memory. Fortunately the economy began to pick up in 1922, and in 1923 annual production of the Morgan three-wheeler reached 2300 cars. Profits were equally buoyant and stood at a respectable £40,851, the equivalent of over £1 million in today's values.

Little wonder that in 1922 'HFS' had been able to buy himself a Mulliner-bodied Rolls-Royce Silver Ghost tourer. Soon afterwards, in 1925, he

and his growing family moved from Chestnut Villa, his home since 1905, to Fern Lodge, Malvern, still in Worcester Road but a much larger property set in spacious grounds.

In the longer term the 1923 production and profit figures represented an all-time high for the business during the inter-war years. Thereafter Morgan production settled into a gentle decline, a process that was marked by the arrival, in July 1922, of the Austin Seven. A large car in miniature, with a small 747cc four-cylinder engine rather than the usual 'twin', Sir Herbert Austin's baby was conceived in the depression year of 1921 when his Longbridge factory was operating under a receivership. Not only did it prove to be the salvation of the Austin Motor Company, but those remnants of the cyclecar movement which had survived the war soon succumbed, as buyers were wooed by the Seven's relative sophistication. Although Morgan, as the best of them,

Chris Booth's 1930 Super Sports Aero, powered by an 1100cc overhead-valve water-cooled JAP unit. (LAT)

did endure, it could only be a matter of time before potential customers would turn their backs on a three-wheeler with its origins so clearly rooted in pre-WW1 days.

When the Austin Seven was announced, it was expensive at £225; but at the 1922 Motor Show, Austin took a gamble and reduced the figure by £60, bringing the price down to £165, even though this was the car's cost price. The corner had been turned. A saloon version joined the original open car in 1926, and as the Seven's popularity grew, accelerated by the arrival of a petrol tax in 1928, so the price dropped. By 1929 the open Chummy sold for £125 – against £102 for Morgan's by-then-ageing Family model.

Still, in motor sport Morgan maintained the three-wheeler's high

A 1932 Aero on the move. Note the stork mascot that today enhances many Morgan three-wheelers. It was offered as an accessory from 1924 until 1933, priced at 7s 6d (37p). (LAT)

competitive profile, the benefits of which were transferred to the production cars. In August 1922 Douglas Hawkes had entered a Morgan powered by a special air-cooled overhead-camshaft Anzani 'twin' in the 200 Miles Race at Brooklands; unfortunately he was forced to retire on the 22nd lap. Despite this setback, the Aero was revised for the 1923 season with a polished aluminium body having flat sides and a tail similar to that on the Hawkes '200 Miles' car; an external gearlever was another noteworthy feature. Power came from a water-cooled Anzani engine although it was possible to specify sidevalve and ohv Blackburne engines, together with the familiar JAP sidevalves. However, this distinctive Aero body style was only destined to last for a year, as a round-tailed version was introduced for 1924 – the earlier style thereafter being available only to special order.

For 1926 electric lighting was standardised across the range. It was during that year that the bowler-hatted Alfie Hales, who had been Morgan's works manager since the start of trike production, became ill; in 1926 he left the company, and he died from cancer in 1927. His replacement, who had arrived in 1926, was George Goodall, who was ideally qualified, having owned nothing but Morgans since 1912 and having been successfully competing in trials since 1913. At this time Bristol-born Goodall was a garage manager, having joined James Fryer of Hereford after demobilisation. He was destined to offer loyal service to Morgan, both behind a desk and a steering wheel, until his death in 1958.

In the meantime, the three-wheeler range continued to evolve. For 1927 the De Luxe, Family and Aero models

Close-up of the '32 Aero's 60-degree 1100cc water-cooled JAP engine. (LAT)

The 1932 Aero from the rear. Note the steering wheel-mounted hand throttle – the elongated lever on the right with the choke in front of it. The advance and retard ignition control is on the opposing side. (LAT)

were both lengthened and widened by 3in, and front brakes of 7in diameter were standardised, this feature having appeared optionally on many cars from the 1924 season. There was a new Family Aero, while the streamlined special Aero remained available to special order. Improvements were also made for 1927 to the V-twin engines, with Burney and Blackburne offering the KMC, a new overhead-valver developing over 40bhp at 4000rpm. JAP also had a pushrod 'LT' unit being available in the Morgan in three forms, the standard LTOW, the sports LTOWC, and the top-of-range LTOWR racing version.

The public was by now benefiting from a fall in prices throughout the motor industry and Morgan customers were no exception. The 1927 Standard now cost a mere £89, while the water-cooled Family model, billed as 'Cheap to Buy, Cheap to Run, Easily Housed', cost £121. That year some 1700 trikes left the Pickersleigh Road factory – and profits of £21,060 were about half those of 1923.

For 1928 the Standard was only available in dark red. Selling for £85, it was discontinued at the end of the year. At the other extreme was the low, purposeful Super Sports Aero – 'a very demon on wheels', said the company – which was 6in wider and 2½in lower than the previous-generation Aero. It was inspired by a car that the factory had prepared for racing driver Ron Horton in 1927, but while he had used a KMB Blackburne engine, the production version was powered by a specially-tuned version of the latest JAP 1096cc LTOWC 'twin'. This permitted the radiator to be mounted lower than previously, which allowed a sloping bonnet; the price was £150.

In 1929 'Ubique' in *The Motor Cycle* set down his impressions of what he believed to be the first example of the Super Sports line, which he had christened Mabel. 'One of the charms of the Morgan Aero is that it feels even faster than it is . . . speeds over the sixty mark provide a delightful sensation of record-breaking velocity; and 60mph is child's play to Mabel's engine', he enthused. 'Ubique' had heard rumours of 'upsets' but countered 'I daresay that it is possible to turn one over; but I have seen more than one four-wheeled car upside down'. However, he found the clutch 'unpleasantly fierce', a problem resolved by the application of engine oil, while the V-twin possessed 'an unpleasant vibration period between 50 and 60 mph'. It was returned to the factory for rectification but there was 'still a vibration period between the figures mentioned: it resembles propeller-shaft whirl'. Nevertheless, he had never regretted his choice of machine. 'The joy of a high power-to-weight ratio and instant surge of power when the throttle is opened . . . provide a fascination which never fails'.

Standardised for 1928 were self-starters, an extra since 1923, the starter being located adjacent to the engine in a position previously occupied by the dynamo, which was now gear-driven from the cross-shaft. The starter's arrival was applauded by *The Motor Cycle*, which regarded the by-

Three-wheelers in transition. A 1934 Sports two-seater powered by one of the last JAP engines, a 60-degree overhead-valve water-cooled 1100cc unit. Alongside is a 1933 example with one of the first Matchless MX sidevalve 'twins'. (LAT)

then universally popular fitment as 'an inestimable boon at all times'.

In 1930 the same publication road tested a Family model and this account provides a revealing contrast to 'Ubique' and his experiences of the Aero Super Sports published the year before. For while that model provided performance motoring for the enthusiast, the Family offered more utilitarian transport. The magazine's evaluation – candidly and refreshingly, in those editorially deferential days – exposed both the strengths of weaknesses of Britain's best-selling three-wheeler.

Powered by the 980cc sidevalve air-cooled JAP engine, the Family proved to have a maximum speed of just over 50mph, and a comfortable cruising speed on moderate roads of 40mph, increasing to 45mph if conditions permitted, without overtaxing the unit. Such performance had its price, even if the writer expressed this in a somewhat roundabout way: 'Only after a great deal of low-gear work was there any unpleasant smell in the driving compartment, and then it was only noticed when the Morgan was

stationary', he commented.

More positively, there was plenty of body room: 'unless grown-ups are put in the children's quarters, there is nothing cramped about it'. In all, the Morgan was 'simplicity itself, was easy to handle, and provided a standard of comfort almost on a par with that of the small four-wheeler – with a far better performance on hills under full load'.

But there were drawbacks which indicated that the model was beginning to show its years. What had been acceptable in the boom year of 1923 was by 1930 becoming less so. The clutch was deemed to be 'on the harsh side', the high-geared steering showed 'a tendency . . . to be a little uncertain at speed, owing to tail movements', while the driver had to accustom himself to 'a certain hardness in the springing'. Then there were the brakes. 'Those on the Family Morgan were adequate and no more, though the front ones could have had more bite with perfect safety', noted the report, observing that after 150 miles it had been necessary to adjust the rear brake, 'as the pedal reached the floorboard before it was properly in action'. But at £97 10s (£97.50), you paid your money . . .

As already noted, the 1928 model year had seen the departure of the Standard, which had intermittently been a feature of the range since

1911. Its place was taken by an improved De Luxe for £86, with lower-geared and thus easier steering. Yet despite Morgan's attempts to update his three-wheeler, demand was ebbing away. Annual production slumped in 1929 to just 1002 units. Then came the Depression. Morgan was to record a £4080 surplus in 1930, but the business toppled into the red in 1931 and would not regain profitability until the Second World War.

Fortunately the Morgan Motor Company was to survive the turbulence of the 1930s, thanks to the financial sagacity of the Morgans, both father and son. When the market for three-wheelers had been buoyant, they had embarked on a policy of careful and highly profitable external investment, the returns from which offset the losses incurred by car business throughout a difficult decade. Had this crucial underpinning not existed, Morgan, like so many of its contemporaries, would have surely succumbed to the harsh realities of the times. Such, indeed, was the success of their stewardship that by 1935 the company's assets stood at an impressive £260,000, the equivalent of some £8.2 million in today's prices. That year 'HFS' and his family moved from Fern Lodge to the Thames Valley and to Cannon Hill, Braywick, near Maidenhead, a palatial 18th century

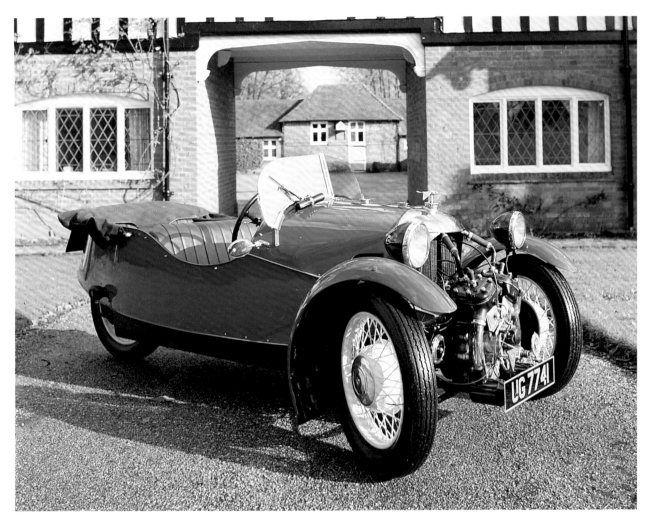

A 1933 Family Sports with sidevalve water-cooled 990cc Matchless engine. (LAT)

mansion with no fewer than 21 bedrooms, set in 25 acres of parkland. A greater contrast to the utilitarian three-wheelers is difficult to imagine.

In such circumstances the Inland Revenue began to take an interest in the affairs of the Morgan Motor Company and finally, in 1940, it questioned whether it was really a business which manufactured motor cars. Was it in reality more a manager of financial resources? That year, after all, when the car side recorded a £1826 loss, gross investment income stood at an appreciable £9209. But in

The Family Sports from the rear. Clearly only children can be accommodated in the back seat! (LAT)

A museum for three-wheelers

Three-wheeler enthusiast Chris Booth's museum in the village of Rolvenden in Kent is devoted to the Morgan three-wheeler. Opened in 1972, it contains some 11 trikes, the oldest of which dates from 1913 and the most recent, an F4, from 1935. The collection includes two Grand Prix models, one Anzani-powered and the other with a MAG engine, a pair of Standards from 1913 and 1927, a 1928 Family model, a trio of Aeros, and an SS

Aero. Booth purchased his first Morgan in 1960 and he has not stopped buying and restoring them since. Most of the exhibits are in working order and he regularly uses them in vintage rallies and road runs. In addition to these three-wheelers there is a 1929 Model A Ford, a Post Office Flatnose Morris van and a 1936 Bampton caravan.

The collection, which is based at Falstaff Antiques, 63 High Street, Rolvenden, Kent, is open throughout

Part of Chris Booth's Morgan motor museum at Rolvenden, Kent, where 11 three-wheelers, dating from 1913 to 1935, are usually on display. In the foreground is an Anzani-engined 1927 Aero. (LAT)

the year from Monday to Saturday, between 10.00am and 5.30pm. If you are intending to travel a long distance, it is advisable to telephone 01580 241234 beforehand. The museum's website is www.morganmuseum.co.uk.

December judgement was made in Morgan's favour.

So although the 1930s were overshadowed by Morgan's continuing losses, its supplementary income allowed 'HFS' to continue to refine his three-wheelers. For 1931, the lowered chassis which had first appeared on the Super Aero of 1929 was extended by 2in on the Family and by 6in on its Sports variant. This M-type frame

required the introduction of a two-piece propeller shaft. There were further improvements for 1932, when a gearbox with three speeds and reverse was introduced, with transmission by a single chain, and accompanied by detachable wheels. Previously all models had used a simple two-chain drive giving two speeds. It was now possible, too, to crank a Morgan from the front rather than from

the cross-shaft at the side: the starter dog now engaged with one of the revised JAP engine's two camshafts, while the other drove the distributor for a coil-ignition system which replaced the long-running magneto.

These were noteworthy new features of the 1096cc unit, which was available in sidevalve and ohv format, and with either air-cooling or water-cooling. Changes were also made to

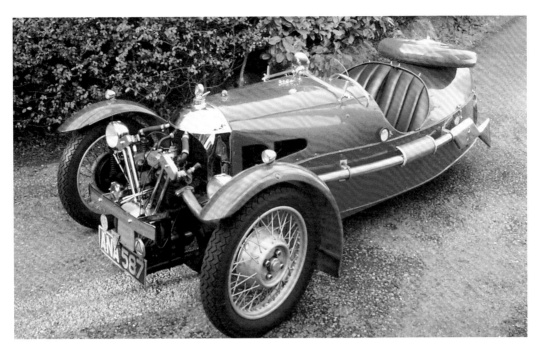

A 1934 JAP-*engined Super Sports, the D-shaped engine intakes on the bonnet identifying the model year.* (LAT)

The 1934 Super Sports from the rear; the spare-wheel cover is a latter-day refinement. (LAT)

the cylinder angle, this being increased from 50 to 60 degrees to improve refinement. The revised engines were designated LTOWZ, the last letter indicating improved lubrication, this now incorporating a dry-sump system.

The Super Aero and the Sports Family were the principal users of this new chassis, designated the R, the two-speeder specification continuing to be available on the Family and Aero models into 1933. Wheels were now interchangeable, across the range, the introduction of these Dunlop 18in Magnas meaning that the Morgan driver could now carry a spare. But accommodating the extra wheel meant that the Sports model lost its distinctive boat tail, this being replaced by a flat rear panel. The Family model was also redesigned, with its flattened rear related to that of the restyled Sports.

The company's stand at the 1933 Motor Cycle Show was one of significance for the company because it marked the arrival of the F-type, which was the first production four-cylinder Morgan three-wheeler. This model is important to our story because it represents the starting point for the four-wheeled line announced late in 1935.

Return of the trike

When the Morgan three-wheeler ceased production in 1952, it was regarded as a utilitarian, outdated vehicle, a pre-WWI anachronism which had clearly outlived its usefulness. But there can be few who would have then predicted that, some 30 years later, the concept of the Malvern-built three-wheeler would be in the midst of a revival.

This reversal of fortunes, it should be said, sprang not from Morgan itself but was prompted by a variety of mostly kit-car producers. Many of these were Morgan three-wheeler owners and enthusiasts responding to their like-minded contemporaries who liked the idea of the Malvern Link trike but lacked the funds to acquire the genuine article. Visual inspiration invariably came from the Super Sports 'twins' of the 1920s and the final flowering of the line, the conventionally Ford-engined four-cylinder F-type.

The individual who can be credited with triggering this revival was Morgan trike enthusiast and draughtsman Tony Divey of Marlingford, Norfolk. In 1979 he offered his own version, the Triking, with a backbone chassis to which were attached alloy body panels. Power appropriately came from a motorcycle engine, in this instance a frontally-exposed 844cc Moto Guzzi V-twin with shaft drive to the rear axle. Performance was sizzling and even more so when the 950cc version was fitted – this giving the three-wheeler a top speed in excess of 120mph!

The price of a completed Triking was £4500, while the more powerful version was £250 more. However, with increasing competition in the early 1990s the vehicle was also offered in kit form at a cost of £3113. The 100th example of what is arguably the best of the modern Morgan lookalikes was built early in 1992 and the Triking remains in production at the time of writing.

The Triking is powered by an 844cc V-twin Moto Guzzi engine and its body lines are unmistakably Morgan three-wheeler. (LAT)

The Lomax, which appeared in 1983, is made in even more respectable numbers, about 180 to 200 kits being sold each year. The work of glassfibre consultant Nigel Whall of Willouton, Lincolnshire, appearances are deceptive because the Lomax is driven by its front wheels, it being ingeniously based on the Citroën 2CV chassis, with the cylinders of its flat-twin engine nostalgically exposed to view. The Morgan-style body is made from glassfibre but the use of the Citroën frame initially meant four rather than three wheels for the original version, designated the 224. Soon after its announcement, however, a supplementary and ultimately far more popular three-wheeler, the 223, appeared. Sold in kit form, it cost £581, with buyers providing their own 2CV chassis. A number of variations on the same theme have followed, the Lambda of 1993 being the most significant, as it has a Lomax-designed frame. By this time the factory had moved to its current home in Cradley Heath, West Midlands.

By contrast, Dick Buckland's B3 is relatively rare. Buckland, of Llanwern, Wales was, like Tony Divey, a Morgan three-wheeler enthusiast who wanted to update the concept, and his interpretation appeared in 1985. Also based on a backbone chassis, the B3 was more closely related to the F-type, in that it had a conventionally-located 1.3-litre Ford 'Kent' engine. However, its drive ultimately had more in common with the original as it was conveyed through the Escort's gearbox via a bespoke torque tube to a Reliant crown wheel and pinion and thence to the single rear wheel by sprocket and chain. The grp body hinged upwards at the bulkhead to reveal the mechanicals. Just seven were built before ill-health forced Buckland to cease manufacture, although production later resumed and the three-wheeler remains available in kit form.

Built in Ellesmere Port, the coffin-nosed Renault-engined wooden-bodied DRF three wheeler of 1987 had only a tenuous visual relationship to the Morgan. The all-wood body

A Triking on the move, in company with its inspiration, in the form of a 1932 JAP-powered Aero. (LAT)

concealed a metal chassis for the front-wheel-drive Renault mechanicals and the price of £2400 meant that the customer supplied the Renault 4 or 6 running gear.

Rather different in concept was the fwd Skip of 1988, for instead of a bonnet was an exposed Mini power unit. The car featured a spaceframe chassis cloaked in a glassfibre body, and was the work of Durham-based Jeffrey Calver, who had a passion for trials. Aimed at like-minded enthusiasts, the Skip was only available in kit form.

Another Morgan enthusiast, machine-tool engineer and restoration specialist John Ziemba, of Darwen, Lancashire, also wanted to produce his version of the trike. Named the JZR, for John Ziemba Restorations, his 1989 design was based on the Honda CX V-twin unit which was exposed Morgan-style at the front of the square-tubed chassis. The body was glassfibre. Priced in kit form below £1000, it was available for

£4000 ready for the road. By 1995 some 250 examples had been built; the JRZ ceased production in 1998.

The BRA CX3 Super Sports, meanwhile, was the work of a company better known for its AC Cobra replicas. In 1992 it announced its Morgan-like CX-powered trike and four or five had been built by the time that the project was discontinued in 1993. A similar fate befell the 2CV-based JBF Boxer, which also appeared in 1992 but did not even reach production.

The Honda CX 'twin', in 500cc or 600cc guise, also formed the basis of the Heathfield Slingshot of 1993, which hailed from Chesterfield, Derbyshire. Built around a round-tube spaceframe, the barrel-sided body was of generous dimensions and made of glassfibre although an alloy version was available at extra cost. There was an aluminium engine-turned dashboard and leather trim. Such features reflected a kit price of £3113; the Slingshot ceased production in about 1996.

The front-wheel-drive Trico similarly dated from 1993, and looked more like a Morgan three-wheeler from the

rear than from the front. This was because the front end housed a Mini subframe complete with A-series engine. The car's Dorset-based creator, Ken Hallett of Wareham, only offered the vehicle as a set of plans.

The Citroën 2CV sub-structure also formed the basis of the Tripacer of 1994. The work of Classic Car Panels of Frome, Somerset, it had an alloy body clearly owing something to the Grand Prix Bugatti as well as to the Morgan.

Bernard Beirne's Dragonfly, finally, also dates from 1994 and is noteworthy because its plywood and steel body came closest of all these three-wheelers to having the look of the F-type Morgan. There was even a Z-section chassis and Morgan-style sliding pillar ifs. Beneath the bonnet was an 848cc Reliant Robin engine driving the rear wheel via a Honda CX shaft-drive. Produced at Toton, Nottinghamshire, the Dragonfly's all-too-brief life came to an end in 1995.

The Lomax has been steadily developed over the years. This Lambda 3 has Lomax's own chassis; 2CV mechanicals are retained. (Lomax)

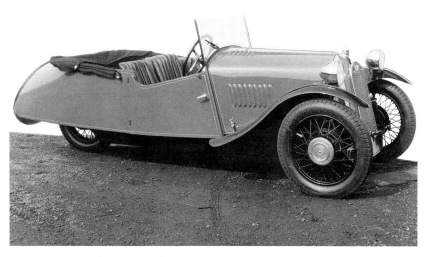

A four-seater F4 of 1937, as available with a choice of Ford engines. Note the stoneguard: the three-wheelers subsequently adopted the vertical slats of the 4-4. (LAT)

Although Morgan retained the familiar backbone chassis, he dispensed with the tubular sidemembers that had served him since 1910. These were replaced by a pair of ingenious Z-shaped steel pressings that were made by Rubery Owen to his design. Not only was this lighter than a channel-section or box-section frame, but the bottom flanges of the pressings faced inwards, allowing the floor to be attached to them, while the body could be secured to the angled top.

'HFS' had begun work on this project in 1929, and the prototype was powered by a four-cylinder sidevalve 750cc Coventry Climax engine that was mounted behind the front axle instead of ahead of it. The familiar independent suspension was retained, but the front of the car looked more conventional than previously because of the presence of a radiator, as the power unit was water-cooled.

The F-type was destined for a protracted four-year gestation, the delay caused by Rubery Owen tooling up for the all-important chassis sidemembers. But 'HFS' put this hiatus to good effect, because the production model emerged with a Ford rather than a Coventry Climax engine – marking an association between the

international motor manufacturer and Morgan which endures to this day. In fact, the 933cc sidevalve unit that powered the F-type had not existed in 1929. Having an RAC rating of 8hp, it had been rapidly designed by Ford in America to power the Dagenham-built Model Y saloon of 1932. As used in the Morgan it had a VW Derrington 'Silvertop' aluminium cylinder head with a higher compression ratio than the cast-iron original, but was otherwise virtually identical to the engine used in the Ford – except for the absence of the Y-type's dynamo-driven fan, on account of the F-type's generously-sized radiator which contained 2½ gallons of coolant. Not only did the robust Ford unit prove to be more powerful than the Climax

'four': it was also significantly cheaper to buy. The transmission, meanwhile, remained pure Morgan, with a rear-mounted three-speed-and-reverse gearbox and chain drive. Magna spoked wheels were fitted, and an innovation was that there was now an accelerator pedal.

The open four-seater bodywork was also new, having a conventional louvered bonnet, cycle wings (soon to be replaced by more elongated ones), cutaway doors, and a round tail that contained the spare wheel. Although the prototype had an angular BSA-style radiator, the production version featured a fashionably sloping prow which was destined to survive, in essence, until 1952. The price was £120 and the top speed 65mph.

The first of the line, chassis FD1, left Malvern in April 1934 and the company was quick to stress on its introduction that the new model 'in no way replaces the twin-cylinder models on which the Morgan name has been built'. But inevitably this proved to be the case – although not before further changes had been made to the two-cylinder line in time for the same 1933 Show.

The 1934 Super Sports was thus shown with a new body, similar to that of its Sports stablemate apart from the spare wheel residing in the tail

A 1938 model F2 two-seater photographed by the factory in August 1937. There was a choice of 8hp or 10hp Ford engines. (LAT)

rather than sitting proud of it. This was the so-called 'barrel back' rear, the earlier tail being known as the 'beetle-back' style. The Family model simultaneously received a new radiator. Whilst JAP engines continued to be available, with new 990cc Matchless engines, the sidevalve water-cooled MX and the ohv air-cooled MX2, were also listed.

Although the 'twins' would continue in production until 1939, the 1934 Motor Cycle Show marked the spiritual end of the old order: Morgan had forsaken raucous performance for refinement, because – for the first time since 1910 – none of the two-cylinder models on display featured JAP engines. In their places were the Matchless 'twins', available in pushrod or sidevalve format and with air-cooling or water-cooling. At the same time out went the beetle-backed Super Sports.

If the appeal of the trike was dwindling, then the knockout blow was provided by the government, which in 1935 reduced the cost of Road Fund Licences on all vehicles except those for three-wheelers, the owners of which continued to pay the £4 levy that had been in force since 1921. But an Austin Seven driver, for instance, instead of being charged £8 per annum to tax his baby now paid £6, so eroding the differential between three and four wheels. That year a total of five manufacturers of three-wheelers were listed in Britain but by 1938 there was just one: Morgan. In June of that year it could rightly claim to be 'The foremost Three Wheeler for over 27 years . . . and now the *only* Manufacturer'.

In the meantime the four-cylinder line was expanding. A two-seater designated the F2 was introduced at the 1935 Motor Cycle Show, at which point its predecessor became the F4. The F2 was available optionally, for 7 guineas more, with Ford's 1172cc 10hp engine, a bigger-bored derivative of 8hp unit. This imbued the F2 with a top speed of 74mph. Further adding spice was the availability of adventurous two-tone colour schemes, the most memorable being a

striking white and scarlet livery.

The enlarged engine was the only power unit available in yet another variant, the two-seater F Super Sports introduced for 1938. Visually this was a cross between the front of the F2 and the rear of the two-cylinder Super Sports, and it had a claimed top speed of 70mph. It also possessed better brakes, Girling units being fitted, albeit actuated by Bowden cables rather than by rods. This arrangement was extended to all three-wheelers for the 1939 season.

Morgan production ceased in that year with the outbreak, in September, of the Second World War. But by this time the three-wheelers had been joined, in 1936, by a supplementary model in the shape of the 4-4, which was the firm's first production four-wheeler. Its arrival not only heralded the opening of a new chapter for Morgan: it also proved to be its salvation.

Despite this re-orientation of the company, trike production resumed after the war, with the 8hp F4 and 10hp F Super four-cylinder Ford-engined models – the 'twins' having been a casualty of the conflict, as Matchless had ceased manufacture of its big MX4 unit. By the 1949 season only the F Super was on offer. In spite of the Matchless engine having been discontinued, an interesting anomaly is that Morgan produce a run of 12 post-war Super Sports cars from spare parts, all but

three being exported to Australia.

But while there was a small albeit diminishing market for the three-wheelers, by no stretch of the imagination could the trike be regarded as having any great export potential – and steel supplies in these difficult early post-war years were geared to overseas sales. The end came on 29 July 1952 when the last Morgan three-wheeler left Pickersleigh Road. After 42 years, what in 1910 had begun life as HFS Morgan's 'runabout' was no more. Fortunately, by this time the four-wheeler model was selling strongly.

Californian three-wheeler enthusiasts John and Bridget Leavens are commemorated in this 1997 stained-glass window in the porch of the church of St Peter and St Paul, Stoke Lacy. (Author)

The First Four-*Wheelers*

The current Morgan car line, Aero 8 excepted, can trace its ancestry back to the 4-4, Morgan's first four-wheeled model, introduced in 1936. HFS Morgan later put the arrival of this all-important car into perspective: 'For some years, competition from light cars had been getting very severe, owing to the improved performances and lower cost of these four-wheelers', he recounted in the *The Light Car* article quoted in the previous chapter. 'Our output dropped, and to keep the works busy I decided to produce a small four-wheeler, light in weight and with plenty of power . . . Taking the successful four-cylinder three-wheeler as the basis of the design, I produced the four-wheeled model . . . It was called the 4-4'.

Morgan later confirmed that this name, to indicate four wheels and four cylinders and so differentiate it from the three-wheelers, had been coined by works manager George Goodall. He had played an increasingly important role in the company's affairs since

Morgan's prototype Coventry Climax 4-4, shod with special trials tyres. Allocated the number 49, it was driven by 'HFS' in the Veteran Class in the 1935 Motor Cycling Club's London to Exeter Trial – when he collected a Premier Award. Note the now rare 'Flying M' mascot. (LAT)

1935, when he had taken over the day-to-day running of the business. This followed Morgan's move to the Thames Valley – although 'HFS' continued to visit the Pickersleigh Road factory once a week, driving himself down from Berkshire. In 1937 Goodall would be promoted to the position of managing director, when 'HFS' took over as chairman following the death of his father at the end of the previous year.

Morgan had built a Ford-powered 8hp four-wheeler prototype in 1934; as he said, this was based on the F-type. Drive was conveyed, via an abbreviated torque tube, to a Meadows gearbox, then passing, via a short propeller shaft, to a live Moss rear axle suspended on quarter-elliptic springs. The bonnet, scuttle, windscreen and front wings were all F-type, to which a makeshift rear portion of bodywork was added. A flat-fronted radiator with a chrome surround was fitted, the core concealed behind a stoneguard, the overall appearance differing somewhat from the later production version.

This car paved the way for a second prototype that was bodied by mid-1935, which was both longer and wider than the original and powered by a 1018cc overhead-inlet/side-exhaust Coventry Climax engine; it also had half-elliptic rear springs, with the chassis members fashionably passing beneath the rear axle to ensure low body lines. The inspiration for this feature was the Hillman Aero Minx of one of Morgan's daughters.

The open two-seater bodywork bore little relationship to that of the finished product, being fitted with rather graceless separate front and rear wings which shared the same economy-conscious contours; nor were there any running-boards. This car in turn led in August 1935 to the construction of a third prototype, with running-boards and with a rather tidier rear end incorporating the petrol tank and the soon-to-be-familiar two spare wheels.

The second prototype, meanwhile, was rebodied with far more graceful all-enveloping front wings, which were now extended to partially cover the wheels and merge in with the running-boards now fitted. Completed by the end of 1935, here was a wholly integrated body that was destined to stand the test of time – although 'HFS'

might have been surprised to find that its essentials were still going strong some 70 years later.

So how did this radical change of appearance come about? Such an evolution, from ugly ducking to graceful swan, is not uncommon within the motor industry and 'HFS' was no mean stylist, as the bodywork of his three-wheelers bears witness. It is not possible to say with certainty if a single car provided the all-important final inspiration for the 4-4's lines; it may indeed represent an amalgam of influences that combined to produce what has proved to be a timeless shape.

However, I would like to provide one candidate, and that is the rare, costly and visually stunning 1½-litre Squire (see box), announced in September 1934. At this point the Squire was only available in chassis form and in fact the works demonstrator was only completed in March 1935. Its breathtakingly elegant open two-seater body, built to Adrian Squire's design by Vanden Plas, was finished in ice-blue paint with silver upholstery. It alone cost £195, which was to be roughly the price of a 4-4, with the complete car costing £1220, the equivalent of *two* 1½-litre Aston Martins. Not surprisingly, it

Morgan 4-4
1936–1939

ENGINE (Coventry Climax):
Four cylinders in line, cast-iron block and cylinder head

Capacity	1122cc
Bore x stroke	63 mm x 90mm
Valve actuation	Pushrod inlet and side exhaust (IoE)
Compression ratio	6.8:1
Carburettor	Single Solex 30HBFG
Power	34bhp at 4500rpm

TRANSMISSION:
Rear-wheel drive via torque tube to separate Meadows four-speed gearbox with synchromesh on third and top gears; thereafter by open propshaft.
Moss gearbox with synchromesh on top three gears also fitted from 1938

SUSPENSION:
Front: Independent, sliding stub axles and coil springs with telescopic hydraulic dampers
Rear: Live axle with half-elliptic springs; friction dampers

STEERING:
Burman Douglas cam-and-peg

BRAKES:
Girling 8in drum, mechanically operated

WHEELS/TYRES:
16in steel disc (drophead);
17in Easiclean pressed-steel (later open cars)
Tyres 5.00 x 16in or 4.50 x 17in; 5.60 x 16in on drophead

BODYWORK:
Coachbuilt, with steel panels on ash frame.
Separate Z-section chassis
Open two-seater, open four-seater, drophead coupé

DIMENSIONS:

Length	11ft 8in
Wheelbase	7ft 8in
Track, front and rear	3ft 9in
Width	4ft 6in
Height, two-seater	4ft 4in, hood raised
Height, coupé	4ft 2in, hood raised

WEIGHT:
Open two-seater 14.2cwt

PERFORMANCE:
(Source: *The Autocar*)

Max speed	77.59mph
0-50mph	28.4sec

PRICE WHEN NEW (NO TAX THEN PAYABLE):
£210 (Two-seater, August 1937)

NUMBER BUILT:
850 (plus further 4 cars built after the war)

Morgan 4/4
(Standard-engined)
1939–1951

As Coventry Climax-engined except:

ENGINE (Standard Special):

Bore x stroke	63.5mm x 100mm
Capacity	1267cc
Valve actuation	Pushrod
Compression ratio	7.0:1
Carburettor	Single Solex DD
Power	39bhp at 4200rpm
Torque	61.6lb ft at 2500rpm

NUMBER BUILT:
578

Four-wheeled forebear

The 4-4 of 1935 did not represent the first attempt at producing a Morgan four-wheeler. In 1911 'HFS' wrote that he had 'almost completed' such a machine, according it the contemporary name of quadricycle. At the time his motivation was that three-wheelers were excluded from some trials – although he was also very much aware that the £1 flat rate road tax the trike enjoyed (see page 13) was a major advantage as far as its marketing was concerned.

The experimental two-cylinder vehicle was finished in 1912, and a patent on a four-wheeler was duly filed on 5 September 1914 and granted on 13 May 1915. The patent drawings shows a tubular chassis of a similar width to that of the trike although the extra wheel meant that the track of both sets of wheels

could be reduced. At the rear a crossmember was introduced ahead of the two-speed gearbox, quarter-elliptic springs attached to this crossmember supporting the back axle. As with the production three-wheelers, the final drive was by two separate chains. The remains of this car survive at Chris Booth's Morgan motor museum (see page 28).

In 1914 'HFS' also experimented with a four-cylinder sidevalve 1024cc Dorman engine in a four-wheeled chassis, a project which could have led to a Morgan light car. But he seems to have set the idea aside, as demand for the three-wheelers showed no sign of abating. It was only when a sales slide became apparent that in 1929 he once again returned to the four-wheeler concept.

transpired, he was to be the sole recipient of a Premier Award. It was on such an upbeat note that the 4-4 entered production in 1936.

The model was fully described in The Light Car of 3 January 1936 and its issue of 31 January carried an item by the editor, who had tackled 'HFS' about the future of the three-wheeled line. 'His reply was reassuring', commented the magazine. 'The new four-wheeler is simply an additional Morgan venture and will not in anyway affect the future of the famous three-wheeled range. What Mr Morgan had done was simply to carry into effect the oft expressed wish "of those who admire the Morgan but have a prejudice against anything with less than four points of contact with the road" . . .'.

Once again 'HFS' had aimed for as high a power-to-weight ratio as possible and the 4-4, weighing a little over 14cwt, was powered by an engine which developed 34bhp. 'Thus it is natural that the performance should be lively', declared the magazine, pointing out that the Coventry Climax engine had 'already proved itself well able to deal with cars of twice the weight'. For the record, MG's newly-introduced TA open two-seater would turn the scales at 17cwt, some 3cwt more than the 4-4. Morgan's first four-wheeler was arguably the lightest open two-seater sports car on the British market. It was also competitively priced, at 185 guineas (£194), making it a significant £28 less than the Abingdon offering.

The 4-4 was initially only available in open two-seater form and there was a choice of three colour schemes, British Racing Green throughout, all-black, or blue with black wings – although a customer's preferred colour scheme was available at extra cost. The first 50 cars had rear-opening doors, but thereafter they were hinged from the front.

The inclined flat-fronted radiator, its core masked, as on the prototype, by a stoneguard, was topped with a mascot, the so-called 'flying M'. Die-cast in mazak, a zinc-based alloy, it was easily damaged and in

proved to be extremely difficult to find buyers, and only seven cars were completed before the company ceased trading in 1936.

Back in 1965 I interviewed Reginald Slay, then the only surviving director of the Squire Car Manufacturing Company, and he recounted the following story to me, that also appears in his autobiography, Haps Mishaps & Fun, published in 1993. Adrian Squire had recruited Aston Martin's former sales manager JJ Boyd-Harvey to try to sell his car. As Slay recalled, Boyd drove the works Vanden Plas demonstrator all over the country. 'I always remember he came back and said he'd been to see his old friend |HFS| Morgan – the Morgan car people at Malvern'. He said "What do you think |Morgan| did? He liked the car very much . . . .|and| he sat down and drew it". I said "I don't believe you". But he said "He did!" I thought, well, we shall see what happens.'

Of course we do not know the precise date of this encounter, but it seems likely that it took place some time in 1935, just as the 4-4's body was evolving. Indeed the visit might

have taken place after the Morgan's lines had been finalised. But the point could be an academic one because, in any event, photographs of the Squire had appeared in the motoring press throughout 1935. Having said that, there is a striking visual similarity between the two cars, in particular in the distinctive lines of their wings, as the accompanying photographs testify.

So much for speculation. What is certain is that by July 1935 a representative of The Light Car had been able to drive the second prototype 4-4 at Brooklands, where it had exceeded 70mph. The magazine later carried a photograph of the finished product and a brief description of the as-yet unnamed model in its issue of 27 December 1935. It reported that the engine was a Coventry Climax unit and that the 'first production car will be driven by HFS Morgan himself in the London-Exeter Trial'.

There were echoes here of his participation in the inaugural 1910 event and 'HFS' was duly entered in the Veterans class which was only open to those survivors of the original run of 25 years before. As it

The 4-4's independent sliding-pillar front suspension has its origins in that adopted for the Morgan Runabout back in 1910. The engine is the 1.2-litre Standard Special which replaced the original Coventry Climax unit in 1939. (LAT)

The 4-4's Z-frame chassis, clearly showing the separate gearbox and underslung side members. This photograph was taken in 1939, when the Standard engine was introduced. (LAT)

The Squire – Morgan's visual inspiration?

Diametrically opposed to the 4-4 in concept, the costly, exclusive 1½-litre Squire was the dream of former MG design draughtsman Adrian Morgan (!) Squire. One of the most stylistically memorable British sports cars of the inter-war years, the Squire was built at Remenham Hill, near Henley-on-Thames. Power came from a supercharged twin-overhead-camshaft 1496cc four-cylinder Anzani engine which drove a pre-selector gearbox in the manner of MG's K3 sports-racer. The Squire's top speed was a guaranteed 100mph, performance that demanded the fitment of powerful Lockheed hydraulic brakes.

Styling was Squire's particular forte and the works demonstrator that JJ Boyd Harvey showed HFS Morgan differed from usual Vanden Plas designs in that it was of all-metal construction, rather than using a traditional wooden frame. Happily this car survives in America. There were two other Squires with Vanden Plas bodies, differing slightly in detail from the original, and a pair of visually unrelated cheaper Markham-bodied cars. Two long chassis Squires were also built but these had Ranalah coachwork.

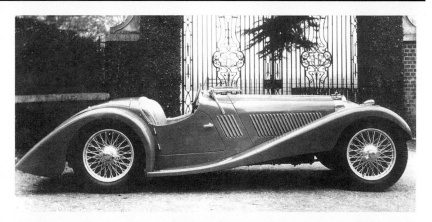

Above: The Squire works demonstrator completed in 1935, with body by Vanden Plas to Adrian Squire's design. 'HFS' inspected it during the 4-4's evolution. Below: A 1995 Plus 8. Were the Morgan's sweeping lines inspired by the Squire? (Both author's collection)

consequence few survive. It was, in any event, a casualty of the Second World War, not reappearing in the more financially stringent post-war years. Beneath the bonnet, with its louvred side panels, was the Coventry Climax IoE unit, now of 1122cc.

The 4-4's sliding-pillar independent front suspension was in essence inherited from the three-wheeler, although it was more robust in execution and incorporated Newton-Bennett hydraulic dampers. The trike's influence was also apparent in the position of the gearbox. As on the first prototype, the four-speed Meadows unit – with synchromesh on top and third gears – was located amidships, 1920s-style, some 2ft from the power

unit. Drive, conveyed via a Borg and Beck clutch, was by an enclosed driveshaft. This distinctive layout was destined to endure until 1972. The clutch mechanism was particularly noteworthy, the pedal being attached via a linkage to an aluminium piston which slid inside the tube that separated the engine from the gearbox. Although this configuration was archaic even by 1930s standards, on the plus side it provided ample legroom and footroom and meant that the gearlever fell readily to hand without the need for a remote control. Because the floor was attached to the lower lip of the Z-frame, the gearbox and attendant driveline ran – unusually – *above* the wooden boards,

rather than below them.

The Hardy Spicer propshaft drove a Moss rear axle, subsequently replaced by a Salisbury unit, this being suspended by five-leaf half-elliptic springs located along the insides of the chassis frame. The springs were shackled at their forward end but ran in trunnions, MG-style, at the rear. Multiplex Hartford Type 502 friction dampers were fitted.

The wheels were 16in steel-disc type, shod with 5.00 x 16in tyres, with two spares carried at the back of the car, their weight being taken by boards which rested, like the floor, on the inner lips of the chassis. Brakes were 8in Girling units actuated by Bowden cable. Steering, as on the three-

This 1939 Le Mans Replica is owned by Morgan historian Ken Hill. Priced at £250 when new, some £50 more than the mainstream two-seater, it is powered by a 1098cc Coventry Climax engine and is instantly identifiable by its cycle front wings and the absence of running boards. (LAT)

Morgan promotional material, 1938-style: a factory postcard of the four-seater. The caption on its reverse, interestingly, calls the model a '4/4', in the post-war manner, rather than a '4-4'! The car is described as being 'Finished in the best style, and upholstered in leather'; the price was £225. (LAT)

A 1939 Le Mans Replica, which spent the war
at Pickersleigh Road and was one of three 4-4s
acquired by Central Garages (Barnstaple) in
March 1947. It is accordingly fitted with a
1098cc Coventry Climax engine and was
successfully campaigned after the war by Jeff
Sparrowe. The rear treatment of the Le Mans
Replica model also differs from the production
versions, in that instead of two vertically-
mounted spare wheels, a single wheel is located
in the reshaped tail. (Both LAT)

The instrument panel of the Le Mans is
essentially standard, apart from the rev-
counter that occupies the glove compartment
on the driver's side. (LAT)

The blown 4-4

During the 1930s, when the supercharger reigned supreme in Grand Prix racing, a number of manufacturers of British sports cars experimented with the device. SS was one and Morgan another, although neither ever marketed a production version in the manner of the MG J3 or the Austin Seven Ulster.

The conversion of the 4-4 in question was completed in 1939, using the car that had previously been fitted experimentally with a Ford V8 unit (see page 96).

Under the bonnet was a 1021cc Standard Eight sidevalve engine which had been fitted with a special high-compression aluminium cylinder head. The intention was to compete in the popular but by then neglected 8hp sports class, once dominated by the MG Midget and the Singer. A low-pressure Arnott supercharger and attendant Arnott carburettor were installed by Carburettors Ltd of Willesden Green, London, the blower running at about 3–4psi of boost. Mounted above the cylinder head on the offside of the engine, the supercharger was belt-driven from the front pulley and had its own oil reservoir, lubricant being supplied from a tank mounted under the bonnet.

Unfortunately this blown 4-4 succumbed to Peter Morgan's driving when, on his way back to the family's Berkshire home, it ran a main bearing

on the Oxford by-pass while he was travelling at 85–90mph!

The car seems to have been repaired, because in 1941 a representative of The Autocar tested it. While wartime petrol rationing prevented any detailed speed times, the writer reported that 'it took gradients on the Maidenhead–Oxford route at a cracking pace, not relying for opinion upon the speedometer,

In 1939 this works 1937 4-4, then fitted with a Ford V8 engine, had it replaced by this Arnott-supercharged 1021cc four-cylinder sidevalve unit rated at 8hp – courtesy of Standard's Flying Eight. Photographed in 1941, the car's wartime headlamp mask is readily apparent. (LAT)

which on a useful but level stretch of road on this section I noticed once at the 80 mark'.

wheelers, was via a reduction gear incorporated within the column near the scuttle, but this was soon changed in August 1936 to a conventional Burman Douglas cam-and-peg steering box.

Despite the 4-4 being a relatively cheap sports car, the instrumentation was more than adequate. The dashboard itself was of ash, produced in the Pickersleigh Road sawmill, and had glove pockets on either side and a

central black-crackle instrument panel dominated by a 90mph white-on-black speedometer enhanced by a trip-meter and an integral clock. There were single twin-function gauges either side, for oil pressure and amps on the nearside and water temperature and fuel on the offside. A plain four-spoked steering wheel was fitted although a Bluemels 'Brooklands' item was available as an optional extra. The fly-off handbrake,

meanwhile, was positioned ahead of the gearlever, beneath the dashboard. The driver and passenger, meanwhile, each sat on pneumatic individual cushions with a one-piece backrest behind which was limited space for luggage and the hood.

The first 4-4 was delivered in March 1936, and Morgan displayed a polished chassis at that year's London Motor Show, the first it attended: as a manufacturer of three-wheelers it had

Like many other British car makers of the early post-war years, Morgan was encouraged to export its cars. In this instance the speedometer is graduated in kilometres per hour, which suggests this 1949 car is destined for continental Europe, despite the retention of right-hand steering. (LAT)

A four-seater 4-4 also intended for Europe. In contrast, the pre-war model's instruments have white figures on black faced dials. (LAT)

not previously been eligible and had accordingly been a regular attender at the motorcycle equivalent.

By then some changes had been made to the 4-4's specification. Engine power was up slightly and, in the words of one commentator, 'several components of the engine are arranged to better advantage'. Additionally the suspension had been tweaked, the diameter of the kingpins being increased from ¾in to 1in and phosphor-bronze bushes being introduced above and below the stub axle.

Weekly magazine *The Autocar* published its first road test of a Morgan in December 1936, and appeared much impressed with the car – which was the third prototype, registered WP 7490 and now rebodied. 'This Morgan is outstandingly steady, and corners exceptionally well, has light, accurate steering, effective braking and a lively, willing

performance', it enthused.

The 4-4's seating position was clearly noteworthy for the day and the tester commented on the car's 'exceedingly low build, it being possible to touch the road surface from the driving or passenger seat'. However, the writer regarded this as something of a mixed blessing. 'This construction no doubt has a good deal to do with the remarkable feeling of safety that is speedily induced in the driver, though it does result in seating positions which, from the point of view of entry and exit, are best suited to younger and more agile members of the fraternity'. The suspension, meanwhile, was found to be 'admirable' on normal roads although 'on the firm side' for less good surfaces and plain 'hard' on potholed sections. What was not in dispute was the new Morgan's performance. 'The engine is a unit that pulls particularly well at low speeds on top gear or will keep the car swinging along happily at 50 to 60mph, third being valuable for extra acceleration and fast hill-climbing', commented the magazine, which obtained a best timed speed of 74.38mph with the fold-flat windscreen in the raised position and 77.59mph over a timed quarter-mile. The latter was identical, even down to the last two decimal figures, to that achieved by the MG TA that *The Autocar* had tested three months before. However, the Morgan's 0–60mph time of 28.4 seconds was 5.3 seconds slower than that of the Midget, despite its engine being 172cc bigger.

In spite of such plaudits, 4-4 production got off to a relatively slow start and it was not until 1937 that demand began to outstrip supply. The two-seater was soon joined by a four-seater, introduced in August 1937, and an example was accordingly displayed on that year's motor show stand. It was built on the same chassis but had 17in

Morgan's display of 4/4s at the 1948 Motor Show at Earls Court was directly in front of the stand of The Autocar. *'Bright colours befit the sprightly performance of the small sporting Morgans', commented the magazine. In the foreground is a drophead coupé, with a four-seater on the right and a two-seater beyond. (LAT)*

perforated Easiclean wheels, later extended to the two-seater, although the original 16in disc wheels could be fitted on both versions at extra cost. Precious space-saving on the four-seater was achieved by including only one spare wheel. *The Autocar* found the four-seater's rear legroom 'generous', there being a 'proper backseat for two people, not an occasional one'; the occupants sat well down in the car, observed the magazine, and benefited from footwells. The new model was priced at £225, which was £15 more than was then asked for the two-seater.

These two versions were joined a year later by a drophead coupé, announced in August 1938, which sold for 225 guineas. This was Morgan's

answer to the Tickford-bodied MG T-type drophead and, as with the MG, the hood could be either fully folded (disappearing into a well at the back of the car) or half-furled to a coupé-de-ville position. The new model was available in a choice of two colour schemes: cream and black and Nile blue and chromium. Once again bespoke hues could be specified.

While the wing line was shared with the two-seater, styling was the work of Warwick-based Avon Bodies which had been supplied with a chassis that it duly bodied. The production version, built at Pickersleigh Road, outwardly resembled the Avon-built prototype although construction methods were simplified somewhat. Two small differences were the deletion of the Avon car's spare-wheel cover, Morgan giving the production car two exposed spares, as on the open two-seater, and the elimination of the bonnet-top louvres. The wheels themselves were 16in discs shod with 5.50 x 16in Dunlop ELP tyres, as opposed to the 17in rims by then being used on the

two-seater and four-seater.

There was space for luggage behind the Connolly-leather bench seat and, unusually, the windows did not wind but were of the sliding variety; they had chromium-plated frames and could be removed completely and stowed behind the seat. This meant that there was no intrusive winding mechanism, gaining extra elbow room and allowing recessed armrests to be provided. Unlike the open cars, the coupé was fitted with semaphore indicators, located on the rear quarter panels just behind the doors. An uncharacteristic touch of luxury, for a Morgan, was provided by a walnut dashboard and matching door cappings.

The 4/4's vertical radiator slats were well established by the time that this two-seater was built in 1949. Originally a fixed stoneguard sufficed, but when the drophead version arrived for 1939 the open cars followed its example and went over to slats. The Morgan is in company with an MG TC, another car with its lines rooted in the 1930s. (LAT)

Spares: a word about factory support

The evaluation of any Morgan should be prefaced by the knowledge that the company has been in the ownership of the same family since its foundation and has continuously occupied the Pickersleigh Road factory since 1919. This means that full details of a car's original specification will have been preserved and, above all, many replacement parts will still be available, whether the vehicle was built in 1936 or 1986. The latter statement does require some qualification, because the spares in question must specifically relate to those components produced by the factory, most significantly the complete body, the chassis, and the front suspension parts. Mechanical components, namely engines and gearboxes, that were originally supplied by outside contractors, such as Ford or Standard-Triumph, are not held but can invariably be supplied by a specialist or sourced through the appropriate one-make club. Inevitably the newer cars, that is to say those produced after 1950, fare better than the pre-war ones, but overall this enlightened policy towards parts supply is an endorsement, as parts manager Paul Trussler puts it, of 'Mr [Peter] Morgan's philosophy of keeping as many cars on the road as possible'.

But first, a word on those all-important factory records, which take the form of the company's 'Car Register'. It is worth being aware that entries differ significantly, depending whether the vehicle dates from before the Second World War or after it. A pre-war chassis number related specifically to an order and, if for any reason this was cancelled, the number went with it, so producing a gap in the sequence. After hostilities a new system was introduced, whereby the car was allocated its chassis number on being dispatched from the works. It is therefore essential that you quote the number of your car in any correspondence. Armed with that information, Morgan can provide you with the date of the car's completion, any special features, the type of engine fitted and colour of the bodywork and upholstery. The Morgan Motor Company's address is Pickersleigh Road, Malvern Link, Worcestershire WR14 2LL.

So much for the paperwork. When it comes to evaluating a specific car, because essentially the same chassis and body combination has been used on all four-wheeled Morgans over the years, much the same remarks apply throughout. However, each model possesses its own peccadilloes and these are set down in the appropriate chapters.

The body of the 4-4, introduced in 1936, set the constructional and stylistic pattern for the next 70 or so years. It is accordingly of coachbuilt construction, with the panels – in the case of the Series I 4-4, in steel –

being attached to an ash and plywood frame. All of these materials are vulnerable to deterioration.

You should be aware of the fact that, until very recently, Morgans were not expensive cars, and that 'HFS' ran a tight ship and bequeathed his cost-conscious ethos to his son. In these circumstances some of the materials used in their cars might charitably be described as being cheap and cheerful. Nor should you be surprised to find that the ash used for the body frame has over the years varied considerably in quality. The pre-war 4-4s are in any event vulnerable to decay simply on the grounds of age. But beyond this, Morgans made in the 1950s and early 1960s are by far and away the best as far as durability is concerned, since they used naturally seasoned ash rather than the kiln-dried wood subsequently employed. Despite this change, the bodies of the cars produced in the later 1960s are about average but then quality took a nose-dive from the 1970s until 1986, and it has to be said that these later frames rot very easily. Post-'86 Morgans have greatly benefited from the wood being treated with Cuprosol wood preservative.

Fortunately, the factory can supply replacement bodies. The cost, for instance, of the Plus 8's woodwork is currently £2753 less panelling or £3380 complete with metalwork, both prices including VAT. Deliveries to all parts of the world take about 10 weeks.

An added touch of refinement was that the radiator incorporated chromium-plated vertical slats, in contrast to the open cars on which the core was protected by a stoneguard. This feature was standardised on all models after the war. Finally, between but below the line of the headlights was a central pass-light which was activated by a foot-operated switch which simultaneously extinguished the headlamps.

Because the drophead could be run

in closed form, the engine was mounted on Silentbloc rubber bushes to help keep the noise level down. For the same reason, the Meadows gearbox was replaced by a Moss unit with synchromesh on the top three gears. Both gearboxes continued to be fitted to the 4-4 until the late 1940s, when the Moss 'box was standardised; used also on the Plus 4, it continued to be a robust feature of its Plus 8 successor until 1972.

Some mechanical changes which

featured in the new model extended across the range for the 1939 season. In particular the front stub axles and bearings were strengthened, as was the rear axle, which was fitted with a four-star differential. Under the bonnet the engine benefited from valves 'of improved shape' while the engine filler incorporated a canister into which an opened tin of oil could be placed and left to drain into the sump.

As mentioned in Chapter Nine, a lightened 4-4 with cycle wings was entered for the 1938 Le Mans race by Prudence Fawcett, who, to the surprise and delight of the factory, achieved a very creditable 13th placing. In March 1939 Morgan accordingly offered a Le Mans Replica 4-4 prepared to this specification – at a price of £250, some £50 more than the standard version. The most obvious external difference was the fitment of cycle wings and the absence of running-boards, but there were also changes to the rear bodywork. This necessitated the deletion of the twin spares in favour of a single partly-recessed wheel. The petrol tank, meanwhile, had a capacity of nine gallons (although the pukka Le Mans 4-4 carried 24 gallons) and came complete with twin fillers. A smaller 1098cc engine was fitted, and this unit also powered the similarly-conceived unofficial TT Replica. This model, which was never catalogued, was on the lines of cars the factory entered, albeit unsuccessfully, in the 1937 and 1938 Tourist Trophy races. Outwardly similar to the Le Mans, the TT differed in having a different tail with a single spare wheel mounted on top of the bodywork. A total of eight Le Mans

and TT 4-4s were built.

Meanwhile in 1939 the mainstream 4-4 underwent the most radical mechanical modifications since its introduction in 1936. The Coventry Climax engine had been in use since the model's inception but Triumph, which supplied the power unit, had for some years been sailing close to the financial wind and finally capsized in June 1939, going into receivership. That, for the time being at least, was the end of the Triumph car. Later, in 1944, the name was acquired by Standard which since 1934 had been run by Captain John Black. Perversely, this controversial and dictatorial figure was destined to provide Morgan with its salvation. As a manufacturer of mass-produced family saloons, Coventry-based Standard had emerged as one of the 'Big Six' car makers of the 1930s. Its entire range was powered by a variety of four-cylinder and six-cylinder sidevalve engines which varied from 1 litre to 2.6 litres in capacity.

While Standard thrived, Triumph's decline was evident, and HFS Morgan had for some time been concerned about his engine supply, the failure of

which could threaten the 4-4 line. Standard's John Black responded by offering Morgan a bespoke version of his 1267cc Standard Ten engine, a 63mm x 100mm four-cylinder unit, enhanced by the fitment – specifically for Morgan – of an overhead-valve cylinder head.

The first car to be given this engine was the Avon-bodied drophead coupé that managing director George Goodall used for trials during the winter months of 1938/39. The Standard unit was 145cc larger than its predecessor and it developed more power: 39bhp rather than 34bhp. It was initially offered, from June 1939, as an alternative to the Coventry Climax. Top speed was pushed up to 77mph whilst two seconds were shaved from the 0–60mph time, which was cut to 26 seconds.

But on 3 September 1939 Britain

The ash for the 4/4 dashboard was cut in the Morgan sawmill and the two glove compartments on this 1949 car perpetuate pre-war practice. However, the instrument layout is different, the speedometer having previously been mounted centrally, flanked by the secondary dials. (LAT)

Buying Hints

1. In general terms the body frame is susceptible to rot at the points where it is attached to the chassis. But when you are evaluating a Morgan of any age, your first port of call should be the doors. Open each in turn and see if they are loose. This shortcoming is particularly apparent on the drophead, its doors being considerably heavier than those fitted to the open cars. Looseness might be a consequence of worn hinges: these were brass with steel pins up until the 1970s, and replacements are available from the factory. But more likely is that the front door post – and the catch post which holds the door shut – will both have rotted at their bases. A shake of the door will confirm whether this is the case. If the forward post moves with the door, or its opposite number succumbs to a gentle backwards and forwards motion, you're in trouble.

2. Look underneath the car and check the condition of the sill board. You shouldn't be able to push a bradawl into it. If you can, beware!

3. The doors can present problems of their own. This is because while their framing tends to remain sound, the method of construction leaves something to be desired. Four pieces of mild steel were first nailed to the wooden frame to provide reinforcement and to give the door its profile. A second steel sheet was then attached on top of them and this was the door skin. Moisture immediately became trapped between the two, and rusting began.

4. With the door open, remove the seat squab if you can, because the inner side of the Z-frame chassis tends to rust at this point, as a result of water entering under the doors. Unfortunately the horsehair under the trim acts as a very efficient piece of blotting paper and tends to trigger rot in the ash frame.

5. While you are examining the chassis, also check where the crossmembers join the frame, this being another rust point. On the subject of the chassis, it's always worth examining the state of the engine mountings as they can crack, the 4-4 and its successors being prone to vibrate somewhat.

6. A rusting frame is not completely calamitous. The factory can supply a replacement, or just the member in question. However, the new chassis are of the post-1956 type, which is when the rear-spring trunnion tube was deleted. The trunnions themselves wear badly, but the Morgan Sports Car Club can supply replacements.

7. At the back of the car, look at the bodywork adjacent to the half beading that runs down either side of the spare-wheel panel. Much more significantly, if you have the opportunity, and the car's owner is not hovering, grasp the underside of the rear wing and gently lift. If you are able to lift the body off the chassis – yes, it can happen – then avoid! Also examine the 'U' bolts securing the springs to the axle. They should be periodically checked for tightness.

8. The body panels were usually made of steel until the early 1960s, and the front wings tend to rust where they join the rest of the body. The rears are similarly vulnerable at the junction of the wing and the arch. A further shortcoming is that the edges of the wings are wired, forming another rust trap.

9. Spares for both the Climax and Standard engines are limited, but parts are available through the MSCC. The Climax is the more vulnerable of the two as its block is prone to cracking. This usually occurs on the offside of the engine, taking the form of a horizontal fissure about 1½in to 2in below the head gasket. The cause is because the exhaust is on the nearside, and this expands and contracts, producing stresses on the colder offside. The overhead-inlet valvegear is another weak point, being susceptible to excessive cam-follower wear; indeed, it is not unknown for the foot of the follower to break off completely, with calamitous results. A warning sign is excessive tappet noise.

entered the war and Morgan ceased car production almost immediately. A respectable 883 examples of the 4-4 had been built since 1936, of which the overwhelming majority, a total of 667, were two-seaters, the balance being made up by 99 four-seaters and 58 dropheads. Practically all of these vehicles, 854 to be precise, were powered by Coventry Climax engines, with the Standard unit accounting for a mere 29 cars. With the 4-4, HFS

Morgan had above all successfully made the transition from a manufacturer of motorcycle-engined trikes to four-wheelers. With his engine supply now assured, he would be in a strong position to resume production after hostilities.

Announced in December 1945, manufacture re-started in March 1946 and the 4-4s were essentially the same as their pre-war counterparts – although initially only the two-seater and drophead coupé were available. News that the four-seater was to resume production did not break until August. If the cars had not changed much, the prices certainly had. Purchase tax had been extended to cars in 1940 and the two-seater now sold for £454, thanks to £99 tax being added to £355, with the drophead selling for £505 (£395 plus £110 tax).

Despite the trikes continuing in production post-war, clearly the future

10. The Standard unit is far more robust and its only real shortcoming is a tendency to get through its main and big-end bearings in fairly short order. Fortunately the club keeps replacements shells in stock, from standard up to 60 thou oversize.

11. While you've got the bonnet up, open the toolbox. Rain enters here via the rear of the bonnet, if it collects, the bottom of the toolbox can rust and corrosion will spread into the bulkhead.

12. The only trouble you're likely to experience with the transmission is with the Elektron transmission housing used on the 4-4 Series I, the Plus 4 to 1969 and the Plus 8 until 1972. The driveshaft runs in an aluminium sleeve, operating the clutch through a graphite thrust bearing. This requires lubrication every 3000 miles and, if this isn't undertaken, the clutch will become unacceptably heavy. If you find you need both feet to depress the pedal, this is the most likely reason…

13. The Meadows gearbox fitted to the 4-4 until 1939 is an extremely robust unit; despite having synchromesh on third and top gears, you must be prepared to double de-clutch.

14. The Moss gearbox is a rather more sophisticated unit – some would say over-engineered – which lives up to its robust image. Double helical gears are used for all speeds, with the exception of first. In view of this, it is recommended that the oil, which is a hypoid gear lubricant, be changed every 2000–3000 miles. The gearbox is reliable enough, although the selectors can break. Secondhand spares are available through the MSCC. It is worth noting that the unit is essentially the same as that used by Jaguar until 1965.

15. The Moss rear axle is robust and shouldn't present any problems; although its Salisbury successor can present troubles, the Club can supply spares.

16. To check the front suspension, jack up the front of the car and recruit an accomplice to apply the brakes to prevent any play in the wheel bearing showing up. Grasp the wheel at the twelve and six o'clock positions and feel for any movement. If this is discernible, the chances are the kingpins are worn, or more likely, the two phosphor-bronze bushes – which in any event require replacement every 15,000–18,000 miles. The bottom bush is the more vulnerable of the two: wheel wobble at about 50mph indicates a problem and has the effect of transmitting vibration throughout the car from the scuttle backwards. Although parts are no longer available for the Newton dampers fitted to the earlier cars, Spax make a replacement especially for Morgan.

17. The steering track-rod ends have grease nipples and lubrication has often been neglected. Heavy steering will be the result. The Burman worm-and-peg steering box is notorious for developing wear and even when new had an inch or two of play at the wheel rim. Its Cam Gears replacement suffers similarly.

18. The 4-4 was upholstered in Rexine or leather, both of which are vulnerable to neglect and to the climate; a professional re-trim may be the only answer. Nowadays most people opt for leather, and as a rough guide the two-seater will require two hides and the four-seater four hides. Although black was the standard finish, any colour could be specified, so the cockpit of every Morgan was to a greater or lesser extent different.

19. If the radiator of a 'Flat Rad' Morgan has been damaged, it is extremely expensive to repair. Although it might not be apparent, the top part of the shell forms part of the header tank and if the core requires replacement every component part will have to be unsoldered to remove it. This is a time-consuming and skilled process and you're unlikely to receive much change from £2000 if you have this repair professionally undertaken.

lay with the four-wheelers and here a small but significant change was made to the specification. While the car was described as the 4-4 on its return to production, by the time that Morgan was displaying its wares at the 1948 London Motor Show, the first to be held since the ending of the war, the rendering in the event's catalogue was '4/4' – even if *The Autocar* continued to refer to the car as the '4-4'. However, '4/4' became the norm and the model has been so called ever since.

With the British motor industry now the focus of a government-directed export drive, an initiative which is more closely examined in the next chapter, in February 1947 Morgan announced that the first 4-4 to be exported was a drophead coupé that had been shipped to America on the *Queen Elizabeth*.

The cars were by now almost exclusively Standard-engined, just four post-war examples (all two-seaters) being Climax-powered. In all, 553 examples of the 4/4 were made post-war, of which 54 were chassis only, up until the moment when production ceased in February 1951, as will be recounted in the following chapter; this figure included 140 four-seaters and 106 dropheads. But this was far from the end for the 4/4 model, which was destined to reappear in 1955.

The Plus 4

A new face at the wheel. Peter Morgan, who arrived at Pickersleigh Road in 1947, and is seen here in the driving seat of a 4/4 four-seater, was responsible for the Plus 4 being powered by Standard's new four-cylinder wet-liner engine. (LAT)

The world in which Morgan resumed production after the war was very different from that which existed before the outbreak of hostilities. And although Britain and her allies were victorious, there was no post-war boom of the type that had followed the first conflict. Instead, government controls introduced during the war were maintained and there were shortages of materials. The era of red tape had arrived. More crucially, Britain needed to pay for the war – and this was to be achieved by gaining foreign currency through export sales. In truth the British motor industry had sold relatively few cars abroad in pre-war days and Dudley Noble, who had worked for both Rover and Rootes, spoke for many when he recalled that selling to overseas countries was then regarded as little more than 'a damned nuisance'.

A Labour government was elected by a landslide in 1945. Faced with an economy bankrupted by war, it decreed that steel supplies would be geared to export performance. With the world desperately in need of motor cars, and the German industry in particular ravaged by the years of war, Britain was well placed to meet this demand. It was one of the tragedies of the history of the British motor industry that this opportunity was missed and that by the mid-1950s Germany was once again buoyant – spearheaded by its Volkswagen, which was well on its way to becoming a world car. But there was one sector in which Britain excelled, and that was in the market for sports cars.

Before the war our industry was the world's largest manufacturer of open two-seaters, and these found a modest though appreciative market throughout the world. But in the post-war years America, in particular, began to respond with increasing enthusiasm to British sports cars. MG and Jaguar – as SS was renamed after the war – found ready sales in the US, and this also applied to Morgan. In fact the Malvern Link company had been more internationally minded than some of its contemporaries: of the 883 examples of the 4-4 produced between 1936 and 1939, no fewer than 121 – or 14 per cent of the total – had been sold abroad.

In retrospect it can be seen that this government-directed export drive was Morgan's salvation. Exports began in earnest at the beginning of the 1950s, and sales rose steadily to reach a point in 1960 when some 85 per cent of the company's production was crossing the Atlantic. Although this would in its turn produce an over-reliance on a single market, without this steady demand from the United States it seems more than likely that Morgan would have succumbed to market pressures as its products, certainly as far as British customers were concerned, became outdated in a highly competitive marketplace.

Morgan's success in the early post-war years was based on a new model which replaced the 4/4 for the 1951 model year, and which carried the Plus 4 name. Its introduction had little to do with Morgan, but rather was dictated by a shift in policy at Standard's factory in the Canley district of Coventry. After the Second World War Standard had reintroduced its 8hp, 12hp and 14hp models, but all ceased production in 1948. In addition

to directing car makers to export its products, the President of the Board of Trade, Sir Stafford Cripps, also exhorted Britain's car makers to adopt a one-model policy. He found a ready convert in Sir John Black, knighted in

1943 for his services to the war effort. As a result Black scrapped his pre-war range in the course of 1948 and replaced it with a single model, the all-new Vanguard saloon, which was powered by a 2088cc four-cylinder

Morgan Plus 4
1951–1958

ENGINE (Standard Vanguard):
Four cylinders in line, cast-iron block and cylinder head

Bore x stroke	85mm x 92mm
Capacity	2088cc
Valve actuation	Pushrod
Compression ratio	6.7:1
Carburettor	Single Solex DD
Power	68bhp at 4200rpm
Torque	112lb ft at 2300rpm

TRANSMISSION:
Rear wheel drive via torque tube to separate Moss four-speed gearbox with synchromesh on second, third and top gears; thereafter by open propshaft

SUSPENSION:
Front: Independent, sliding stub axles and coil springs with telescopic hydraulic dampers
Rear: Underslung live axle with half-elliptic springs; lever-arm hydraulic dampers

STEERING:
Cam Gears cam-and-peg

BRAKES:
Hydraulic drum, optional front discs from 1959

WHEELS/TYRES:
16in steel disc wheels; 5.25 x 16in tyres

BODYWORK:
Coachbuilt, with steel panels on ash frame
Separate Z-section chassis
Open two-seater, four-seater and drophead coupé

DIMENSIONS:

Length	11ft 10in
Wheelbase	8ft 0in
Track, front and rear	3ft 11in
Width	4ft 8in
Height	4ft 4½in

WEIGHT:
16.07cwt

PERFORMANCE:
(Source: *The Autocar*)

Max speed	85.5mph
0–50mph	11.3sec
0–60mph	17.9sec
0–70mph	28 sec

PRICE INCLUDING TAX WHEN NEW:
£652 (Two-seater, September 1950)

NUMBER BUILT:
799

Morgan Plus 4
(TR2 engine)
1954–1956

As Vanguard-engined except:

ENGINE:

Bore x stroke	83mm x 92mm
Capacity	1991cc
Valve actuation	Pushrod
Compression ratio	8.5:1
Carburettor	Twin SU
Power	90bhp at 4800rpm
Torque	115lb ft at 2600rpm

PERFORMANCE:
(Source: *The Autocar*)

Maximum speed	96.3mph
0–50mph	9.0sec
0–60mph	13.3sec
0–70mph	17.5sec

PRICE INCLUDING TAX WHEN NEW:
£830 (Two-seater, May 1954)

NUMBER BUILT:
344

Morgan Plus 4
(TR3 engine)
1956–1962

As TR2-engined, except:

ENGINE:

Carburettor	Twin SU HS6
Power	100bhp at 5000rpm
Torque	117lb ft at 3000rpm

BRAKES:
Front discs optional from 1959; standard from 1960

WHEELS/TYRES:
15in steel disc wheels from 1959, or optional wires
Tyres 5.60 x 15in

PERFORMANCE:
(Source: *The Motor*)

Maximum speed	101.1mph
0–50mph	6.8 sec
0–60mph	9.7 sec
0–70mph	13.3 sec

PRICE INCLUDING TAX WHEN NEW:
£1018 (Two-seater, January 1958)

NUMBER BUILT:
1808

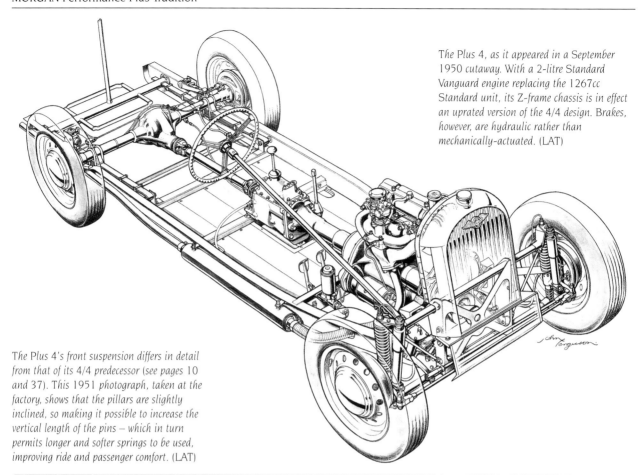

The Plus 4, as it appeared in a September 1950 cutaway. With a 2-litre Standard Vanguard engine replacing the 1267cc Standard unit, its Z-frame chassis is in effect an uprated version of the 4/4 design. Brakes, however, are hydraulic rather than mechanically-actuated. (LAT)

The Plus 4's front suspension differs in detail from that of its 4/4 predecessor (see pages 10 and 37). This 1951 photograph, taken at the factory, shows that the pillars are slightly inclined, so making it possible to increase the vertical length of the pins – which in turn permits longer and softer springs to be used, improving ride and passenger comfort. (LAT)

Morgan Plus 4
(TR4/4A engine)
1962–1969

As TR3-engined except:

ENGINE:
Bore x stroke	86mm x 92mm
Capacity	2138cc
Compression ratio	9:1
Carburettor	Twin SU HS6; from mid-1963 Stromberg 175CD
Power	100bhp at 4600rpm
	104bhp at 4700rpm
Torque	127lb ft at 3350rpm
	132lb ft at 3000rpm

PRICE INCLUDING TAX WHEN NEW:
£816 (Two-seater, May 1964)

NUMBER BUILT:
1582

Morgan Plus 4 Super Sports
1962–1968

As TR3/3A/4/4A except:

ENGINE:
Compression ratio	9:1
Carburettors	Twin 42 or 45 DCOE Weber
Power	115bhp at 5500rpm

BODYWORK:
Aluminium panels (except scuttle and radiator cowl) on ash frame

WEIGHT:
15.5 cwt

PERFORMANCE:
(Source: *The Autocar*)
Maximum speed	122mph
0–60mph	7.6 sec

PRICE INCLUDING TAX WHEN NEW:
£1118 (May 1964)

NUMBER BUILT:
101

Morgan Plus 4
(Fiat-engined)
1985–1987

As TR4A-engined except:

ENGINE:
Cast-iron block, alloy head	
Bore x stroke	84mm x 90mm
Capacity	1995cc
Valve actuation	Twin overhead camshaft
Compression ratio	9:1
Fuel injection	Bosch LE-Jetronic
Power	122bhp at 5300rpm
Torque	129lb ft at 3500rpm

TRANSMISSION:
Abarth five-speed all-synchromesh, in unit with engine

STEERING:
Gemmer recirculating ball

BRAKES:
Front: 11in disc
Rear: 9in drum

DIMENSIONS:
Length	12ft 9in
Wheelbase	8ft 0in
Track, front	3ft 11in
Track, rear	4ft 1in
Width	4ft 9in
Height	4ft 2in

BRAKES:
Front: 11in disc
Rear: 9in drum

WHEELS/TYRES:
195/60 x 15in

WEIGHT:
16.7 cwt

PRICE INCLUDING TAX WHEN NEW:
£11,082 (Two-seater, September 1986)

NUMBER BUILT:
125

Morgan Plus 4
(Rover M16 engine)
1988–1992

As Fiat-engined except:

ENGINE:
Bore x stroke	84.45mm x 89mm
Capacity	1994cc
Valve actuation	Twin overhead camshafts; 16 valves
Compression ratio	10.0:1
Fuel injection	Lucas L
Power	138bhp at 6000rpm
Torque	131lb ft at 4500rpm

TRANSMISSION:
Rover '77mm' five-speed all-synchromesh, in unit with engine

STEERING:
Jack Knight rack-and-pinion optional from 1991

WEIGHT:
16.7cwt

PRICE INCLUDING TAX WHEN NEW:
£17,037 (Two-seater, August 1990)

NUMBER BUILT:
357

Morgan Plus 4
(Rover T16 engine)
1992–2000

As M16-engined except:

ENGINE:
Power	134bhp at 6000rpm

TRANSMISSION:
From 1994, Rover R380 five-speed gearbox

BODYWORK:
Aluminium panels from 1998

PRICE INCLUDING TAX WHEN NEW:
£19,152 (Two-seater, October 1993)

NUMBER BUILT:
[approx 500 to end of 1996]

---

engine. As it happened, in the short term there were plenty of 1.2-litre Standard engines left for Morgan, but it could only be a matter of time before supplies were exhausted. In retrospect it might seem obvious that Morgan would replace one Standard engine with another, but in reality the process proved to be more protracted.

In 1947 HFS Morgan's son Peter had joined the business, and one of his first assignments was to investigate alternatives to the soon-to-be-discontinued unit. He approached General Motors to no effect and was politely rebuffed by Austin when he inquired about the availability of its new A40 engine. In truth, Standard's Vanguard 'four' proved to be ideal for Morgan's needs although 'HFS' took some convincing. He had grown up in the shadow of the horsepower tax (see pages 13) and was apprehensive that the new engine, with its 85mm bore, would be unduly penalised. In fact on 1 January 1948 the old tax was replaced, as a spur to the export drive, by a flat-rate scheme.

Morgan at this time was still losing money. In 1949 it recorded a deficit of £1551, which was reduced to £618 in 1950 before sinking further, to £2683, in 1952. But the company moved back

A drophead coupé Plus 4, as road-tested by The Autocar in April 1951. It was possible to run the car with the hood partially raised in the so-called coupe-de-ville position. (LAT)

The lines of the drophead version of the Plus 4 are essentially similar to those of its 4/4 predecessor – although it is higher and wider. As before, the doors are hinged at the B-post, unlike those of the open cars which are forward-hinged. (LAT)

This hinged flap was offered as an optional extra on the drophead, to permit the storage of extra luggage. (LAT)

into the black in 1953 with a surplus of £543, thanks to the success of the Plus 4, announced in September 1950.

As the new engine was of a larger capacity and of greater power and weight than its predecessor, the Plus 4 had demanded some rethinking of the 4/4 concept. The wheelbase was increased from 7ft 8in to 8ft while overall width, at 4ft 8in, was one inch greater than on the 4/4. The chassis was also stiffened, the five channel-section crossmembers being replaced by more robust box sections. The bulkhead was also reinforced.

Morgan also took the opportunity to make improvements to the long-running independent front

40 years at the helm

Peter Morgan, born on 3 November 1919, joined Morgan in 1947 and was its chairman from 1959 until his death in 2003 – although in 1999, at the age of 80, he passed operational responsibilities to his son Charles.

Peter Henry Geoffrey Morgan, or 'PM', as he was known, was born in Chestnut Villa, the house next to his father's original factory in Worcester Road, Malvern Link. He was educated at Oundle and between 1937 and 1940 he successfully studied for a BSc degree in automotive engineering at Chelsea College of Automobile and Aero Engineering. Wanting to join the Royal Navy but unable to do so because of his eyesight, he went instead to the Royal Army Service Corps and was demobbed with the rank of Captain.

On joining the family business in 1947 as production engineer, Peter Morgan's first assignment was to recommend an engine to replace the Standard Special unit then powering the 4/4. His choice of the Vanguard engine, destined to evolve into the long-running TR unit, proved to be a good decision, as did most of his ensuing ones. Appointed deputy governing director to his father in 1951, he thereafter worked closely with him and became Morgan's chairman following the death of 'HFS' in 1959.

Cautious and fiscally prudent, as his father, he skilfully steered the company through the turbulent waters of the 1960s, when Morgan's products began to appear increasingly dated. He successfully

Peter Morgan (right), the architect of Morgan's post-war survival, who took over full control of the company on his father's death in 1959 and remained at the helm until his own demise in 2003. This photograph was taken at the dinner following the Birmingham Post Rally, organised by the Midland Automobile Club, in September 1953. He is receiving the MAC Challenge Cup from the newspaper's managing director, EM Clayson, for putting up 'Best Performance' in the event. (LAT)

reduced the company's dependence on the American market, soon to be bedevilled with safety and emissions legislation, and shifted the emphasis to European and home sales.

His Plus 4 Plus glassfibre coupé of 1963 was judged a failure but, perversely, it focused attention on the unique if dated appeal of Morgan's mainstream products. During that all-important decade Peter Morgan's

greatest achievement was the creation of the V8-powered Plus 8 of 1968. It was destined to be the longest-running model in the company's history, enjoying a 36-year life.

On a corporate front, Peter Morgan oversaw the restructuring of the Morgan Motor Company during the period between 1962 and 1970, in a series of protracted legal wrangles which finally saw him buy out his two sisters, thus securing the company's future.

The criticisms in 1990 by Sir John Harvey-Jones, in a well-publicised TV programme, highlighted the company's archaic production methods. But Peter Morgan rode out the controversy, thanks to the overwhelming support of Morgan owners and enthusiasts.

Although son Charles Morgan took over the day-to-day running of Morgan from 1999, his father continued to chair board meetings and was a regular visitor to the Pickersleigh Road factory until only a few days before his death on 20 October 2003 at the age of 83.

HFS Morgan is buried in the family plot in the churchyard of St Peter and St Paul, Stoke Lacy. (Author's collection)

suspension. The swivels were now slightly inclined upwards so it was possible to increase the vertical length of the kingpins, which permitted the use of longer and softer springs. Suspension comfort was thereby improved, although it remained traditionally unforgiving. In addition, the sliding sleeves of the swivels were now lubricated with engine oil, the

driver being required to activate a foot pedal every 200 miles. Girling telescopic dampers were used at the front, with piston-type lever-arm units replacing the 4/4's friction dampers at the rear. The steering was also uprated, a more robust Cam Gears cam-and-peg unit being specified.

The Plus 4's layout, with the gearbox separate, followed that of the 4/4. The

2088cc engine was essentially the same 68bhp unit as that used in the Standard Vanguard; the only minor difference was that it was mounted sloping to the rear, which meant that a different flange was required for the single Solex DD carburettor, to keep it upright.

Mechanical brakes were rapidly becoming a thing of the past, so the

A 1954 *Flat Rad drophead coupé. The independent front suspension was exposed to view before the arrival of the cowled radiator.* (LAT)

Plus 4 used full Girling hydraulics. At 5.25in, the Dunlop tyres, meanwhile, were wider than previously although the wheels were slightly smaller in diameter, being 16in pierced discs, as used on the 4/4 drophead, rather than the 17in rims of the open models. These ministrations produced a car which looked rather sturdier than its

predecessor, not only on account of its elongated and wider body but also because of the longer bonnet and higher radiator.

Morgan also took the opportunity to modernise the instrument panel. It will be remembered that the 4/4 had glove pockets on either side of the dashboard, with the black-on-cream

Unlike the open cars, which were usually powered by twin-carb TR engines, the dropheads invariably retained the less potent Vanguard unit. (LAT)

On this car the Plus 4 badge is duplicated on the spare-wheel strap. (LAT)

instruments in their central panel comprising a 100mph speedometer flanked by two smaller dual-function auxiliary gauges. For the Plus 4 in came an oval panel finished in black-crackle paint and containing just two gauges, a 110mph speedometer with integral clock, directly in front of the driver, and a matching combination dial for fuel, oil pressure, water temperature and electrics.

Launched at the 1950 Motor Show, the two-seaters, available in open and drophead coupé forms, sold for £652 and £722 respectively, which was £96 and £89 more than their 4/4 predecessors. These two models were joined for 1953 by an open four-seater.

As might be expected, acceleration was a great improvement on that of the 4/4. Although at 15.75cwt it was 1.75cwt heavier, the Plus 4's greater engine power immediately showed its worth, with *The Autocar* recording a 0–60mph time of 17.9secs and a top speed of 85mph. These figures were in fact obtained with the heavier

The coupé's driving compartment. In contrast to the 4/4, the Plus 4 only has a single glove compartment, for the benefit of the passenger. (LAT)

This curiosity was built in 1953 by Coach Bodies of Western Lane, Nightingale Lane, London SW12. A four-seater Plus 4, with a luggage locker at the rear, it would be interesting to know whether any more were made. (LAT)

Halfway house: a 1954 model-year Plus 4 with the new inclined partially-cowled radiator with an apron concealing the front suspension. Initially the headlamps were lower, but they were raised for new lighting regulations that came into force at the beginning of 1954. The definitive cowled radiator arrived in June of that year. (LAT)

This Plus 4, now sporting its new cowled radiator, was road tested by The Autocar early in 1954: it attained 102mph. (LAT)

drophead, and the magazine was clearly impressed with the Morgan's performance: 'Above all...it *goes*, in the full sense of the phrase. It gets up very quickly indeed to 65mph and does not want much road to see 70 to 75mph', it wrote. As as far as handling was concerned, 'rock-firm stability ensures remarkable liberties can be taken in fast cornering, with enterprising handling methods tyre squeal can be produced even with pressures recommended for fast driving.' To this was allied good tractability and fuel consumption, the magazine returning an overall consumption of 26mpg. On the debit side, the test found that 'the suspension was firm to the point of harshness over some kinds of surfaces', there was 'a good deal of mechanical noise when the car is driven hard', and the Plus 4 was deemed 'relatively stark with regards of one or two items of equipment which have come to be regarded as normal these days'.

Whatever the car's vices and virtues, it had an unashamedly pre-war look, especially from the front. This was addressed by the factory, and the Plus 4 given a new face for the 1953 London Motor Show. The modifications were effected, as Peter Morgan explained in later years, for two reasons. The principal one was that electrical supplier Lucas informed the company that it could no longer afford to produce the separate headlights for Morgan, which by then was its only customer: the motor industry had been recessing headlights into the front wings since the 1930s and the practice had by then become the norm. Secondly, from a visual standpoint the company was well aware that the exposed front suspension and its attendant crossmember were difficult to keep clean. As a result, the front

'Unfamiliar frontal treatment has now submerged the Morgan radiator . . . in keeping with the modern trend', commented The Autocar in May 1954. The new radiator and integral headlamps have produced the definitive Morgan front end which endures to this day. The Lucas Flame Thrower spot lamp is not a standard fitment.

Rear view (left) of the '54 test car. The twin spare wheels, a pre-war inheritance, endured until 1955, while the centrally-located petrol filler survived until 1958. (Both LAT)

A Morgan by Milan, out of Sunbuy-on-Thames

Roy Clarkson, one of Britain's more successful rally drivers of the early 1950s, wanted a British car to enter in the Monte Carlo Rally, held every January when the winter weather was usually at its worst. He was attracted to the Plus 4 but it was only available in open form. However, he already owned a magnificent Ferrari 212 Inter with a coupé body by Touring of Milan. On being supplied in 1952 with a Plus 4 chassis by Peter Morgan, Clarkson commissioned a coachbuilder, Adams and Robinson of Sunbury-on-Thames, Surrey, to produce a closed body inspired by his Ferrari. Crucially, it had to be ready in time for the '53 Monte.

Coincidentally, racing driver Philip Fotheringham-Parker had a similar objective, although he opted for a Jowett Jupiter chassis. Work on both cars was undertaken by Charlie Robinson, an accomplished panelbeater who had learnt his trade in the aircraft industry. But Jowett began to experience financial problems, so resources were concentrated on the Morgan (For the record the Jupiter was not finally finished until 1957!). To have the Plus 4 completed in time

for the Monte, Maurice Gomm, who had previously built two Jupiter saloons for Beverley Motors at nearby New Malden, was recruited to help.

Although Clarkson managed to reach his Munich starting point, he soon retired. However, the Plus 4, memorably registered VNO 600, became a familiar sight in British rallies and Clarkson, with CC Wells as co-driver, attained a creditable second place, at a speed of 64.94mph, in the Motor Cycling Club's National

'No, not a Ferrari!', said The Autocar in its caption. Roy Clarkson in his special-bodied Plus 4 about to leave Lampeter in the Motor Cycling Club's 1953 rally – when he was placed second. (LAT)

Rally of November 1953.

Peter Morgan remembered the results of this unlikely union of a traditional Morgan chassis with coachwork inspired by the latest Italian styling as 'very pretty'. But the production Plus 4 coachwork stayed as it was, all the same . . .

end looked, in Peter Morgan's eyes, rather 'tatty'.

In the event the changes to the front of the car, to reach the definitive style continued to this day, were effected in two unplanned stages. The first stage was the design seen at the 1953 show, which was introduced in December 1953 – although the last of the so-called 'flat rad' models was not completed until June 1954. Having said that, some of these final Plus 4s were retrospectively updated by the factory. For 1954, therefore, the radiator now had a separate core, complete with underbonnet filler, and was fronted by a flat multi-slatted chromium grille set into a curved painted-metal cowl. The front wings were redesigned to embrace the area

between the wheels and the cowl and to hide the hitherto exposed front suspension. As for the headlamps, these were now recessed into cannister-like pods mounted low in the wings just above the front bumper.

These changes significantly altered the model's appearance. However, the new look was destined to last barely six months. One reason was that Morgan had been unaware that new lighting regulations were due to come into force on 1 January 1954, and would require higher-positioned headlamps. Another was that the reworked front end was stylistically uneasy, and a dissatisfied Peter Morgan succeeded in convincing his father of the need for a further redesign. From March 1954, therefore,

the cars were given the distinctive front end with its deep cowl, high-set headlamps and curved-slat radiator grille that effectively endures to this day. A mere 19 cars were fitted with the interim cowl, and the majority of these were retrospectively updated, although two do survive in their original form.

These changes coincided with the arrival of a modified engine. The Vanguard-derived 1991cc Triumph TR2 unit had first appeared on the Plus 4 in December 1953, during the time of the 'interim cowl' model, and the new power unit transformed the Morgan into a 95mph car. It added £20 to the price of the Plus 4; the Vanguard engine continued to be offered until 1958 and was standard wear in the

Interior of the The Autocar's *road-test car. The dished steering wheel was to be replaced by a flat one on an extended column.* (LAT)

A four-seater Plus 4 *photographed in August 1954. Unlike the two-seater, this version was only provided with a single spare wheel.* (Author's collection)

more staid drophead model unless the owner specified otherwise.

The arrival of the Triumph TR2 was a reflection of the fact that Sir John Black had failed in his attempt to acquire Morgan. He had approached Peter Morgan to this end at the 1950 Motor Show, and the offer had been considered by the Morgan board but politely and firmly rejected. Black therefore decided that to benefit from lucrative sales in America he would develop Triumph as his company's sports car line; the result, after a crash development programme, was the TR2 of 1953 – first of a long and famous line.

With twin SU carburettors, the 90bhp Triumph engine, aided by Morgan fitting a close-ratio gearbox, gave the Plus 4 strong acceleration, 60mph arriving in a respectable 12 seconds. In its test *The Autocar* found that the new engine transformed the Morgan 'from a lively sporting car to a definitely potent machine'. The car's 'extraordinary performance', wrote the magazine, was 'proof that the ingredients are right'. However, it recognised that the brakes required a considerable amount of pressure to bring the Plus 4 to a halt.

A further arrival in 1954 was a four-seater version of the drophead. Prototypes had appeared in September 1951 and September 1953 and although the model looked similar at the front to the well-established two-seater version, it differed significantly at the rear. This was because the two additional seats at the back meant that there was only a narrow slot-like boot containing the spare wheel. In consequence there was not much room for luggage.

A 1957 two-seater Plus 4 powered by the 95bhp TR engine; the model was also available with the 68bhp Vanguard unit. (LAT)

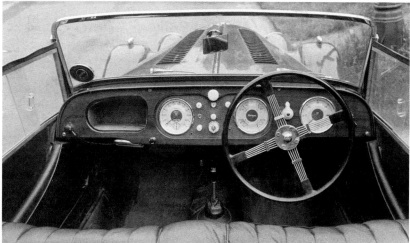

The presence of a rev-counter on the right-hand side of the dashboard indicates the fitment of a TR engine. This instrument panel was used between 1957 and 1960; in 1961 the white toggle switches were replaced by black ones. (LAT)

Unsurprisingly, there was a limited demand for the model, and only 51 had been built by the time the last example was completed in February 1956; of these, 29 cars, all Vanguard-engined, were sold to British customers. Those dispatched abroad were TR2-powered, and the largest overseas customer was the US, which took 18 cars. The balance went to Spain, which took two, and Belgium and Australia, which took one apiece.

When Triumph's TR3 arrived for 1956, Morgan began to offer its uprated 100bhp engine as an option at the end of 1955 – although the TR2 unit continued until October 1957, when stocks were exhausted. Outwardly the Plus 4 was unchanged, although under the bonnet the larger carburettors and manifolding indicated the presence of the improved engine, which pushed the Morgan's top speed to beyond 100mph for the first time.

The 1956 season also saw the rear of the Plus 4 undergo some revision when the second spare wheel, a feature since the 4-4's 1936 introduction, was deleted. The remaining wheel was recessed at an angle within a well in the revised sloping tail. This change was prompted by the fact that the back springs, which slid in trunnions at their rear ends, another 4-4 inheritance, were revised to replace them with conventional shackles. This in turn meant the removal of the trunnion tube which did double duty as the spare-wheel support.

Modest changes continued. Another pre-war inheritance, the fold-flat windscreen, was discontinued for 1957, while the 1958 season saw the arrival of an optional cowl, about 1in lower than the norm, for the open two-seater. There were few takers and the lowline cowl only lasted for about a year.

When in January 1958 The Motor published its road test of a Plus 4 it underlined the fact that, at £969, it was still the cheapest 100mph car made in Britain. The Morgan was found to have handling that was above average for its class and through-the-gears acceleration up to 80mph that was a match for competitors costing up to double the Plus 4's price. In fact that car in question, registered TUY 875, was fitted with optional wire wheels, which brought the price up to £1017.

'To many a driver accustomed to modern comforts, first impressions of the Morgan will inevitably be of rather spartan simplicity, a view that may not be finally abandoned until he embarks upon a journey prepared for the pure fun of driving', commented the magazine. On the plus side, the report continued, this was a 'very British sports car, . . . [and] needs a very exceptional British road to throw it off balance. Stiffly sprung and firmly damped, its roadholding is outstanding and it remains one of the very, very few vehicles (including cars built for racing) which corner with *no* appreciable roll'.

The writer also applauded the Morgan for its acceleration and noted that the 6.8 seconds it took the car to

A four-seater Plus 4 with the hood down, photographed by The Motor *in October 1958. It was then that this version's front seats were widened by 2in. They could now be moved fore and aft. (LAT)*

reach 50mph 'has been beaten only by two sports racing cars, of 3.5 and 5.5 litres respectively'. Bearing in mind the Plus 4's no-nonsense character, it comes as no surprise to find that the tester also found the Plus 4 a noisy car. This was mainly on account of the fact that the Triumph engine's twin SUs lacked their air cleaners because of the Morgan's narrow bonnet. Beyond this, reverberations were transmitted through the bulkhead, and the gearbox whined in the indirect ratios and in reverse, while with the hood and sidescreens in place there was plenty of noise from wind buffeting.

The magazine summed up the appeal of the Morgan thus: 'Taken as a whole, minor criticisms of the Plus 4 might appear rather forbidding: in detail it undoubtedly lacks some of the refinement of the mass-produced saloon of today. To this the complete answer is that a relatively small body of motoring enthusiasts are still prepared to exchange central-heated luxury for driving that is fun and, incidentally, fast'. Fairer than that cannot be said.

Further changes to the Plus 4 body were introduced for 1959. In particular

A left-hand-drive Plus 4 drophead coupé with front disc brakes and wire wheels. A Morgan publicity photograph of September 1961, it shows the deeper windscreen which arrived for the 1962 season. (LAT)

the rear deck of the two-seater and drophead was made more sloping and the petrol filler cap moved from the centre to the nearside, where it was matched on the offside by a chromed 'Morgan' badge. Alterations were also made to the wings, which became slightly narrower. The four-seat tourer, finally, was enhanced by adjustable seats that were also widened by 2in.

In May 1959 Girling front disc brakes were offered as an extra at a cost of £42 10s (£42.50). They were at first only fitted to cars shod with the optional wire wheels, then priced at an additional £32.10s (£35.50), but for 1960 disc brakes could be ordered for cars with standard pierced disc wheels. Also in May 1959 the long-

running 16in wheels were replaced by 15in rims shod with 5.60 x 15 tyres. This change was adopted because at this time the majority of Morgans were being sold in America, where 16in wheels were becoming something of a rarity, which made tyre and tube replacement difficult.

Morgan was due to celebrate its 50th anniversary in 1960 but sadly its founder was destined to miss the celebrations, HFS Morgan having died in June 1959 at the age of 78. 'Looking

What the other drivers saw: a 1964 Plus 4. The 'Morgan' script was added to the rear deck of the Plus 4 in 1958, it being balanced with the petrol filler on the opposite side. (LAT)

back through the years, seeing both errors and triumphs in their current perspective, I feel I have enjoyed it all – so far as I am concerned, a most interesting business', he had said, just nine years before, in the course of his reminiscences in *The Light Car*: His son Peter, who had taken over as managing director following the demise of George Goodall in 1958, therefore became chairman. Peter Morgan was to remain at the helm until his death in 2003, although in 1999 – at the age of 80 – he handed over the day-to-day running of the business to his son Charles.

This is therefore an appropriate moment to pause to consider the Plus 4 in the context of its contemporaries. While the evolution of the TR range has been referred to, this was a market dominated by MG. The MGA had in 1955 replaced the archaic T-type line that was stylistically contemporary with the 4-4. With over 100,000 ultimately built, the 'A' was to become the most popular sports car in the world by the time that it ceased production in 1962. It would be replaced by the MGB, which would

The 1964 Plus 4's instrument panel. The white-on-black instrument faces arrived in June 1962. (LAT)

The TR4 engine was standardised from mid-1962 although for a time the TR3 unit could be specified. This example is fitted with twin Strombergs, as opposed to SUs; the line of the Plus 4's bonnet prevented the use of air filters. (LAT)

First of the Super Sports line, Chris Lawrence's famous TOK 258 – this being a registration which dates from 1956. When used in competition the front bumper was invariably removed and a numberplate stuck to the front wing. Note the functional scoop in the bonnet, revealing the presence of a pair of Weber carburettors. (LAT)

A cockpit that clearly means business. TOK 258's instrument panel, with a rev-counter added directly in front of the driver. (LAT)

be even more successful. Also looking for a share of the lucrative American sports-car market was Rootes, which in 1959 had introduced its Alpine two-seater. Whilst Austin-Healey (latterly) and Jaguar were both six-cylinder cars and out of Morgan's league, they did nevertheless feature modern full-width coachwork, as did all of their contemporaries. This contrasted with Morgan's pre-war lines which remained ever-faithful to separate wings and running-boards. So much for the rival British sports cars. But in 1959 the British Motor Corporation had produced its revolutionary front-wheel-drive Mini. Although the Mini was far from a performance car, in September 1961

TOK 258's twin DCOE 42 Webers which feed the Super Sport's Lawrencetune engine. In 1962 this developed 128bhp, endowing the car with a top speed of 130mph. (LAT)

BMC launched the more potent Mini-Cooper, which was destined for a distinguished rallying career.

What all this amounted to was that with the arrival of the so-called Swinging Sixties the Morgan was beginning to appear positively antiquated. Yet within five years the company would experience so significant a transformation in its fortunes that by 1965 *Autocar* sports editor and former Morgan three-wheeler owner Peter Garnier would report that 'the Morgan cult is still growing . . . .[and] demand for Morgans is now outstripping supply'.

From 1964 the Super Sports was fitted with the lower body lines of Lawrence's Le Mans car. This example is owned by Morgan authority John Worrall. (LAT)

The tail of the Worrall Super Sports. The spare wheel cover, which matches the hood, is a period extra. (LAT)

Opposite: When the Plus 4 was revived in 1985, it closely resembled the 4/4 although it was 1in wider than previously, to accommodate its centre-laced wire wheels with their earless spinners. Under the bonnet was a 2-litre Fiat twin-cam engine. (LAT)

Passenger's view of the Fiat twin-cam, which endowed the revived model with a top speed approaching the 110mph mark. (LAT)

It is to Peter Morgan's great credit that he steered the company through these choppy waters in a period that saw its dependence on the American market diminish. In its place came a gradual switch in emphasis to the requirements of the Old World, in other words the home market and Europe.

Just one factor in this remarkable renaissance was the announcement at the 1960 Earls Court Motor Show of the Plus 4 Super Sports – reviving a famous three-wheeler name. A tuned, competition version of the Plus 4, it was a reflection of the impact that Chris Lawrence was making in the Morgan world. As chronicled in Chapter Nine, Lawrence's successes had begun in 1959 and would be further underpinned by his outstanding class victory at Le Mans in 1962.

The essentials of the conversion were a tuned engine and aluminium bodywork, which respectively cost £120 and £30 plus purchase tax. Work on the Super Sports engine was undertaken at the workshops of Lawrence's Westerham Motors, his Acton-based tuning business. There the engine was stripped and the crankshaft, connecting rods, flywheel and clutch balanced by Jack Brabham Ltd. The combustion chambers and ports were polished, a special camshaft was fitted and the twin SU carburettors replaced by two Weber DCOE 45s with trumpet intakes. The side-mounted Webers meant that it was possible to lower the bonnet line, but they also required their own air scoop, mounted on the offside. A new exhaust system also featured, and the resulting engine developed 116bhp, against 100bhp for the regular Plus 4's production TR engine; an oil cooler could be supplied if required. Finally, wide-rimmed 72-spoke wire wheels were fitted.

The cockpit of the Fiat-engined Plus 4 is essentially the same as that used on its 4/4 contemporary. (LAT)

The 'Sports' alloy body (with steel bulkhead and radiator cowl) was not only lighter but also lower, to the benefit of drag. Indeed, it had more in common with the 4/4, whose smaller Ford engine took up less space under the bonnet. The 'lowline' body also entailed the fitment of a smaller radiator, and to lessen the risk of overheating, a separate header tank was mounted on the bulkhead. More outwardly obvious was the large rev-counter mounted immediately in front of the driver; it was also possible to specify a wood-rimmed three-spoke alloy steering wheel.

The first Super Sports, chassis 4749, was delivered in March 1961. Between then and May 1968, when the last example – chassis 6656 – was completed, a total of 101 were made. All were two-seaters, with the exception of a single four-seater built in 1966.

The 2138cc TR4 engine, developing 100bhp, became an option on the Plus 4 from February 1961, and was standardised in June 1962; in 1965 it gave way to the TR4A engine, which was changed only in detail but had a slightly higher 104bhp output. Super Sports from mid-1962 thus had a 2138cc engine, unless the owner wanted a 1991cc unit in order to compete in the up to 2-litre class in motor racing; in Lawrencetune form

A 1985 Fiat-engined Plus 4 keeps company with a 1939 Le Mans Replica. Both cars share the same Z-frame chassis and the essentials of the sliding-pillar independent front suspension. (LAT)

the bigger engine developed 125bhp.

There was also an intermediary line, which slotted in between the Super Sports and the production Plus 4. This was the Competition model, introduced in October 1965. This shared the same body as the Super Sports, but all the panels were of steel rather than aluminium and the wire wheels were 60-spoke, rather than 72-spoke as on the Super Sports. Engine modifications were less radical, with power being only mildly boosted, by fitment of a four-branch Derrington exhaust system. Armstrong Selectaride

rear dampers, adjustable from the cockpit, were the only other modification. At £938 the Competition cost £97 more than the basic Plus 4 but £211 less than the Super Sports. It did not prove to be a great success, and just 42 were made in the 18 months between October 1965 and April 1967.

In 1967 Triumph introduced its new TR5 sports car, powered by a six-cylinder 2.5-litre engine. This heralded the end of the Vanguard-based 'four', and led to the V8-powered Plus 8 replacing the Plus 4. Accordingly the last Plus 4 four-seater was produced in November 1968, the last two-seater in December and the final drophead coupé, by then a pre-war anachronism, in January 1969.

Thanks mainly to the demands of the American market, the Plus 4 had proved to be the most successful Morgan to date, with 4584 TR-engined cars being built – 344 with the TR2 unit, 1808 with the TR3/3A unit, 1582 with the TR4/4A engine, and 101 of the Super Sports. The Plus 8 would soon move centre stage, but this was far from being the end of the Plus 4 – although 17 years would elapse before

Driving a cowled-rad Plus 4

In a way the TR-powered Plus 4 is the most harmonious of Morgans. It has the modernity of a reasonably up-to-the-minute power unit, yet one that has the ruggedness of a vintage-era 'big four', to the point where it marries perfectly with the car's otherwise pre-war characteristics.

There's torque a-plenty, a strong 100mph performance, and none of the engine's workings sound-deadened away. Add the deliberate Moss gearbox, with its less than wonderful synchromesh, the firm clutch and brake actions, and the steering that demands an effort but is rewardingly precise, and you have

a deliciously rounded drivetrain: all the inputs seem so well matched, although none of them could ever be described as delicate.

Chassis behaviour is of a piece. The handling on smooth roads is nicely neutral, controllability is first-rate, roll is totally absent…and the pay-off is an unyielding suspension once the going gets rough. Compared to a contemporary such as an MGA, the Morgan seems rough but big-hearted, with a stripped-down honesty. Morgan enthusiasts would look at the MG and pronounce it effete. That's the Morgan difference . . .

A 1987 Rover-engined Plus 4 with distinctive wheels and matching trim and body piping. (LAT)

the model reappeared.

As recorded in the following chapter, in 1981 Morgan began to offer the Fiat 1.6-litre twin-cam engine in the 4/4, to replace the Ford unit, and in March 1985 it announced a revived Plus 4 powered by the 2-litre fuel-injected version of the Fiat engine, and its matching five-speed gearbox, as used in the recently-discontinued Fiat Argenta saloon. By all accounts Morgan had contemplated the Saab 2-litre unit and the smaller-capacity BMW 'sixes' before making its final choice; the result was a car that neatly plugged the gap between the 1.6-litre 4/4 and the then 3.5-litre Plus 8.

Although relying on the 4/4 chassis with its 96in wheelbase, the new Plus 4's bodies, in two-seater and four-

Driving a Super Sports Plus 4

The Super Sports shows what sensitive honing can do to the Morgan. With a power increase that is not too extreme, the 125bhp 'big four' keeps its low-down sloggability while gaining in responsiveness, high-revs zing, and smoothness – the engines were balanced, remember, and that's always a big help. Try a Super Sports with Spax telescopic dampers at the rear, as on some special-order cars, and you'll have a further surprise: the ride smooths

out and the car is less thrown off course on bumpy roads. Dial in the excellent behaviour on smooth roads and the robust Moss gearbox – which is far less of a chore than legend has it – and you have a beguiling big-hearted sports car. That's food for thought, if you have a standard-spec TR-powered Plus 4: the Super Sports shows how much potential the regular car has, and how easily it can be extracted. A little bit of judicious tuning goes a long way.

seater forms, were slightly wider than their predecessors on account of the use of 6in-wide Cobra wire wheels. These were shod with low-profile Avon 195/60 VR 15 Turbospeed tyres, for which a bespoke inner tube had been developed, radial tyres

(generally of course tubeless) and wire wheels being an unusual combination. Outwardly the wings were initially cut down Plus 8 items. By this time the suspension had softened somewhat when compared with 1968 standards, and there were now five-

Driving an early Rover-powered Plus 4

The M16-powered Plus 4 is an intriguing marriage of the ancient and the modern – but also a reminder that Morgan will always be constrained by its policy – an eminently sensible one – of buying mainstream power units more generally found in mundane saloons.

Thus the M16, while willing and giving a strong performance, never feels as if it's a sports car engine; it's too smooth by half. Mind you, such questions become academic once you've reached 70mph or so, as the engine is drowned by wind noise and the rattling of the sidescreens.

The SD1-derived gearbox is its usual self: notchy but precise, and operating via a heavyish clutch actuated by Morgan's traditional and very vintage floor-pivoted pedal. Together with the board-hard short-travel brakes, this means the messages your feet are receiving are from another era from those your ears pick up listening to that smooth 16-valve saloon-car engine.

Also on the modern side of the equation is the Gemmer steering, which is quick, well-weighted and fluid – a definite improvement on earlier set-ups. The rack-steered cars,

all, the same, have a dose more precision.

For the rest, one knows what to expect: the arms-bent close-to-the-wheel driving position, the good adhesion on smooth roads and the waywardness on poor ones, the rock-hard ride. But if fast driving on badly-surfaced roads is a scuttle-shaking bone-jarring struggle, that discreet but torquey M16 incites you to back off a bit and settle back. That way you can appreciate the Plus 4's old-world charm – something that would be lacking if all its old-world faults had been antisepticised out of existence.

leaf rather than six-leaf rear springs. Another change was that the Cam Gears cam-and-peg steering box, a feature of the original Plus 4, was replaced by the French-sourced Gemmer recirculating-ball assembly also used on 4/4.

As before, the Plus 4 was available in two-seater and four-seater versions, at £10,901 and £11,711 respectively.

While the car was capable of over 110mph, the lack of aerodynamic efficiency preventing anything more, a 0–60mph time of 8.8 seconds was respectable enough.

The Fiat-engined Plus 4 survived until 1987, when gearbox supplies dried up. By then 122 examples had been completed and although Charles Morgan looked abroad and Fiat for

The instrument panel of this '87 Plus 4 is essentially the same as that used on the 4/4. (LAT)

one was visited, eventually the company turned to Rover, already supplying its V8, for a replacement power unit. Morgan opted for the 2-litre M16 twin-cam used for Rover's front-wheel-drive 820 saloon. To

Quality: it's better today

The frames of a modern-day Morgan are constructed from ash grown in managed forests in Lincolnshire. But before 1986, after which timber of all cars was treated with Cuprosol wood preservative, some frames began to suffer from wet rot by the time the cars had covered as little as 25,000 miles – and that could have been when the vehicle was only five to six years old.

An interesting aside is that in the 1950s and 1960s the frames for Morgan bodies were made from ash imported from Belgium. The trees grew on the sites of some First World War battlefields, and it was not uncommon for the wood to come complete with fragments of metal ordnance. Should you think that this is an urban myth, Morgan specialist George Proudfoot has some pieces of timber on his desk, complete with .303 rounds embedded in the grain!

The year 1986 was also significant because after that date the wings were sprayed off the car, which helped prolong body life. Previously the bodies were painted after the wings had been attached, with the beading in place, so trapping in moisture and providing an ideal environment for rust to take hold. There was also a change of paint, with the cracking-prone ICI cellulose replaced that October by a more flexible acrylic paint from the same manufacturer.

On the subject of paintwork, early examples of the Plus 4 were finished with coach paint, although in 1953 this was replaced with cellulose. The reason you need to know which is which will only occur if you need to re-spray a section of bodywork. The two finishes do not mix and if this inadvertently occurs it can produce some undesirable bubbling. Should you be in doubt, find an unobtrusive area of bodywork and apply a rag dipped in cellulose thinners. If the paint comes off on the rag, then you know you've got cellulose.

The chassis was another important beneficiary of the 1986 changes. Before that date they went unprotected, which is why today some are very badly rusted, but from 1986 they were powder-coated or galvanised. The latter process is, however, vulnerable to chassis flexing. A further all-important chassis date is December 1991, when the Plus 4 adopted the Plus 8's wider frame.

Buying Hints

These should be read in conjunction with the Buying Hints relating to the 4-4, on pages 48–49. This is because, in essence, the Plus 4's body and chassis construction was carried over from the earlier design.

1. Starting with the bodywork, you need to know whether the car is panelled in steel or aluminium. The latter applies to the Super Sports of 1961–1968, and to 'revival' Plus 4s from 1998 onwards.

2. From 1953 the Plus 4's headlamps were integrated in pods that were then welded to the wings. The joints can rust and separate, so check for signs of this happening, or attempts to disguise the fact with filler – although be warned that the presence of the latter can date from the car's manufacture!

3. The front suspension should be lubricated from the cockpit every 200 miles. If a driver has been over-exuberant in this regard, there'll be oil all over the brakes.

4. The steering damper mountings wear. This component, which is made of flat spring steel, is fixed to the chassis at one end and attached to the suspension, via a phosphor-bronze bush, at the other. It is intended to prevent any twisting motion set up by the springs when under compression being transmitted to the stub axles, to the detriment of the steering.

5. The wet-liner Standard/Triumph engines of the 1950–1969 era are remarkably reliable and can easily exceed 100,000 miles without overhaul. For this reason and because of the number built – some 4500 cars – this generation of cars represents an attractive proposition, as spares availability is encouraging, thanks to the good offices of the TR Register and a number of Triumph specialists. Parts for the Standard Vanguard unit are however rather more difficult to source. The only real weak point on these engines is a leaking rear oil seal although fortunately oil seldom seems to reach the clutch. The front seal is similarly vulnerable. Ideally engine oil pressure should be 40psi at 2000rpm, athough examples have been known to run happily at 20psi!

6. The specific power unit used in Fiat-engined cars was never fitted to any Fiat sold on the British market, and the same goes for the attendant five-speed Abarth gearbox. Having said that, there is an active Fiat section within the Morgan Sports Car Club and most spares problems can be resolved. The engine itself has a good reputation for reliability.

7. Parts for the M16 and T16 Rover units are in contrast rather more plentiful. Here it is worth making a conventional Rover spares outlet your first port of call, moving on to a specialist if you draw a blank there. Don't neglect breakers' yards, either.

convert this for rwd, a new endplate was fabricated, and Sherpa van parts incorporated to mate with the versatile '77mm' Rover gearbox also used on the Plus 8. Changes also had to be made to the clutch, because the Morgan's pedals were chassis-mounted and pivoted from the bottom while those on the Rover used a conventional pedal box. A purpose-designed exhaust system by Tube Investments was used, finally, and incorporated no fewer than three silencer units. The 130bhp generated by the Rover unit – compared with the Fiat's 100bhp – required a strengthened back axle, while the rear springs were more flexible than hitherto, thanks to the latest hot-oil tempering technology.

Launched in May 1988, production was subsequently rationalised and in December 1991 the Plus 8's wider chassis was adopted, with rack-and-pinion steering accordingly offered as an option to the Gemmer system. For the 1993 season Morgan was obliged to follow Rover in adopting its T16 engine, a more refined successor to the M16 – although output was modestly reduced from 138bhp to 134bhp.

A further refinement occurred in March 1994 when the Rover '77mm' five-speed gearbox, which had served Morgan since the 1977 season, was discontinued and replaced by the stronger and quieter R380 unit, newly

There is nothing to show that this car is powered by the Rover M16 twin cam engine which replaced the Fiat unit in the Plus 4 from the 1989 season. The width of the wire wheels used on the Plus 4 is more apparent when you look at the spare. (LAT)

introduced on the Range Rover. This was an inch longer than its predecessor, so Morgan had to fit a supplementary underslung crossmember.

From summer 1997 all Morgans were given extended seats, lengthened doors and a deeper dashboard to accommodate airbags. Plus 4 production ceased in 2000, following Rover's abandonment of its T16 engine. After 50 years the Plus 4 was no more.

Return of the
4/4

This 1956 4/4 was road tested by The Autocar *in that year. The magazine found the rear corners of the raised hood 'rather blind'. A separate tonneau covers for the passenger seat and a cover for the luggage space were optional extras.* (LAT)

It was an anticipated threat to supplies of Standard engines that prompted Morgan to revive the 4/4 in 1955, rather than a desire by the company to introduce a cheaper, secondary line alongside its Plus 4 model. Selling for £638 on its introduction, the new 4/4 cost a significant £206 less than its more powerful TR2-engined stablemate.

Morgan's association with Standard had been rooted, to some extent, in the goodwill extended to it by

managing director Sir John Black. Renowned for his dictatorial behaviour and unpredictability, Black's often unpalatable conduct eventually prompted his entire board of directors to demand his resignation at the end of 1953, a request to which he reluctantly acceded. He was replaced on 1 January 1954 by his deputy, Alick Dick, who was to steer the fortunes of this smallest member of Britain's 'Big Six' until 1961.

Whilst Morgan was assured that

deliveries of Triumph engines would not be jeopardised, soon after Black's departure they began to be in short supply. Rather than having all his eggs in one corporate basket, Peter Morgan decided to re-establish his company's connections with Ford, which had lapsed in 1952 with the demise of the three-wheeler line.

At the 1955 London Motor Show Morgan consequently displayed what it anachronistically designated the '10hp Series II' – RAC horsepower not having been a factor since 1947; today the model is universally known as the 4/4. Outwardly the body lines of this open two-seater, the only version at first produced, were lower than those of the Plus 4, on account of the physically smaller engine. Otherwise the 4/4 resembled its stablemate, except that there were no bonnet-top louvres – although these could be specified at extra cost – and the windscreen was fixed rather than fold-flat. The rear end incorporated a single spare wheel, a detail introduced at the same time on the Plus 4, and the 5.00 x 16in disc wheels were the same as those used on the Plus 4.

The design of dashboard differed somewhat from that of the Plus 4: instead of the main instruments being centrally located, the 90mph speedometer was positioned on the right of the steering wheel, with a matching combination dial to the left. This meant that there was no room for a rev counter, although this was listed as an optional extra. Additionally the familiar bench-type seat with its one-piece backrest was revived, but this time with leathercloth upholstery – although leather was available at extra cost, as was a so-called 'fug stirrer' heater. Morgan had yet to acquaint itself with carpeting, so the floor covering remained rubber matting.

As for the power unit, this came from Ford's boxy, no-frills 100E saloon of 1953, the 1172cc sidevalve 'four' developing a modest 36bhp. Unlike the Triumph engine of the Plus 4, the Dagenham-built unit came complete with its three-speed gearbox, with synchromesh on second and top gears. On the Morgan the change was

Morgan 4/4 Series II (100E engine) 1955–1960

ENGINE:

Bore x stroke	63.5mm x 92.5mm
Capacity	1172cc
Valve actuation	Side
Compression ratio	7.0:1
Carburettor	Single Solex
Power	36bhp at 4400rpm
Torque	54lb ft at 2500rpm

TRANSMISSION:
Rear-wheel drive. Three-speed Ford gearbox with synchromesh on second and top gears, in unit with engine

SUSPENSION:
Front: Independent, sliding stub axles and coil springs with telescopic hydraulic dampers
Rear: Underslung live axle with half-elliptic springs; lever-arm hydraulic dampers

STEERING:
Cam Gears cam-and-peg

BRAKES:
Hydraulic 9in drum

WHEELS/TYRES:
16in steel disc
Tyres 5.00 x 16in

BODYWORK:
Coachbuilt, with steel panels on ash frame
Separate Z-section chassis
Open two-seater only

DIMENSIONS:

Length	12 ft 0in
Wheelbase	8ft 0in
Track, front and rear	3ft 11in
Width	4ft 8in
Height	4ft 2in

WEIGHT:
14cwt

PERFORMANCE:
(Source: *The Autocar*)

Max speed	70.5mph
0–50mph	18sec
0–60mph	29.4sec

PRICE INCLUDING TAX WHEN NEW:
£714 (September 1956)

NUMBER BUILT:
387

Morgan 4/4 Series III (Ford 105E engine) 1960–1961

As Series 11, except:

ENGINE:

Bore x stroke	80.96mm x 48.41mm
Capacity	997cc
Valve actuation	Pushrod
Compression ratio	8.9:1
Carburettor	Single Solex 30ZIC2
Power	39bhp at 5000rpm
Torque	52.9lb ft at 2700rpm

TRANSMISSION:
Four-speed Ford gearbox with synchromesh on second, third and top gears

WHEELS/TYRES:
15in steel disc
Tyres 5.20 x 15in

PRICE INCLUDING TAX WHEN NEW:
£738

NUMBER BUILT:
59

Morgan 4/4 Series IV (Ford 109E engine) 1961–1963

As Series III except:

ENGINE:

Bore x stroke	80.96mm x 65.07mm
Capacity	1340cc
Valve actuation	Pushrod
Compression ratio	8.5:1
Carburettor	Single Zenith VN2
Power	54bhp at 2500rpm
Torque	74lb ft at 2500rpm

BRAKES:
Front: 11in disc
Rear: 9in drum

WHEELS/TYRES:
Steel disc wheels
Tyres 5.60 x 15in

PERFORMANCE:
(Source: *The Motor*)

Max speed	80.3mph
0–50mph	11.9sec
0–60mph	18.6sec
0–70mph	27.1sec

PRICE INCLUDING TAX WHEN NEW:
£730 (April 1962)

NUMBER BUILT:
114

The 4/4 was outwardly similar to the Plus 4, with the exception of the bonnet which lacked its top set of louvres – although these could be specified as an optional extra. This is a 1956 car. (LAT)

The 4/4's driving compartment in all its stark simplicity. The gearlever is a simple pull-push device and the seat cushions pneumatic. (LAT)

The Autocar found the 4/4's luggage accommodation 'rather limited' – although there is more space with the hood removed, the irons being retained either side by straps. (LAT)

effected by a crude remote pull-push control that projected from below the dashboard – meaning that there was more room between the seats than on the Plus 4.

With this banal powertrain the 4/4 was capable of about 75mph flat-out,

with 60mph arriving in a pedestrian 27 seconds. However, there were plenty of tuning kits available for the seemingly unburstable Ford unit, allowing Morgan owners to push the top speed of their cars to beyond the 80mph mark.

There was a compensation, however, for the car's relative sloth: when in 1956 *The Motor* evaluated a 4/4 it remarked that the model entered a short list of cars it had tested that could attain 60mpg (at 30mph) in the magazine's constant-speed consumption tests; the overall figure over a distance of 745 miles was 35.1mpg.

The testers found the 4/4 had a happy vibration-free cruising speed of 65mph but that acceleration tailed off appreciably thereafter. The magazine unsurprisingly also recognised the limitations of the three-speed gearbox. 'Undoubtedly a four-speed gearbox would be an advantage for opportunist overtaking on winding or busy roads,' it commented, while observing that at £713 the Morgan 4/4 was not only the cheapest open two-seater on the market, but undercut other sports cars by a healthy £200–£300 or so.

Weekly rival *The Autocar* also tested the 4/4 and, on balancing pros and cons, declared that the main items on the debit side were 'performance which is not exciting in standard form, difficulty in getting in and out, the laborious hood mechanism and the lack of accommodation for luggage'. On the credit side were 'low price, fuel economy, handling of a high order, the ease with which engine power could be increased, and the accessibility of those parts subject to routine attention'.

A performance package was formalised for 1958 as a supplementary 'Competition Model'. Outwardly similar to the mainstream 4/4, the newcomer had an Aquaplane aluminium cylinder head which raised the compression ratio from 7:1 to 8:1, while the single Solex carburettor was replaced by twin 1½in SUs. With 40bhp at 5100rpm, Morgan claimed an increase in top speed of 10mph, to about 80mph, this for an extra cost of

Morgan 4/4 Series V
(Ford 116E engine)
1963–1968

As Series IV except:

ENGINE:
Bore x stroke	80.96mm x 72.74mm
Capacity	1498cc
Valve actuation	Pushrod
Compression ratio	8.3:1
Carburettor	Single Zenith 33 VN
Power	60bhp at 4600rpm
Torque	81lb ft at 2500rpm

TRANSMISSION:
Ford four-speed all-synchromesh gearbox

WHEELS/TYRES:
Disc wheels
Tyres 155 x 15in

PRICE INCLUDING TAX WHEN NEW:
£659 (May 1964)

NUMBER BUILT:
639

Morgan 4/4 1600
(Ford 'Kent' engine)
1968–1982

As 4/4 Series V except:

ENGINE:
Four cylinders in line, cast-iron block and cylinder head
Bore x stroke	81.0mm x 77.6mm
Capacity	1598cc
Valve actuation	Pushrod
Compression ratio	9.0:1
Carburettor	Single Zenith
Power	74bhp at 4750rpm
Torque	97lb ft at 2500rpm

WHEELS/TYRES:
Disc wheels: 5.00 x1 6in tyres
Wire wheels: 165 x 15in or 195 x 15in tyres

BODYWORK:
Additionally available as open four-seater

DIMENSIONS:
Length	13ft 2in
Width	5 ft 0in
Height	4ft 4 in

PRICE INCLUDING TAX WHEN NEW:
£988

NUMBER BUILT:
3513

Morgan 4/4 1600
TC (Fiat engine)
1981–1985

As 4/4 1600 except:

ENGINE:
Four cylinders in line, cast-iron block and alloy cylinder head
Bore x stroke	84 mm x 71.5mm
Capacity	1584cc
Valve actuation	Twin overhead camshaft
Compression ratio	9.0:1
Carburettor	Single Weber 32ADF 53/250 or Solex C32TEE/10
Power	98bhp at 6000rpm
Torque	96lb ft at 4000rpm

TRANSMISSION:
Fiat five-speed all-synchromesh gearbox

WHEELS:
Disc or wire wheels
Tyres 195/60 x 15

PRICE INCLUDING TAX WHEN NEW:
£8766 (Two-seater, November 1983)
£9628 (Four-seater, idem)

NUMBER BUILT:
96

Morgan 4/4
(Ford CVH engine)
1982–1991

As 4/4 1600 except:

ENGINE:
Four cylinders in line, cast-iron block and alloy cylinder head
Bore x stroke	79.52mm x 97.5mm
Capacity	1597cc
Valve actuation	Single overhead camshaft
Compression ratio	9:1
Carburettor	Single Weber 32/34
Power	96bhp at 6000rpm
Torque	98lb ft at 4000rpm

TRANSMISSION:
Ford four-speed or five-speed all-synchromesh gearbox

STEERING:
Gemmer recirculating ball from 1984

PRICE INCLUDING TAX WHEN NEW:
£8569 (Two-seater, November 1983)
£9431 (Four-seater, idem)

NUMBER BUILT:
2222

Morgan 4/4 1600
EFI (Ford engine)
1991–1992

As 1600 CVH except:

ENGINE:
Compression ratio	10:1
Fuel injection	Weber electronic
Power	100bhp at 6000rpm
Torque	102lb ft at 2800rpm

WHEELS/TYRES:
Wire wheels
Tyres 165TR x 15in

PRICE INCLUDING TAX WHEN NEW:
£16,102 (Two-seater, February 1992)
£17,452 (four-seater, idem)

NUMBER BUILT:
195

Morgan 4/4 1800
(Ford Zetec engine)
1993 to date

As 1600 EFI except:

ENGINE:
Four cylinders in line, cast-iron block and alloy cylinder head
Bore x stroke	80.6 mm x 88m
Capacity	1796cc
Valve actuation	Twin overhead camshaft
Compression ratio	10:1
Fuel injection	Multipoint
Power	121bhp at 6200rpm
Torque	119lb ft at 6250rpm

TRANSMISSION:
Ford five-speed all-synchromesh gearbox

WHEELS:
Wire wheels
Tyres 195/90 VR15

BODYWORK:
Aluminium panels from 1998

PRICE INCLUDING TAX WHEN NEW:
£24,193 (Two-seater, March 2004)
£28,864 (Four-seater, idem)

NUMBER BUILT:
[approx 400 to early 1997]

A 4/4 of 1969 vintage, ready for rain. The engine in this instance is a 1.6-litre Cortina unit. (LAT)

The dashboard of this '69 car is similar to that of the late Series V cars; it was redesigned for the 1970 season. The 4/4 then had PVC upholstery but leather was available at extra cost. (LAT)

£78, taking the price to £826. The Competition 4/4 was to remain available until 1960.

A Series III version of the 4/4 arrived for the 1961 season, dictated by Ford's discontinuing of its long-running sidevalve four-cylinder engine, a design that dated back, in essence, to 1932. From thereon the pace of the 4/4's development was determined by Ford's progressive refinement of its new generation of 'Kent' overhead-valve engines. The first of these, in 997cc guise, powered the all-new 105E Anglia saloon introduced at the 1959 Motor Show, and it was this unit that was used in the 1961 model-year 4/4. With it came a new four-speed gearbox, still without synchromesh on

first gear, and smaller 15in disc wheels with wider 5.20 tyres. Although of a slightly smaller capacity, the pushrod engine's greater efficiency meant it developed 39bhp, some 3bhp more than the trusty 1172cc sidevalve. As a result the Series III was a faster car than its predecessor, having a top

speed of 78mph, some 7mph more, whilst about 3.2 seconds was shaved off the 0–60mph time – which was a still lowly 25.8 seconds.

The body tub was 1½in to 2in wider than the previous generation of 4/4s and in consequence had slightly narrower wings with less overhang, so

A study in 4/4 hoods: a two-seater on the move . . . (LAT)

. . . and a four-seater (middle), better windowed than the two-seater, prepared for the worst the English climate can offer. (LAT)

When it can take four people, the 4/4 (bottom) really is family transport. This is a 1979 car. (LAT)

as to avoid increasing the car's overall width. Perversely some of the last 100E-powered 4/4s were fitted with this body which was designed for the new model's smaller 15in wheels. This produced some visual unease, as more of the wheel was concealed than might be expected.

But the Series III was destined for a relatively short life because in 1961 Ford enlarged the 'Kent' engine for its new Consul Classic saloon. This unit, with a capacity of 1340cc, was noticeably more powerful, developing 54bhp. Once installed under the Morgan's bonnet, for the 1962 season, it pushed the new Series IV 4/4's performance to the 80mph mark. To cope with the extra performance, 11in

Bird's-eye view of the four-seater 4/4. The instrument panel with the same diameter speedometer and rev-counter was introduced in 1977. (LAT)

disc brakes were fitted at the front, whilst the rear drums were increased to 9in in diameter. Physically the only identifying feature of the Series IV was the introduction of a 'Morgan' script on the top right-hand corner of the rear deck.

Again the Series IV was to be relatively short-lived, lasting for a mere 18 or so months before being replaced in February 1963 by the Series V with Ford's newly-enlarged 1498cc 'Kent' unit, as used in later Consul Classics. Although the Morgan's top speed remained about the same, at 80mph, acceleration improved, 0–60mph now taking 16.5 seconds, 1.1 seconds better than its predecessor. This meant that, for the

first time, the 4/4 had a performance edge on its Triumph Spitfire, Austin-Healey Sprite and MG Midget rivals.

Along with the new engine came its four-speed all-synchromesh gearbox. While this could be fitted with the factory's rudimentary remote-control mechanism, there was the option of a more conventional Wooller remote, as was then proving popular with Cortina owners. However, Morgan was rather coy about the unit's origins and machined off the 'Wooller' lettering when fitting the device to the 4/4!

The Series V's improved performance saw the standardisation of a rev-counter, while wire wheels became an option. Less outwardly apparent was the extra-cost option of Armstrong Selectaride rear dampers. These were standardised on a Competition version of the Series V which appeared for the 1964 season, powered by the 78bhp Ford Cortina GT (118E) engine. This enabled the car to sprint to 60mph in a shade under 12 seconds, while top speed went up again, this time to 95mph.

The year 1968, when the Series V ceased production, proved to be a seminal one in Morgan's affairs. In September the Plus 8 made its appearance, at a price of £1477 which was a significant £562 more than that of the Plus 4 which it replaced. This move upmarket, both in engine capacity and price, meant that the 4/4 was allowed to flourish in its own right; hitherto it had been overshadowed to some extent by the Plus 4. Helping the process was Ford's stretch of the 'Kent' engine to 1597cc for later versions of the MkII Cortina; fitted to the 4/4 from February 1968, this revised and now crossflow 74bhp unit provided the 4/4 with a welcome dose of extra muscle.

This change, announced at the October 1967 Motor Show, was accompanied by the car being renamed the 4/4 1600. The basic 4/4 had a price at launch of £825, while the Competition 4/4 1600 with the Cortina GT engine cost £856. Now delivering 95bhp, the GT unit took performance of the Morgan to just beyond the 100mph mark for the first

Rear view of a 4/4 four-seater. (LAT)

time. The net result was that the Competition model was soon outselling the original by about four to one, so in May 1971 the standard 4/4 was discontinued and thereafter all cars conformed to the Competition specification.

As the Plus 8 was only produced in two-seater form, a four-seater 4/4 was reintroduced for the 1969 season, inititially only with the standard 1600 engine. The body of the 4/4 1600, meanwhile, was essentially similar to that of its Series V predecessor and exterior modifications over the years were to be relatively modest. Inside changes, however, were more noticeable, with in particular the arrival from 1970 of a redesigned dashboard with the rev-counter to the right of the steering wheel and the larger speedometer and matching white-on-black combination dial being set in a radiused oblong central panel; switches were now the rocker type demanded by US regulations, and for 1971 a collapsible steering column was fitted for the same reason.

The 1972 model year saw the introduction of anti-burst locks, courtesy of Land Rover, in deference to new EEC regulations. Traditional twin-eared wheel spinners were similarly outlawed, and so were replaced by the earless variety.

While Morgans have never been known for their creature comforts, from May 1972 the optional heater, introduced back in 1955, was replaced by a standard-equipment Smiths

A 1981 four-seater at the factory, now sporting the wire wheels offered as an option since 1977. The long-running Ford 'Kent' engine would be discontinued in March of the following year. (LAT)

fresh-air unit, relocated from the passenger's footwell to the transmission tunnel. Intriguingly, the demist facility was not activated until the 1975 season.

In the middle of 1975 legislation

A 1982 *four-seater with the upholstery matching the body colour.* (LAT)

Below: *Rear lights and flashers on an X-reg* 4/4. (LAT)

Tony Bostock, *editor of the now defunct* Sports Car Mechanics *magazine, removes the hood of an X-registration 4/4 two-seater.* (LAT)

came into force requiring that the passenger's seat be made independent of the driver's seat, which spelt the end of the 4/4's long-running single-piece seat backrest. In its place came bucket seats, with a folding and reclining version optional on the two-seater and standard on the four-seater.

Further revisions were made to the dashboard in 1977, with the rev-counter and speedometer now being the same size and positioned in front of the driver and the auxiliary dials becoming separate 2in units set in a more square central panel. The dashboard itself was covered with vinyl or leather, the choice being dictated by the trim.

As far as exterior presentation was concerned, chromed wires became an option from 1977 and in January of the same year it became possible to order a 4/4 with an aluminium body. At the same time the chrome bumpers gave way to aluminium components which were semi-square in section. Additionally, a rear bumper was standardised for the first time, whereas hitherto a pair of chromed overriders had sufficed.

Since its introduction in 1955 the 4/4 had been shod as standard with disc wheels with circular piercings but in 1980, in the face of dwindling demand, Dunlop decided to discontinue this charming but archaic

style. Morgan responded by acquiring a stock of German 15in Rostyle-type wheels produced by Lemmerz for a special edition of the Volkswagen Beetle, German production of which had ceased in 1978. Although these wheels became the standard fitment, most 4/4 owners chose wires, and it was not until 1990 that stocks of the Lemmerz wheels were finally exhausted. It was at that point that wires were standardised.

By this time the 4/4 had undergone a change of engine supplier. Being so closely geared to Ford engines had its advantages, certainly in terms of spares availability. But it also had its downside, because Dagenham was progressively switching to transverse-engined front-wheel drive. The Fiesta

A 4/4 four-seater displaying the wooden instrument panel with lockable glove compartment offered as an option from 1988. The red 'Morgan' script on the steering-wheel boss arrived in 1987. (LAT)

A 4/4 of 1997 complete with bonnet strap, sidescreens in place and lights on. (LAT)

supermini, first of the line, appeared in 1976 and the Escort followed for the '81 season, powered by a new 'CVH' ('Compound Valve-angle Hemispherical combustion chamber') overhead-camshaft engine. More significantly, the pushrod 'Kent' unit could not meet EEC emissions regulations coming into force in April 1982.

Morgan therefore had no choice but to look around for an alternative 'four' for north-south locatation. It came up

with the 1.6-litre twin-overhead-camshaft Fiat engine, then powering the Fiat 131 Supermirafiori saloon in tandem with a five-speed gearbox. Morgan duly announced the impending arrival of the Fiat unit, the company's first twin-cam, at the 1981 Earls Court Motorfair.

What then happened has since entered the realms of Morgan fable, and I can do no better than quote from *Autocar* of 21 December 1981 – although

its report is complicated by the fact that it was only partially correct! By all accounts a Ford executive had, in the mid-1970s, ordered a 4/4 which was then, of course, Ford-powered. Because of Morgan's much-publicised waiting list, he had still not received his car by the 1981 event . . . .which is when he heard of the proposed switch of power unit, and was reported as saying that he 'could not stomach driving behind a Fiat engine'. However,

Driving a 1600cc Ford-engined 4/4

The Ford-engined 4/4 is the sensible Morgan, imbued with all the essential and traditional marque characteristics but without the flamboyant excess-all-areas performance of the Plus 8, the bite of the Fiat-engined Plus 4 or the easy refinement of the Rover-powered Plus 4. Obviously the performance varies depending on the engine – although you'd be hard-put to notice much difference between a 1600cc 'Kent' 4/4 and one with the frankly pretty prosaic CVH unit. A tuned 'Kent' engine is a different matter: cook up 125bhp of twin-Webered '1700', and you'll have a car that begs to be driven hard…

That doesn't mean that a regulation 1600cc 4/4 isn't fun. Performance is lively enough, and mid-range pulling power respectable – although four-up in a four-seater you might find yourself changing gear more often to keep the Morgan on the boil. Older cars with the Cortina/Corsair gearbox have a slicker change than the more ponderous Sierra unit on later cars, but whatever the gearbox you'll have Morgan's traditionally heavy clutch – with a similar effort demanded by the brakes. But the 4/4 wouldn't be a Morgan without those vintage floor-pivoted pedals with their odd over-centre action.

Smooth-road behaviour is exemplary, with sharp turn-in, no body roll (perish the thought!) and easy adjustability on the throttle; the steering is not heavy, and is surprisingly informative for a non-rack arrangement, but does load up when you start applying lock. Rough roads are another matter: the 4/4 is easily thrown off course and the harsh ride can have one clinging to the steering wheel rather than carressing the car from curve to curve. If you're not prepared to buy into this modern-day vintagery, you're better off looking for a Lotus Elan …

Buying Hints

1. The 4/4 was offered with the option of an aluminium body. This represents a very real advantage over steel panels. A magnet will confirm which material is used.

2. The 1172cc sidevalver, although often described as unburstable and indestructible, is vulnerable to main-bearing wear; these being of the old-fashioned white-metal variety, expensive re-metalling will be involved, unless the mains are converted to modern shell bearings. The old warrior also has a tendency for the top piston ring to break up; should the 4/4 you are contemplating smoke badly, this is the most likely cause. If the car is fitted with the standard Ford cylinder head, as opposed to a proprietary aluminium one, this does have a tendency to crack around the web adjacent to the thermostat housing. This manifests itself by a water dribble which looks as though it might come from the hose but in fact can be rather more serious.

3. The sidevalve engine came complete with its three-speed gearbox, and while this tends to keep going in most circumstances, be prepared for worn second-gear synchromesh.

4. The Ford pushrod engine is extraordinarily reliable and parts are readily available. The 1600cc version of 1971–82 powered more 4/4s than any other, and is regarded as the most successful of the Ford ohv units. Indeed these days there are very few 100E-engined 4/4s around, most having been converted to 1600 'Kent' power, together with the matching four-speed gearbox. The most likely mechanical ailment with these pushrod units is noisy valve gear, usually caused by wear in the rockers, cam followers and camshaft. A top-end rebuild is the only answer – although the engines will continue to run without one! Timing-chain wear – revealed by a rattle at the front of the engine – is not unusual, any more than worn rings and bores: look for fuming from

the oil-filler cap and excessively blue exhaust smoke. If you have any doubt about the state of the bearings, the best indication is oil pressure: a gauge reading of 15–20 psi (hot) on tickover is acceptable, and anything below that figure should be viewed with suspicion. After a modest run, 35–40psi is the norm. Spares do not present a major problem.

5. If you're running a Zeta-powered 4/4 then practically all engine spares are available across the counter from Ford main dealers. Because of its age, parts for the CVH unit are likely to be less instantaneously available from Ford: you may wish to opt for a specialist supplier. Timing belts on these later Ford engines should be changed regularly, of course.

6. The second-generation 4/4 has always had a gearbox in unit with the engine. As the overwhelming majority are of Ford origin, they benefit from having reasonably plentiful spare parts, and are relatively cheap to replace or rebuild.

From 1986 the build quality of all Morgans was much improved and this is no more apparent than when one casts an eye on the interior of this 1997 car, a world away from the Series II of 1956! (LAT)

– while from the following year it was possible to specify the 4/4 with the Plus 4's wider body.

Peter Morgan's son Charles arrived at the Malvern factory in 1985 and from 1986 build quality across the board improved appreciably (see page 72). Undersealing, previously an option, was standardised in 1988 and wire wheels became the conventional fitment in 1990.

The 4/4 went briefly out of production in 1992 because of delays in the supply of Ford's new Zeta twin-cam engine. It reappeared, Zeta-powered but only in two-seater form, in March. A claimed output of 128bhp looked promising but this was subsequently adjusted to 121bhp and finally stood at 114bhp. The arrival of the new engine required some chassis modifications, while in 1993 came a switch from Girling to Lockheed brakes, these front discs and rear drums being standardised across the Morgan range. A further change followed in 1996 when the Salisbury rear axle on the 4/4 and Plus 4 was replaced by an Australian-built BTR unit.

In July 1999 the four-seater version of the 4/4 returned – although it differed from its predecessors, which had a bench back seat, in being fitted with individual rear buckets which could be folded down separately to improve luggage accommodation. The doors were also longer, to aid access.

In 2003 Morgan revived the Runabout name for its entry-level 4/4, which sold for £21,771 – some £2500 less than the mainstream model. Only available in three patriotic colours of Bulldog Blue, Whitehall White and Regal Red, it is outwardly distinguished by having ten bonnet louvres instead of the usual 24. Demand for the 4/4 range, now powered by Ford's Zetec twin cam, shows no sign of abating, an impressive endorsement of a line that began back in 1936.

Detail of the wire wheels, standardised in 1990, on the 1997 car shown above. Earless spinners have been fitted since 1971. (LAT)

the magazine maintained that the Italian-powered 4/4 had been in production for the last two years – which was of course not the case, and it hurriedly published a correction in the following week's issue. The net result of this encounter was, said the *Autocar* account, that 'with Ford collaboration, Morgan have more recently fitted the 1600 ohc CVH Ford Escort XR3 engine, adapted to suit north-south installation, and the Type B Cortina four-speed gearbox'. Subsequently, in 1983, the car was to acquire the Capri/Sierra five-speed gearbox.

The Ford-powered 4/4 was to be supplementary to the Fiat version, rather than a replacement for it. The first Fiat-engined 4/4, designated the 1600 TC, was delivered in December 1981, but the CVH-powered car did not follow until April 1982, the last 'Kent' 4/4 having been dispatched in March. There was a price differentiation in favour of the Ford-engined 4/4, which in November 1982 cost £7861 for the two-seater – a full £905 less than the Fiat-engined car. Ultimately, though, it did not make sense to make two versions of the 4/4, so in 1984 the Fiat version was discontinued. In compensation the 2-litre version of the Fiat twin-cam was used to power the revived Plus 4 which appeared in 1985

The Plus 4 Plus

The prototype, bearing its familiar registration number. The doors – both lockable – contain deep storage pockets. (LAT)

All of us, of course, in hindsight possess 20/20 vision. And in retrospect the arrival of the Plus 4 Plus coupé in October 1963 was a mistake on the part of Morgan. But at the time there were wholly logical reasons for its introduction. It should be remembered that in the early 1960s Morgan was being chided for its increasingly old-fashioned products, in the light of sure-footed opposition from its MG, Triumph and Rootes rivals. Sales in the all-important American market had taken a nosedive and European demand, which would play an increasingly important role in Morgan's affairs, had yet to materialise.

Lotus, in particular, had shown the potential of glassfibre bodywork and Peter Morgan began to think about the material as a possible alternative to the traditional coachbuilt methods that the company had employed since its foundation. He discussed the matter with his father but 'HFS' was against the idea, believing that the Morgan's flexible chassis was unsuitable for the material and would have led to bodyshell cracking that was unacceptable from a structural and visual standpoint.

It should be said that Peter Morgan was not alone in his thinking. At Abingdon, John Thornley, his opposite number at MG, was already predicting that the impending MGB would be the marque's last metal-bodied car. The answer to ever-rising tooling costs, considered Thornley, was glassfibre bodywork – although in the event he was proven wrong.

With HFS Morgan's death in 1959 his son decided to press ahead with the idea. Interestingly, according to The Autocar it had been an enquiry from Greece about mounting a special streamlined body on the Morgan chassis that has sparked off the new design.

By the 1960s the accent was on the exciting and innovative. Morgan was viewed as being positively antiquated, although attitudes would change by the time that the decade came to an end. Peter Morgan recognised that some action was necessary, especially with an eye to the hitherto untapped European market – although later, in 1966, he claimed that he had never wanted to make more than 50 cars and that development costs had been tailored to this figure.

There was no question of introducing glassfibre to Pickersleigh Road, so Morgan turned to a specialist in the material, EB (Staffs) Ltd. Run by the Edwards Brothers, it was one of the many businesses which supplied

glassfibre sports bodies for the robust but crude Ford Popular chassis – making in all more than 2000 of its EB50 and EB60 shells, some being sold as far afield as Australia. EB went on to produce its own chassis, with rack-and-pinion steering, wishbone front suspension and quarter-elliptic rear springs, and announced this in 1960, along with a more up-market shell, the Debonair, designed to take either the new chassis or the trusty Ford frame. It was also sold with another proprietary chassis, the CRS, and was additionally offered as LMB-Debonair, with the LMB chassis. Stylistically bearing some resemblance to Aston Martin's newly-introduced DB4, the shell came complete with door locks, wind-up windows and even a mahogany-faced instrument panel. EB made efforts to reduce crazing of the glassfibre by strictly limiting the amount of resin in the body to 20 per cent, the mouldings being based on 1.5 oz of resin per square foot of mat. The panels were self coloured but nonetheless finished in cellulose. Production of the Debonair shell was planned at four a week with a price of £200 and it was officially launched at the 1961 Racing Car Show. The Autocar commented favourably on its 'very attractive coachwork and first-class finish'.

Peter Morgan was also impressed, and following a careful study of the various bodies available he approached EB Plastics in 1962 with a view to it designing and building a body for Morgan. He needed a body that could be fitted with the minimum of modification to the Plus 4 chassis and in the event the only significant changes to the frame were to be two sheet metal extensions bolted to either side of the engine. These also provided reinforcement between the front suspension and bulkhead and had the effect of strengthening the front of the car.

As far as the body itself was concerned, there was no written contract, but Peter Morgan stipulated that the shape should echo in part traditional Morgan lines and should retain the marque's radiator grille in a

Plus 4 Plus
1963–1967

As TR4/4A-engined Plus 4 except:

BODYWORK:
Glassfibre coupé

WHEELS/TYRES:
Wire wheels
Tyres 5.60 x 15in

DIMENSIONS:

Length	12ft 8in
Width	5ft 1in
Height	4ft 3in

WEIGHT:
16.25cwt

PRICE INCLUDING TAX WHEN NEW:
£1275 (October 1963)

NUMBER BUILT:
26

recognisable form. John Edwards, EB's founder and managing director, was responsible for the styling and for developing the body's construction. He came up with a distinctive and competent design that bore no visual relationship to the EB Debonair; in truth it had more in common with the Lotus Elite, and wore a grille that had vague shades of the Jaguar XK150 about its shape. Perhaps the most distinctive aspect of the design was the winding side windows, which were almost semi-circular in shape – and which did not wholly disappear into the doors when lowered. This then was the design adopted by Morgan and, once approved, EB built a wooden former which was then panelled in alloy. Moulds were then taken from this metal shell. Morgan delivered a TR4-engined Plus 4 chassis (A5379) to EB's Keele Street works and the first body was mounted, trimmed and finished there although all the production cars were to be built in the Malvern factory. This first Plus 4 Plus also differed in having a single back squab to service two separate seats, whereas production cars were to have individual bucket seats.

Completed in March 1963 at a cost of some £3000 and given the

Morgan's publicity photograph of the Plus 4 Plus. This is the prototype, registered 869 KAB. (LAT)

The Plus 4 Plus styling still looks good some 40 years on. The curvature of the door prevents the glass from descending completely. (LAT)

Worcestershire registration number of 869 KAB, the prototype was taken by Peter Morgan and his wife on a 14-day tour of France and Spain. During the 3000-mile run only minor problems were experienced and repairs to a damaged front wing were speedily carried out by a French garage. Later Morgan used the car in Motor Cycling Club trials and by 1966 it had clocked up a respectable 50,000 or so miles.

The Plus 4 Plus – interestingly, the original rendering was 'Plus *Four* Plus' although today the model is invariably described as 'Plus 4 Plus' – was launched at the 1963 London Motor Show. It was priced at £1275, which was a considerable £459 more than the mainstream open Plus 4 which by then sold for £816. But it was some £347 less than Lotus's admittedly much more sophisticated Elite.

Externally the familiar Morgan radiator grille was retained, although it was slightly smaller and was flanked by small horizontal grilles. These remained in situ when the bonnet, which hinged at the scuttle, was raised. The adjoining bumper and overriders were essentially the same as that used on the Plus 4. At the rear such limited production clearly did not justify tooling up for a bespoke bumper, and so a cut-down Ford 100E blade, as also used on mainstream 1958–78 Morgans, was therefore adapted, with ingenious wraparound end-pieces made of glassfibre and then chrome-plated. Another item that Morgan never got around to producing was a special badge for the new model. Located just above the grille, it was the usual Plus 4 one.

Both doors were lockable, and the interior was closely related to the open cars – albeit with a vinyl-covered dashboard. A bonus was some storage space behind the seats, enough for a single suitcase; additionally the Plus 4 Plus possessed a boot, the first Morgan to do so, even if luggage space had to be shared with the spare wheel.

Considering that in commercial terms the Plus 4 Plus was a failure, it received a good press, even allowing for the fact that motoring magazines were then rather more deferential than

The opened door underlines the distinctive shape of the aperture. (LAT)

they are now. A*utocar* commented favourably that there was the impression of more interior space than the exterior might suggest, and spoke of the Morgan's 'really invigorating performance'. In a quick run around the Malvern Hills, the writer was able to 'rush up to 75 or 80mph on short stretches of straight, using the excellent third gear, underlining the low weight of the new body'. In fact, the glassfibre-shelled Morgan was barely a quarter of a hundredweight lighter than the regular Plus 4 . . .

The magazine also commented favourably on the high standard of exterior finish and the good door and body fit – although there were some concerns about sound levels. 'There was rather more engine and transmission noise than there should

Detail of a very un-Morgan-like tail light cluster. The extremities of the bumper are made of glassfibre. (LAT)

The EB Morgan

This is a Morgan might-have-been. With the Plus 4 Plus entering production in 1963, EB Plastics boss John Edwards suggested to Peter Morgan a modern open body for the 4/4. A Series V Cortina-engined rolling chassis was duly procured, and late in 1963 the prototype was ready, a sleek glassfibre-bodied open two-seater with more than a little Italian flavour about its lines.

Without its aerodynamically inefficient coachbuilt body, the grp-shelled Morgan performed well, to such an extent that John Edwards blew a tyre on the M6 when he was exceeding 100mph. It was only then that he realised that the crossply tyres, which were the usual fitment on the 4/4, were not recommended for speeds above 85mph!

The omens for putting the EB Morgan into production looked good but the project was overtaken by business changes. Truck makers ERF Ltd, of Sandbach, Cheshire, for whom EB produced cabs, acquired the Edwards concern and that put an end to the Morgan project.

The single car, which bore the 1964 Cheshire registration number of ELG 428B, was sold in the following year and in 1978 was rediscovered in Surrey, clearly showing the passage of years. A new owner took the car over and restored it, fitting a Cortina 1.6-litre crossflow engine.

The EB Morgan prior to restoration, as photographed by E Winfield in 1978. (Morgan Sports Car Club)

Buying Hints

1. Should you be contemplating the purchase of a Plus 4 Plus, its mechanicals are shared with the TR4/4A-engined Plus 4; refer to pages 72 for information.

2. While a potential owner will not have to encounter any body problems with rotting wood or rusty

steel, after some 40 years the glassfibre shell is likely to have cracked and crazed. This is the result of a flexible body being mounted on a chassis with an unforgiving suspension – despite the respectable thickness of the panels, not least the bonnet, which is surprisingly heavy.

be with production models', it commented, 'but the level of wind noise was low and there was an absence of squeaks or rattles'.

Harold Hastings in *The Motor* predicted that the Plus 4 Plus 'should make many new friends for the marque Morgan'. He found the Plus 4 Plus 'more solid yet more softly suspended' than previously and was 'delighted to find that performance and handling were, if anything, better than ever, with the "ton" showing on the speedometer on any straight of moderate length'. His only gripe was that the positioning of the driver's seat resulted in the fly-off handbrake being too far away.

Despite expectations on the part of both the maker and the press, the Plus 4 Plus did not sell, and in all only 26 were made. Peter Morgan's claim in 1965 that '60 or so had been sold' thus deserves a quizzical raising of the eyebrows. Perhaps the Plus 4 Plus was a too radical departure; maybe it was too expensive. Possibly it was too 'civilised', although conversely it was also rather noisy for a closed car, a shortcoming highlighted by some commentators who drove Peter Morgan's prototype. Equally to the point, hoped-for European sales failed to materialise. Of the cars produced, only three found continental customers, and North America took the bulk of cars – a total of 10 – with just nine remaining in Britain. In truth sales only reached double figures in 1964, the first full year of production, when 16 examples of the Plus 4 Plus were sold. Although the model continued to be listed until the 1966 season, only one example found a buyer in that year, with the final car being delivered in January 1967.

As is often the way with models that were not in demand when they were new, today the Plus 4 Plus has a rarity value and, in consequence, is sought-after as a collector's item. This is probably on account of the fact that the years have also dealt kindly with its lines – something that underlines the competence with which EB's John Edwards went about his work.

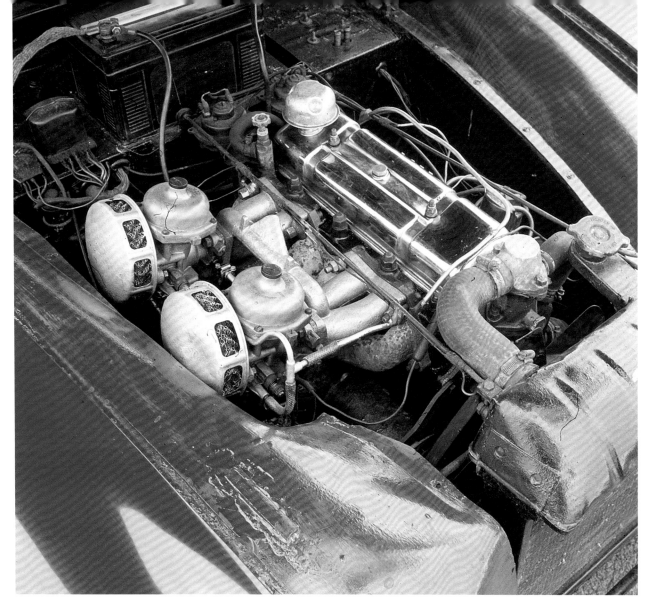

Perversely, the appearance of the Plus 4 Plus may in fact have had a catalytic effect on sales of the mainstream Morgans, in the same way that, in later years, when Coca-Cola launched its poorly received 'New Coke', it succeeded only in reinvigorating sales of the original. What can be said is that in 1965, just two years after the announcement of the Plus 4 Plus, demand for the open two-seaters began for the first time to outstrip supply. Although America remained Morgan's principal market, French sales in particular suddenly took off: Jacques Savoye in Paris ordered 18 cars in 1964 and by the autumn of 1965 had taken delivery of a further 60 cars. Other European outlets were Holland, Germany and Sweden, which were precisely the countries targeted by Peter Morgan when he conceived the Plus 4 Plus . . .

Engine specification was unaltered on the Plus 4 Plus, with the TR4 engine fed by twin CD Strombergs. (LAT)

Once inside, one is confronted with a familiar instrument panel although it is vinyl covered and a new counter is standardised. (LAT)

Plus 4 Plus: where they went

As mentioned in the text, of the 26 examples of the Plus Four 4 built, the majority – no fewer than 10 – were sold in America. The first of these (chassis A5544) was delivered in November 1963 with the next example (A5606) not leaving Malvern Link until February 1964. All the remaining cars exported to the States were also sold in 1964. A5619 went in March with A5657 following in April and A5678 in

May. Production, if that is the word, peaked in June when two further cars, A5686 and A5702, were dispatched. A5723 was completed in July and A5758 in August. Morgan displayed an example (A5794) on its stand at the 1964 London Motor Show and this car was also the last to find a buyer in the States. However, a US serviceman serving in Japan purchased A5989, it being dispatched in May 1965.

Next came Britain, where eight Plus 4 Pluses were sold, excluding the prototype, registered 869 KAB, that was retained by the works. The first production car (A5504), which was Morgan's 1963 Earls Court car,

This particular car is chassis A5722, and left the factory, destined for a UK customer, in July 1964. (LAT)

The Plus 4 Plus looks equally good from the rear. The large rear window contributes to a sense of space inside the car. (LAT)

completed in September 1963, went to a UK customer, as did A5530 when it left the factory in November of the same year. As with the US, most cars – all three of them – were sold in 1964. In January A5575 was delivered, with A5625 and A5650 following in March and April respectively. A further car (A 5722) found a British buyer in July. The final two cars to find British customers followed in 1965: A5908 in March and A6124 in December.

Canada took three cars, A5558 in December 1963, A5592 in January 1964, and A6373 in November of that year. A further trio was sold in continental Europe: A5612 was dispatched to Switzerland in February 1964, A5737 to Belgium in August 1964, and the final Plus 4 Plus (A6436) to Holland in January 1967.

The Plus 8

Morgan's hardworking 'MMC 11', which was road-tested by Autocar *and* Motor *magazines on the model's launch in September 1968. (LAT)*

Although the Plus 8, discontinued in 2004, is instantly recognisable as the car that Morgan announced at the 1968 London Motor Show, the model underwent considerable alteration and refinement over the years. With a 36-year life, it was also in production for longer, and was built in larger numbers (some 6000), than any other Morgan.

As with so many Morgans, the Plus 8 came about because of a change in the requirements of the company's engine supplier. It will be recalled that the Triumph TR2 and its TR3 and TR4 derivatives had been powered by Canley's robust wet-liner four-cylinder engine that had been created for the Standard Vanguard saloon. But Standard-Triumph, which in 1961 had been acquired by Lancashire truck manufacturer Leyland, wanted to move its products upmarket. The result was the 2000 saloon, announced in 1963. In injected 2.5-litre form its six-cylinder engine made Triumph's Michelotti-styled TR5 of 1967 into a 115mph sports car.

These developments, beneficial though they were for Triumph, presented Morgan with a problem because the in-line 'six' would not fit under the Plus 4's bonnet. Although it would have meant placing all its eggs in one corporate basket, the company did experiment with Ford's 3-litre V6. Not only did the unit sit too high in the engine compartment but it was also made of cast iron, which would have played havoc with the Morgan's power-to-weight ratio. The company also briefly toyed with the idea of using the Ford-based Lotus twin-cam unit, but soon dismissed it as too fragile.

Then, thankfully, fate intervened. In May 1966 Peter Morgan received a visit from Peter Wilks, technical director of Rover. A new younger generation was taking over at Solihull, Wilks and his cousin Spen King being key players. The well-received Rover 2000 saloon of 1963, a rival to the Triumph 2000 in the increasingly significant executive market, had opened a new era for the firm. There were even thoughts about building a Rover sports car . . .

In conversation, Wilks informally suggested a possible takeover of Morgan and as an inducement he offered the Malvern Link company the opportunity of using a General Motors 3.5-litre V8 engine that Rover was in the process of reworking for its own use. Peter Morgan courteously rejected the takeover suggestion but responded positively to the idea of the V8. Despite the rebuff, Peter Wilks was as good as his word and agreed to supply Morgan with the as-yet-unseen engine. This meeting thus marks the first link in a chain of events that led to the announcement, in October 1968, of the Morgan Plus 8.

In the short term Rover did not have any available engines, only working drawings, so Morgan installed a privately-obtained Buick unit in a modified Plus 4 chassis. This was because in 1966 a new recruit had joined the Pickersleigh

Morgan Plus 8
1968–1972

ENGINE: (Rover)
V8, aluminium cylinder block and aluminium cylinder heads

Bore x stroke	88.90mm x 71.12mm
Capacity	3528cc
Valve actuation	Pushrod
Compression ratio	10.5:1
Carburettor	Twin SU HS6
Power	160bhp at 5200rpm
Torque	210lb ft at 2600rpm

TRANSMISSION:
Rear-wheel drive via torque tube to separate Moss four-speed gearbox with synchromesh on second, third and top gears; thereafter by propshaft

SUSPENSION:
Front: Independent, by sliding stub axles, with coil springs and telescopic hydraulic dampers
Rear: Underslung live rear axle and semi-elliptic springs; lever-arm dampers

STEERING:
Cam Gears cam and peg

BRAKES:
Girling servo-assisted
Front: 11in disc
Rear: 9in drum

WHEELS/TYRES:
Cast magnesium alloy wheels;
Tyres 185VR x 15in

BODYWORK:
Coachbuilt, with steel panels on ash frame
Separate Z-section chassis.
Open two-seater only

DIMENSIONS:

Length	12ft 8in
Wheelbase	8ft 2in
Track, front	4ft 1in
Track, rear	4ft 3in
Width	4ft 9in
Height	4ft 2in

WEIGHT:
17.7cwt

PERFORMANCE:
(Source: *Autocar*)

Max speed	124mph
0–50mph	5.2sec
0–60mph	6.7sec
0–70mph	8.6sec

PRICE INCLUDING TAX WHEN NEW:
£1487 (September 1968)

NUMBER BUILT:
484

Morgan Plus 8
1972–1977

As before except:

ENGINE:
From August 1973:

Compression ratio	9.5:1
Carburettor	Twin SU H1 F6
Power	143bhp at 5000rpm
Torque	202lb ft at 2750rpm

TRANSMISSION:
From April 1972 Rover four-speed in unit with engine
From October 1976 Rover five-speed

WHEELS/TYRES:
From September 1976 6 x 14in alloy with 195 x 14in tyres

DIMENSIONS:
From August 1973:

Track, front	4ft 3in
Track, rear	4ft 4in
Width	4ft 11in

WEIGHT:
16.8cwt

PRICE INCLUDING TAX WHEN NEW:
£3375 (August 1975)

NUMBER BUILT:
702

Morgan Plus 8
1977–1984

As above except:

ENGINE:

Compression ratio	9.25:1
Carburettor	Twin Stromberg 175CD from 1982
Power	155bhp at 5000rpm
Torque	202lb ft at 2750rpm

STEERING:
From 1983 optional rack-and-pinion

BRAKES:
From October 1981 servo deleted

WHEELS/TYRES:
From February 1982 6.5 x 15in alloy; tyres P6 205/60 x 15in

DIMENSIONS:

Length	13ft 0in
Wheelbase	8ft 2in
Track, front	4ft 5in
Track, rear	4ft 6in
Width	5ft 2in – 5ft 3in from 1982
Height	4ft 0in

WEIGHT:
18.5cwt

PRICE INCLUDING TAX WHEN NEW:
£11,651 (November 1983)

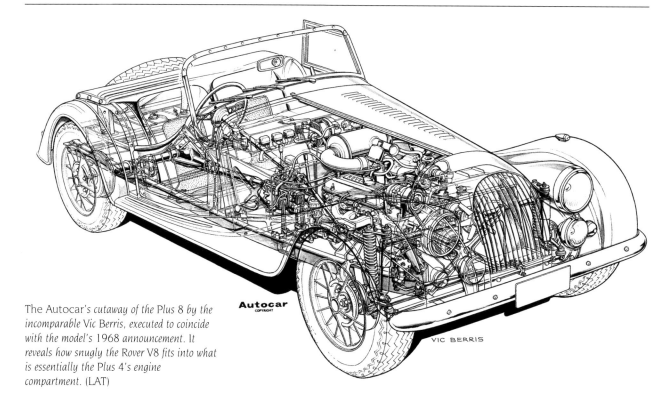

The Autocar's *cutaway of the Plus 8 by the incomparable Vic Berris, executed to coincide with the model's 1968 announcement. It reveals how snugly the Rover V8 fits into what is essentially the Plus 4's engine compartment. (LAT)*

Road engineering staff in the shape of Maurice Owen, who had come from the disbanded UDT-Laystall racing team.

Quite coincidentally, Owen had acquired three surplus Buick V8 engines from the bankrupt Gordon-Keeble company. One of these went into a hillclimb Cooper for a client and the second he used in a Rover 2000TC saloon – before Solihull in 1968 unveiled the results of doing precisely the same thing! The third V8 was destined for a Morgan and Owen, as he later recalled to *Classic and Sports Car*, asked Peter Morgan if he'd sell him a Plus 4 without an engine. 'He asked what I was up to, then told me that he was talking to Rover about using their V8 when it was ready. Eventually he decided he wouldn't sell me a Plus 4, but asked me to come and do the V8 job for him'.

Out of sight of the Morgan workforce and tucked away in a small brick building at the factory, Owen created what was to be the prototype Plus 8. The Plus 4 frame needed some surgery, but the modifications were not extensive and it only required a 2in extension to accommodate the

V8-powered 4-4

The Plus 8 was not the first occasion that Morgan had attempted to market a V8-engined sports car. In 1933 the concept of installing a large-capacity American engine under the bonnet of a British sports car had been pioneered by Railton, who chose a 4-litre Hudson unit. Outstanding performance was achieved at low cost, although on the debit side was high fuel consumption and the penalty of a high RAC horsepower rating.

In 1937 HFS Morgan fitted a 2.2-litre Ford V8 engine, which had been specifically designed for the European market, into a 4-4 which Peter Morgan later recalled being finished 'in a sort of battleship grey'. The car was extensively tested by Morgan and his son and performed

American unit. The V8 proved to be only a little heavier than the Triumph cast-iron 'four' and although barely longer was significantly wider; despite this, the Cam Gears cam-and-peg

well enough, being capable of over 90mph – even if the brakes, which had not been modified, were not really up to task.

But the experiment came to an end in 1939 when the government announced that with effect from 1940 the horsepower tax would be increased from 15s (75p) to £1.5s (£1.25) per fiscal horsepower. At the time the Ford unit was rated at 22hp, thereby requiring an annual Road Fund Licence of £16 10s (£16.50). The increase would have demanded an additional £11, bringing the total to £27.50, and the financially sagacious 'HFS' scrapped the idea. The V8 unit was removed and a supercharged Standard engine (see page 41) fitted in its place.

steering gear was retained, although the original intrusive steering column was replaced by a collapsible universally-jointed AC Delco unit.

The Buick engine's non-standard

Alloy wheels instantly identify a Plus 8; otherwise the lines are pure Plus 4. This 1969 car is the 54th example to be completed. (LAT)

Holley carburettor had been mounted on an Offenhauser manifold for an Oldsmobile. This was discarded in favour of twin SUs, but these necessitated two bonnet-top bulges. Underbonnet space was indeed at such a premium that there was no room for the fan, so a thermostatically-controlled electric Wood-Jeffreys unit was fitted.

When it came to the transmission, it proved possible to retain the separate but rough-and-tough Moss gearbox although some modifications were necessary to the V8's flywheel, to the Borg and Beck clutch and the primary driveshaft. As a result the mechanical clutch gave way to hydraulic actuation, another first for Morgan. Wire wheels were retained, although the stub axles were strengthened.

The car, registered OYE 200E, took to the road in February 1967 and Peter Morgan hoped to launch the new model at that year's London show. But in the event it would be another 18 or so before the Plus 8 could be announced.

Two obstacles needed to be overcome. Firstly, it was necessary for General Motors to give permission for

Morgan Plus 8
1984–1990

As previously except:

ENGINE:
Compression ratio	9.75:1
Fuel injection	Lucas L
Power	190bhp at 5280rpm
Torque	220lb ft at 4000rpm

STEERING:
From August 1986 rack and pinion standardised

PRICE INCLUDING TAX WHEN NEW:
£15,436 (August 1987)

Morgan Plus 8
1990–2004

As above except:

ENGINE:
Bore x stroke	94.0mm x 71.12mm
Capacity	3946cc
Compression ratio	9.35:1
Fuel injection	Lucas L-Jetronic
Power	185bhp at 4750rpm
Torque	235lb ft at 2600rpm

TRANSMISSION:
From 1994 R380 Rover five-speed gearbox

BRAKES:
From 1993 Lockheed brakes replace Girling

WHEELS/TYRES:
From 1991 optional 6.5 x 15in wire
Tyres 205/55 x 16in

BODYWORK:
From September 1997 aluminium panels

DIMENSIONS:
From September 1997:
Length	12ft 9in
Wheelbase	8ft 2in
Width	5ft 9in
Height	4ft 2in

WEIGHT:
19.2cwt

PRICE INCLUDING TAX WHEN NEW:
£25,814 (February 1992)

TOTAL NUMBER BUILT:
Approx 6000

Morgan Plus 8 4.6
1997–2004

ENGINE (optional fitment):
Bore x stroke	94mm x 82mm
Capacity	4555cc
Compression ratio	9.35:1
Fuel injection	Lucas 14 CVX
Power	220bhp at 5000rpm
Torque	260lb ft at 2600rpm

PERFORMANCE:
(Source: Morgan Motor Co)
Max speed	128mph
0–60mph	6.0sec

PRICE INCLUDING TAX WHEN NEW:
£32,489 (May 1998)

The earlier Plus 8s were considerably narrower than their descendants and were until mid-1973 just 4ft 9in wide. The headlamps are also noticeably closer to the radiator cowl than the later cars. (LAT)

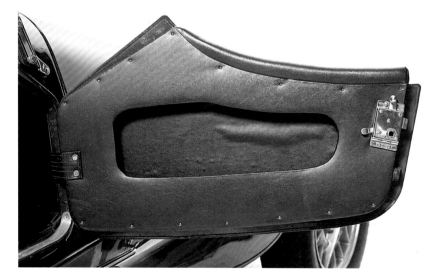

The absence of winding windows means that there is extra storage space in the doors. The padded top provides a convenient armrest for the driver. (LAT)

its engine to be used in a sports car, and this was duly forthcoming. The second concerned Rover's corporate status – for its independent existence came to an end in March 1967 when it joined the Leyland Motor Corporation. Then, in January 1968, Leyland went on to absorb the British Motor Corporation, which was then the country's largest indigenous car maker. The resulting British Leyland Motor Corporation effectively brought the entire British-owned motor industry into single ownership.

In view of BLMC's calamitous future, Peter Morgan's earlier rejection of Rover's marriage proposal would be vindicated by history. In retrospect he would also be proved right when he rejected an alternative offer to reactivate the Triumph connection by adopting the new 3-litre single-cam Triumph Stag V8: the reputation of this potentially successful model soon

Tight fit! The Rover V8 just slots under the Plus 8's bonnet – but it necessitated some attention to the air filter, which was modified by the judicious application of a hammer to provide the necessary clearance. (LAT)

became clouded by the unreliability of its engine.

With the advent of British Leyland there was now a further hurdle to be overcome before Morgan could adopt the Rover V8. British Leyland's technical director Harry Webster, who as Standard-Triumph's former chief engineer knew Morgan of old, together with George Turnbull, also ex-Triumph, but by then managing director of the Austin-Morris division, had to sample the prototype Plus 8. Owen remembers their astonishment when they had a run in the prototype: 'They couldn't believe how we'd got hold of an engine. It made us look very on the ball, and certainly helped to swing the deal'.

So the union of the Malvern chassis and body with the Detroit-designed and Solihull-refined V8 was approved and two further prototypes were completed in time for the London Motor Show, held at Earls Court in October 1968. The first of these, registered MMC 11, was subsequently road-tested by the motoring press while a second car bore the number plate AB 16, which dated from 1904! For the record the original prototype was used by Owen for a time and then passed to American arch-enthusiast Bill Fink (see page 110), whose sterling efforts with an LPG-powered Plus 8 helped to keep the marque's name alive in the US.

The wires used on the prototype had given way to five-stud rough-cast magnesium-alloy wheels finished in silver paint, the first time that alloy wheels had been used on a Morgan. They emphasised the Plus 8's flagship status but their adoption was far from being cosmetic: they were necessitated by the 160bhp generated by the V8, in contrast to the more modest 127bhp of the last of the Triumph-powered Plus 4s. As with the

Plus 4, the spare was left exposed on the rear deck, below the twin chromed filler caps used instead of the single filler that had previously sufficed; it was advisable to open both caps when filling up, to avoid splash-back. The presence of two filler caps meant that the Morgan script on the offside of the rear deck was deleted. The 13½-gallon petrol tank itself was slightly larger than previously, 12 gallons having sufficed for the Plus 4.

The Z-section chassis, which continued to pass under the axle at the rear, was essentially unchanged, with the exception of the footwells. Here the time-honoured wood was dispensed with and replaced by metal,

to give the frame some extra rigidity.

Bodily, the Plus 8 closely resembled its predecessor – although it was only ever to be produced in open two-seater form. It was however 1in wider and 8in longer, with a 1½in wider front track and a 2in wider rear track. The running-boards featured a single rubber strip on either side, although a popular option was to fit a second one which was available at extra cost. There were twin spot lights and a chromed front bumper, while the customary twin overriders sufficed at the rear; a back bumper was an optional extra.

Beneath the bonnet, heavily louvred along its top and sides, was the Rover V8. It developed maximum torque of 210lb ft at the comparatively modest figure of 2600rpm, and Morgan was the first British manufacturer to employ the engine in conjunction with a manual gearbox, albeit one which lacked synchromesh on first gear, and was archaically separated from the engine by a short driveshaft.

The engine appeared a remarkably good fit, despite its bulk, and was destined to power the Plus 8 for the next 36 years. In fact Morgan continued to install the V8 long after Rover had ceased to use the unit in its passenger cars with the 1986 demise of the SD1 model. The engine continued in use in Land Rover products, however, and its manufacture only ceased in 2004, taking the Plus 8 with it.

Although the V8's state of tune in 1968 was essentially the same as when used by Rover, the production Plus 8 did differ in some respects from Maurice Owen's prototype. The most obvious under-bonnet difference was that the twin SU HS6 carburettors now snuggled close to the top of the unit. In its original Buick guise the engine had a single four-barrel fixed-jet Rochester carburettor. Rover had given some consideration to retaining the Rochester but decided against it because the engine would be subjected to cornering surges of a type familiar to European motorists but not to their less energetic transatlantic counterparts.

Rover's installation thus used two semi-downdraught SU carburettors, each positioned at an angle and feeding its opposite cylinder bank. The

The Plus 8 dashboard as it appeared at the car's 1968 launch. The presence of rocker switches, in accordance with American safety regulations, reflects the importance that Morgan then attached to the US market. (LAT)

carbs were mounted on a bespoke steel manifold which was unusual in that it was extended to cover the vee of the cylinder banks.

One careful modification was however required at Pickersleigh Road so that Rover's circular air filter would fit beneath the bonnet. A wooden block was placed directly on the top of the cover which was then smartly whacked with a hammer to produce the necessary indentation . . .

So tight was the installation that another modification was to remove an elliptical section of front wing to accommodate the alternator. In these circumstances it will come as no surprise to hear that the unit can be the very devil to change. The cooling system was also a squeeze. The presence of the electric fan has already been referred to but there also

wasn't room for a radiator header tank so a separate reservoir was used, positioned between the radiator and the engine.

Finally, lest the Plus 8 owner should think that this engine made the car a thoroughly modern Morgan, the tool kit still resided in a full-width scuttle-mounted box, a location that harked back to the 1930s.

The interior was new but basic, with the wooden dashboard covered in Ambla and a central instrument panel with the speedometer on the left and a combination dial on the right, the rev-counter being positioned on the dashboard itself, to the right of the driver. Rocker switches were used, to conform to American safety regulations current from January 1968. The steering wheel, finally, was a three-spoked black-finished Astrali,

The distinctive combined rear light and reflector unit as fitted to the Plus 8 from 1968 until 1971. (LAT)

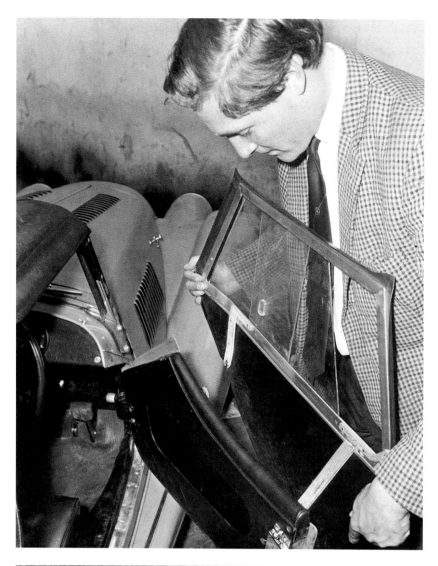

Michael Bowler, then a road tester on Motor and subsequently editor of Classic Car and now The Automobile magazine, demonstrates the Plus 8's sidescreens. He is credited with coining the word 'Transmogrification' to describe the Plus 8. (LAT)

while the floor covering was no-nonsense fluted rubber matting.

The triple wipers for the fixed windscreen were another first for Morgan, as were the Restall bucket seats, replacing the long-running fixed bench; designed by Maurice Owen, they drew on his racing experience. Ambla upholstery was standard but pleated leather was available at extra cost, as were folding and reclining seats.

But modernity only went so far: drivers still had to lubricate the independent front suspension every day by pressing a pedal, which duly delivered engine oil to the working parts.

Weather equipment was as basic as ever, with a simple hood, located by three hoops and secured to the top of the windscreen by press-studs. Perspex sidescreens, complete with sliding panels, were retained.

Morgan deemed that the brakes would only require modest enhancement. The front 11in discs, assisted by a Girling Powerstop servo, used 16P Girling callipers with greater resistance to fade than the 14P units used on the Plus 4, while the 9in rear drums were unchanged.

Similarly the rear axle was carried over, although the Salisbury 7HA unit now had a 3.58:1 ratio, the highest available, and a Powr Lok limited-slip differential was fitted. Rear suspension was by the traditional five-leaf springs, although a stiffer six-leaf set-up was used for a time; Armstrong lever-arm dampers were retained.

Selling for £1477, which was a substantial £562 more than the £915 the last Plus 4 had cost, the Plus 8 was capable of over 120mph, which was an impressive enough top speed. But the

The seats differ from those of the Plus 4 in being Restall units. (LAT)

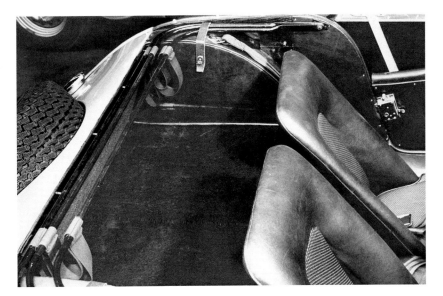

really memorable aspect of the model was its acceleration, the result of a light, powerful V8 being installed in an equally light chassis. The Morgan was able to reach 60mph in just 6.7 seconds, which was better than the MGC, Lotus Elan and Triumph TR5 – and even the E-type Jaguar, which cost £651 more.

The first Plus 8 road test was published in A*utocar* on 12 September 1968. The summary pithily distilled the Morgan's appeal: 'Superb performance and very great flexibility. Poor synchromesh on top three gears; precise but stiff gearchange. Fade-free brakes. Hard bumpy ride. Very good smooth-surface roadholding, not as good on bad roads. Heavy, accurate steering; poor lock. Great fun.'

The testers recorded a top speed of 124mph, achieved, for aerodynamic considerations, with the hood raised. This made the Plus 8 noisier than when the car was driven in open form. The hood also took some time to erect, and suffered from irritating blind spots. The rear-view mirror was not much good either, as the windscreen vibrated in sympathy with the suspension. But when the hood was lowered, the Morgan's top speed dropped to 118mph. Despite such limitations, the magazine reported that 'maximum speed runs on a bumpy Belgian *autoroute* were far more exciting at 124mph in the Morgan than they have been in modern Grand Touring cars at over 150'.

There was no doubt that its performance was the key to the Plus 8's appeal, and A*utocar* praised its 'wonderful flexibility'. But there was a down side. Once at the wheel it was necessary to become acclimatised to steering 'from the elbows rather than with the finger tips'. The suspension was predictably unyielding, needless to say, and the ride was judged 'decidedly uncomfortable over second-class roads', despite well-padded seats.

'One cannot help thinking that even more remarkable results could be

Bowler unrolls the Plus 8's hood, essentially the same as that on the Plus 4. (LAT)

achieved with more up to date suspension and a better gearbox without losing anything of the car's tremendous character,' concluded the test. But the final words of the evaluation betray the testers' underlying affection for the Morgan, flaws and all: 'Perhaps the spontaneous remark made when slowing hard after an acceleration run at MIRA does the job adequately – "There's a lot which could be better, but there's an awful lot right".'

Rival M*otor* was not able to take the

same car abroad to extend it fully but achieved a speed of 120.8mph at the MIRA circuit. Fuel consumption was 20.3mpg, which gave a range of about 250 miles. The Morgan's performance and its smooth-road handling was praised, but other aspects of the Plus 8 were trenchantly criticised. 'On grade two surfaces,' wrote the magazine, 'the ride is so bad that roadholding suffers more than do the

14" X 11" X 5"

17½" X 13" X 6"

21" X 15" X 7"

MMC 11

appeared a natural candidate for the US market. But the model only ever enjoyed switchback fortunes in the States, as a result of safety and emissions legislation. In 1960 some 85 per cent of Morgan's production had crossed the Atlantic. However, the US economy went into recession in the early 1960s and, although Peter Morgan's personal sales drive saved the situation, it did highlight the company's vulnerability to having such a high proportion of its sales vested in one country.

As a result Morgan switched the emphasis to continental Europe and the home market. America then provided a further obstacle by announcing in 1965 its first wave of emissions and safety regulations, due to come into effect on 1 January 1968. As a small company, Morgan was given a two-year extension to comply but in the event it chose instead to pull out of the US market. Such had been the growth of demand in the Old World that by 1968 American sales had dropped considerably, and Peter Morgan could feel fairly relaxed about a withdrawal – although he respected the loyalty of his American customers.

But when Rover entered the US market in 1970 with a version of its 3500 saloon, Morgan decided to return, as it was able to benefit from Rover's emissions certification for the V8 engine. Unfortunately the Rover received a decisive thumbs-down from the American public, although, by contrast, the Plus 8 was well received. Faced with this rebuff, in 1972 Rover pulled out of the US, and Morgan was left with the obligation of applying for its own type-approval documentation. In view of the small numbers of cars involved, it decided against this, and withdrew again from the US. The Morgan standard was upheld in America by Bill Fink of Isis Motors in San Francisco, who in due course introduced his own propane-powered Plus 8 (see page 110).

Raising the hood did take a little time and was ideally a two-person task. (LAT)

passengers; moreover protection from the weather in an otherwise comfortable and civilised cockpit is about as primitive as you can get and the gearbox is about as Vintage as the styling'.

A few minor changes were

introduced to the Plus 8 in 1969. The single exhaust pipe was found on occasions to foul the rear wheel when the car was cornered fast on right-hand bends, and so it was replaced by twin outlets. Later in the same year the distance between the chassis sidemembers was increased by 2in.

On paper the Plus 8, with its American-designed V8 engine,

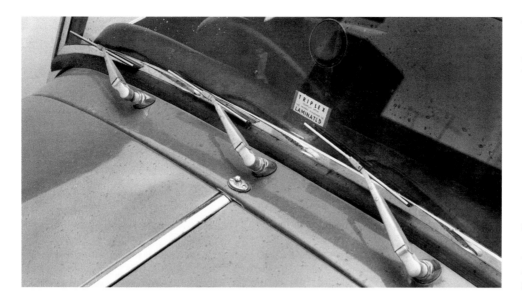

The triple windscreen wipers were a first for Morgan, a feature that was subsequently extended to the 4/4 and Plus 4. (LAT)

Safety padding was added to the top of the Plus 8's cockpit in 1971. Note the rubber mats, which were replaced by carpeting in 1974. (LAT)

The Plus 8 had in the meantime continued to evolve. In 1970 the metal footwells, themselves an innovation on the Plus 8, were replaced by wooden boards on account of rust problems with the metal panels. In 1971 the model underwent a more visible change, dictated by increasingly stringent American safety requirements, when the scuttle top received a layer of padding matching the interior trim. Similarly, the hard plastic used for the boss of the steering wheel was replaced by a softer material, easily identifiable by the presence of the Morgan script. But it was European regulations that required the fitment at the same time of anti-burst door locks.

Further albeit modest changes came in the autumn of 1971. Wider 15 x 6.5in wheels were fitted, these also having the virtue of being better-quality castings than the originals. At the same time the triangular stop/tail lamps and the round rear indicators were replaced by matching round units mounted on chromed plastic pods, a square reflector on a painted plastic plinth being mounted below

There is only one factory-built Plus 8 drophead coupé, constructed in 1971 for Peter Morgan's wife, Jane; it is also the only works automatic Plus 8. It inspired this intriguing one-off, built in the late 1990s by Morgan specialist Bob Harper – hence the personalised registration number. (LAT)

A P-registered car endowed with the twin exhaust pipes that replaced the single outlet from the 1972 model year. (LAT)

the stop/tail unit.

A more radical change occurred in April 1972 when the rugged but unrefined Moss gearbox was replaced by Rover's all-synchromesh 2000-based manual transmission developed for its 3500S model. This meant that the Moss unit, a Morgan feature since 1939, was discontinued after only 702 Plus 8s had been so equipped. Whilst the new gearbox's operation was certainly an improvement on its noisy predecessor, positioning it in-unit with the engine meant there was less footroom in the Plus 8 cockpit.

Further improvements included the arrival of a larger-capacity radiator to improve cooling. This followed complaints of overheating from some customers in warmer climates. In response to occasional breakages, a mechanical modification at the same time was to fit stronger stub axles and steering arms.

The engine underwent a modest change in specification in 1973 when the compression ratio was reduced from 10.5:1 to 9.35:1. This was undertaken in the face of increasingly stringent emissions legislation and the impending demise of five-star petrol. The carburettors were changed for the same reason, Rover switching to the latest H1 F6 type of SU. But there was a downside to these modifications because output was reduced by 17bhp.

March 1973 saw the old recirculating heater, which had first appeared in 1955, replaced by a fresh-air unit. This was now located on the bulkhead under the bonnet, which reduced the dimensions of the toolbox somewhat. In August the same year the front wings were widened and the track increased to 4ft 3in at the front and 4ft 4in at the rear, while the final-drive ratio rose from 3.58:1 to 3.32:1; engine power, as a result of detoxing, was now quoted at 143bhp rather than the preceding 160bhp. On a non-technical tack, Morgan began to recognise the creature comforts of its customers in 1974 when the all-too-basic rubber matting was replaced by a nylon/wool carpeting.

At the 1975 London Motor Show a variation on the Plus 8 theme was unveiled in the shape of the limited-production Sports Lightweight, of which only 19 were built between late 1975 and early in 1977. The mechanicals were essentially unchanged but the wider bodywork (at 5ft 2in) in 'broken white', differed in being made of 18-gauge aluminium. The Lightweight was more obviously distinguished by 14in oval-slotted, black-finished Millrace alloy wheels.

The 1976 Motor Show saw the

A 1976 car at speed, a photograph which clearly indicates the noticeable gap between the front bumper and wings. (LAT)

Rear view of a 1976 Plus 8, even if the all-too-appropriate registration number dates from 1964! Round rear lamps werte introduced for 1972, with a separate rectangular reflector on a plinth. (LAT)

The year 1976 was the last in which the original rough-cast alloy wheels were fitted to the Plus 8. (LAT)

While the dashboard of this 1976 car is essentially the same as its 1968 forebear, the gearlever now actuates a Rover rather than a Moss gearbox. (LAT)

The Plus 8 dashboard was redesigned for the 1977 season, with the rev-counter and speedometer relocated in front of the driver and four auxiliary dials in a reshaped centre panel. Although the steering wheel was carried over, it was soon replaced by one with plain spokes. (LAT)

The '68 look remains intact on this later car – apart from the 14in Millrace wheels, which replaced the original rough-cast alloy wheels in 1977. These were fitted for five years, being discontinued early in 1982. (LAT)

The open road…with the Millrace spare wheel and redesigned dashboard clearly visible. (LAT)

Morgan's press demonstrator, showing the improved quality of alloy wheel, similar in design to the originals and back to 15in, as introduced in 1982. The wheels bear the legend 'Morgan Motor Company Ltd' on their periphery. (LAT)

Classical gas

From 1976 until the early 1990s the Morgan name was more or less single-handedly upheld in America by the irrepressible Bill Fink of San Francisco. In 1972 Morgan had been forced to withdraw from the US market in the wake of Rover's retreat. But personally-imported cars were subjected to less swingeing regulations and Fink was accordingly able to circumvent this legislation.

The multifaceted American collected university degrees in the way in which some people collect cars, reading English Literature at Yale and Business Administration at Stamford, while on the other side of the Atlantic he attained a diploma in social studies at Keble College, Oxford, where he was also a successful oarsman. This is why his American car sales business was named Isis Motors, after the river which runs through the city.

It was through his sale of secondhand Morgans that Fink established contact with Peter Morgan and when official exports to the US ceased, he immediately sought ways to sidestep the legal barriers. A dialogue with the US Department of Transport and members of the environmental lobby produced the information that propane-powered cars were exempt from the usual restrictions. Armed with this knowledge, in 1973 Fink approached Peter Morgan for factory co-operation. As a result he was promised 24 cars a year, but because of protracted delays in obtaining the necessary permission from the US authorities, deliveries did not begin until 1976.

The Plus 8s dispatched to America were specially modified to meet safety regulations, being fitted with the windscreen from the four-seater 4/4 and having an unobtrusive reinforcing steel hoop bolted to the chassis behind the dashboard. There were also inertia-reel seat belts, while gas-filled dampers replaced the usual lever-arm units.

On arrival at Fink's premises the cars' wings were modified to accept 5mph impact bumpers and steel beams introduced into the doors as side protection for occupants. Modifications then had to be made to the ignition, carburettors, fuel lines, petrol tank and fillers so that the engine would run on propane. As if that were not enough, Fink had to compile a 45-page dossier illustrating and setting down the modifications. But he persisted, and there were even a few turbocharged cars, for those Americans for whom Morgan had become a way of life.

When in 1989 Sir John Harvey-Jones visited Morgan, he reported that the company had a lean-burn engine under development for the American market. In fact the company was fortunate that when the Range Rover began to be sold there from the 1990 season, the Plus 8's V8 engine was once again US-eligible. This coincided with the arrival of the catalytic converter model, which allowed albeit low-key sales to begin. This obviated the need for Bill Fink's propane-powered cars, but it took until September 1998 for the model to be sanctioned for sale in America in its own right.

Leyland's '77mm' unit, so named after the distance between the mainshaft and layshaft centres. It had been created for use in a range of corporate products, from the Triumph TR7 sports car to Jaguar's XJ-12 luxury saloon, and its adoption by Morgan reduced fuel consumption and gave the car a welcome extra dose of refinement. Fitting it in the Plus 8 required the gearbox mounting rails to be moved further apart and the attendant crossmember moved back in the chassis; this was accompanied by the engine being moved back a little, improving weight distribution and making front-end accessibility better. The chassis was also widened by 2in, bringing with it an increase in the track, this time to 4ft 5in at the front and 4ft 6in at the rear.

Marking the powertrain changes was a move to small-diameter 6.0 x 14in Millrace alloy wheels similar to those on the Sports Lightweight: a subtle difference was that the angular slots had raised rather than flat edges.

During 1977 changes were made to the dashboard, with the speedo and rev-counter now in front of the driver and four separate auxiliary dials in a reshaped central panel; this configuration lasted in its essentials until the end of production, with the option from 1989 of a walnut dashboard.

Externally, the steel front bumper was replaced by an aluminium-alloy one, with a matching bumper at the the rear. Although the low-volume Sports Lightweight ceased production in 1977, its wings, both in width and profile, became standard wear on the Plus 8 proper during the course of that year. Aluminium bodywork could now be specified, too, although in the interests of rigidity both the scuttle and cowl continued to be produced from steel.

Refinements for 1979 were minimal, with door mirrors now fitted as standard, while 1981 saw right-hand-drive cars using Cibie headlamps. This was the last year of the Girling brake servo, and the system thereafter lacked any assistance. One-piece carpeting was also introduced, with

arrival of a more radical improvement to the Plus 8 when it received the five-speed gearbox and revised 3.5-litre engine from Rover's new SD1 saloon, introduced in June 1976. The 155bhp engine had better low-range torque and was easily identifiable by its smaller air cleaner – which meant that

Morgan no longer had to tin-bash the casing to make it fit. In addition there was a new four-branch exhaust system with a tubular manifold for better gas flow, while a deeper radiator meant that the separate header tank was no longer needed.

The new gearbox was British

In June 1984 the Plus 8 was fitted with the 190bhp V8 engine that Rover used in the Vitesse, the high-performance version of its SD1 saloon. (LAT)

The all-important refinement of rack-and-pinion steering was offered as an option on the Plus 8 from the 1984 season. Costing £1100, it was standardised in August 1986. (LAT)

at Pickersleigh Road; in any event, the Plus 8's increasingly wide track was beginning to make the steering unacceptably heavy. Morgan therefore commissioned a bespoke rack and steering gear from Jack Knight Developments of Woking, Surrey; this was initially offered as a £1100 option, but was standardised in August 1986.

The 1984 season also saw the optional fitment of the 190bhp Rover Vitesse fuel-injected engine, from June of that year. By 1986 most Plus 8s were leaving the factory with this unit, which was eventually standardised in 1987. The injected engine was a tight squeeze in the Morgan, being dominated by a plenum chamber which made it necessary to cut away a

the seats now being bolted directly through the pile. From February 1982, the Plus 8 reverted to the original style of 15in wheels, but with a smoother casting and with a 'Morgan +8' logo on their centre cap.

Further engine changes arrived for the 1982 season, when the twin SU carburettors featured on the model since its 1968 introduction gave way to a pair of Stromberg 175 CDs, complete with automatic choke, to the benefit of exhaust emissions.

In 1984 there were fears within the industry that Cam Gears, a long-time Birmingham-based supplier of steering boxes to Morgan, was about to go out of business. This concentrated minds

May the sun never set on Morgan. A fine photographic study of a 1985 Plus 8. (LAT)

section of the bonnet hinge. Outward changes to the Plus 8 during 1983 included the fitting as standard of twin round reversing lights on the rear numberplate plinth; previously these had been an option. At the same time two rear fog lamps were mounted on the rear deck, latterly being replaced, in 1986, by a single lamp attached to the bumper.

For 1987 the dual exhausts were replaced by a single pipe, complete with three silencer boxes, while the tubular manifold gave way to a cast-iron Land Rover item. More significantly, in April 1990 Morgan was able to benefit from an enlarged 3.9-litre 190bhp engine, as used in the

Range Rover Vogue SE. Initially available without a catalytic exhaust, subsequent examples were fitted with three-way cats, resulting in increased torque. As a consequence of the increasingly complex specification of the Rover engine, Morgan ended up being forced to re-work the drive to the ancillaries, when V8s started to arrive at Pickersleigh Road complete with pumps for air-conditioning and power-steering. Such refinements were clearly surplus to requirements, and their deletion meant re-routing the engine's beltwork. One unexpected benefit resulted in the relocation of the alternator, making its replacement a far quicker task than had hitherto been the case. With the Range Rover being sold on the American market, another side-effect

of the new engine was that Morgan was able to return to the US, albeit in a low-key way, with the Plus 8 not gaining type approval in its own right for a further eight years.

February 1991, meanwhile, marked a significant change to the Plus 8's rear suspension with the disappearance of the lever-arm dampers in favour of Gabriel telescopic units. These required the introduction of a transverse tube to which the tops of the new dampers were fixed; they were attached at their lower ends to triangular plates secured to the rear axle casing.

When *Autocar* came to test the 3.9-litre Plus 8 in May 1991 it reported that there was a six-year waiting list for the £22,849 model – which with the options of aluminium wings and

A 1985 car ready for an English summer! The chromed plastic rear light plinths are readily apparent in this shot. Introduced in 1971, they survived in this form until 1987, when the plinths were painted the same colour as the body. (LAT)

Fuel injection was gradually introduced to the Plus 8 from the 1984 season and most cars were so equipped by 1986 – although this '86 example retains carburettors. Note the twin Strombergs which replaced the SUs in 1981. (LAT)

A 1989 car. By this time the Plus 8's width had increased from the 4ft 9in of the original car to 5ft 3in, with effect from 1982. (LAT)

The immaculate 'office' of a 1986 Plus 8. That year the T-shaped warning-light cluster was replaced by a similar arrangement made up of separate units. (LAT)

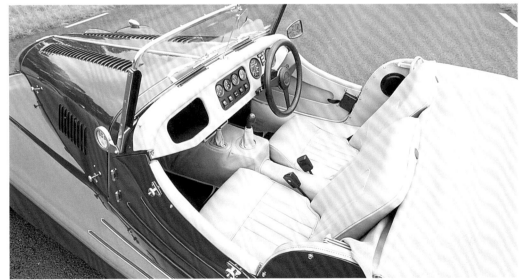

Perfect open-air motoring: a 1991 car in profile. (LAT)

The walnut-faced dashboard of this 1991 Plus 8 was offered as an option from 1989 and subsequently standardised. (LAT)

The 3.9-litre Range Rover engine in a 1991 car; equipped with fully mappable hot-wire fuel injection, it was fitted to the Plus 8 from mid-1990. (LAT)

Driving a Plus 8

No Morgan is more defined by its engine than the Plus 8, the Rover V8 giving the trad-Morgan flagship a unique colouring and a truly seductive character. But it's not quite as simple as that: evolution of the breed over its long life means that each significant development of the Plus 8 has brought to the car a subtly different flavour.

Common to all Plus 8s is gorgeous flexibility, a beguiling exhaust note, and sufficient power to have the rear end stepping out of line any time you want to play hooligan – not least in the wet.

Early cars feel zingier, thanks to their close-ratio Moss gearbox and the purely physical messages sent out by the narrower body and the more abrupt suspension. The gearbox might have sluggish synchromesh but the crisp action and short throw have an immediacy lacking in later Rover-'boxed cars, while the steering has more weight, relatively little self-centring, and an inevitable element of play at the straight-ahead.

Move up to a four-speed Rover-gearbox Plus 8 and there's a less mechanical feel to the gearchange but a blessed improvement in synchromesh efficiency. With higher ratios and a taller back axle, cruising is more relaxed, while cars with the Gemmer steering box have lighter and more accurate steering, with stronger self-centring. The skittish behaviour of the car on bumps is unchanged, as are such Morgan constants as the arms-bent driving position, the weighty clutch and brake actions, the bottom-hinged pedals that some find awkward, and the delightful little fly-off handbrake.

With the five-speed gearbox there is disdainfully laid-back top-gear cruising as a new facet of the Morgan, while cars with the Jack Knight steering rack point with all the accuracy you'd expect of a rack, yet without any heaviness. Add a 3.9-litre engine to the pot and you have more beef, translating into engagingly broad-chested mid-range pulling power: the way the Plus 8 surges forward without the need for a down-change is truly impressive. Consider that a cat-equipped 3.9 punches out 235lb ft of torque at 2600rpm, against the original car's 210lb ft at 3000rpm, and you can understand why. Another change you're also sure to appreciate is that after the 1991 move to telescopic rear dampers the rear end is better tied down on poor roads – although the board-firm ride remains. Finally, the 1993 switch to twin-pot callipers signalled not only greater braking efficiency, but a less bicep-enhancing pedal action.

These later cars are broader in beam – by a full 8in, if you compare the first Plus 8s with the last; they are also heavier, and more plush in their interior trim. But they are also more comfortable (especially in late long-cockpit form), grippier on poor roads, and have not lost any of their V8 muscle: the 4.6-litre is in fact the fastest Plus 8 of the lot, with even more effortless overtaking abilities. Some of the bought-in cockpit hardware might disappoint, but the final generations are also the best-built Plus 8s ever to leave the factory. As an example of how to hone a design without losing its essential character, the Plus 8 doesn't do too badly.

in-gear grunt at normal speeds (in other words, less than 80mph) you won't catch the Morgan'.

These figures showed a big improvement on the times compared with a Plus 8 tested in 1987 although the top speed of 121mph remained about the same – and slower than the 1968 original. 'The old car sprinted to 60mph in 5.6sec and to 100mph in 16.4sec. Now, it can't quite break the six-second barrier to 60mph and is two seconds slower to 100mph,' lamented the road-testers.

From March 1993 the Plus 8's looks were enhanced by the optional fitment of wire wheels. These wires were imported from India, and were to be standardised from 1998. For the 1994 season the wheels, whether wire or alloy, hid a new Lockheed disc/drum braking system with four-piston callipers for the front discs. In the same year the Plus 8 was fitted with Rover's improved R380 gearbox – as indeed was the Plus 4. Designed for the new-generation Range Rover, it was quieter and had better change quality.

In 1996, Morgan bade farewell to another long-running component when the Salisbury rear axle was replaced by an Australian-built BTR unit. Traditionalists might have been disposed to whine, but warranty claims dropped markedly . . .

The 1998 models, announced in September 1997, witnessed some radical although at a first glance imperceptible changes to the specification. The most significant of these was the introduction of all-aluminium bodywork in place of steel or a steel and alloy combination. The alloy body also had the dashboard moved slightly forward, doors that were longer by 1½in, and more rearward seat movement to allow the introduction of optional twin air bags, with the passenger bag ingeniously located behind a folding aluminium cover disguised with walnut veneer. The dashboard itself was also redesigned, with the four supplementary dials now stacked two-by-two rather than strung out in a line. Less apparent was a stainless-steel bar behind the dash, to limit body

bonnet, leather trim, mohair hood and walnut dashboard ended up costing a steep £25,229 in total.

As a result of the power-sapping catalytic converters the enlarged engine was no more powerful than its

predecessor. But torque was up seven per cent to 235lb ft at a lower peak of 2600rpm and the 0–60mph figure had by then been shaved to 6.1 seconds. 'Porsche 911 Turbo drivers eat your hearts out,' advised the magazine: 'for

The cockpit of an immaculate 1994 car. The thickness of the seat squabs indicates that these are of the folding and reclining variety. (LAT)

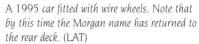

The 1994 Plus 8s were offered with the option of a 4.2-litre engine alongside the 3.9-litre unit. (LAT)

A 1995 car fitted with wire wheels. Note that by this time the Morgan name has returned to the rear deck. (LAT)

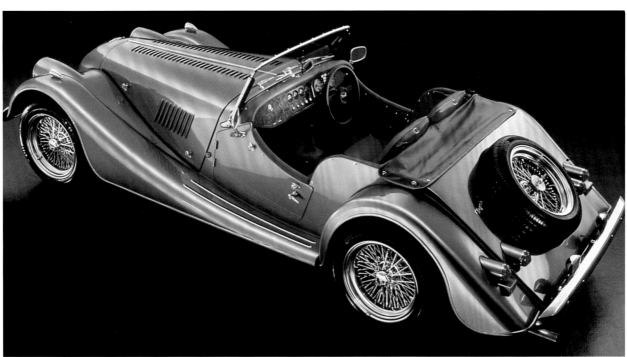

Buying Hints

1. As the Plus 8 effectively inherited the Plus 4's body and chassis, see the Buying Hints relating to that model and the 4-4 (pages 48–49 and 72). However, it is worth underlining the fact that aluminium bodywork was available on the Plus 8 from 1977 onwards. This is obviously preferable to steel, although that material was retained for the radiator cowl and scuttle and so you should look out for signs of corrosive electrolytic action where the two metals meet.

2. Where aluminium rather than steel wings have been fitted, check for stone damage. The factory's response was to coat the wing undersides with underseal, something that owners of cars not so treated can do for themselves.

3. As with the 4/4 and Plus 4, the really important date as far as the Plus 8's bodywork is concerned is 1986, when significant improvements (see page 72) were made to the build quality. One aspect of this was that with the arrival of all-aluminium bodies in 1998 the front wings were made in one piece, apart from the headlamp pods, rather than in four sections welded together. But perversely the wings continued to be edged using steel wire; again, this uneasy combination of metals can prompt electrolytic corrosion.

4. The Rover V8 engine is a remarkably reliable and long-lived unit and will run for 100,000 miles without attention; oil and filter

changes at the specified intervals are essential, because of the presence of hydraulic tappets. As an all-aluminium engine, the use of the correct anti-freeze is important.

5. Despite its wide use in Rover cars, parts for earlier engines can be surprisingly difficult to find – especially items such as the exhaust manifolds. Between 1976 and 1986 the Plus 8 used variations on the Rover SD1 engine and there were some 107,000 of those built, plus 3900 or so Vitesses, so in theory there should be many more secondhand parts available.

6. Cars built before 1977 have distributors with contact-breaker points. Keeping the correct dwell angle is a problem and this can cause misfiring. Many Plus 8s have consequently been converted to the later more efficient electronic ignition system.

7. The fuel pumps on post-1977 cars (up until the mid-90s) have a reputation for failing without warning. Many owners carry a spare.

8. The Moss gearbox fitted until 1972 is notchy with poor synchromesh. It is also susceptible to damaged teeth on first and reverse cogs. The Rover four-speed unit of 1971–76 is an improvement, not least as it has first-gear synchromesh. However, the selectors tend to weaken and introduce an element of chance into the business of

gearchanging. Today reliability is a problem and parts are difficult to find. By contrast, the Rover five-speed unit combines consistency with ease of use. The fuel-injected Vitesse engine came complete with a revised five-speed gearbox, and spares are no longer easily availabile. It was replaced in 1994 with another five-speeder, courtesy of the Range Rover, and parts for this present less of a problem.

9. The Plus 8's dual-circuit brakes are good and were originally servo-assisted although the servo was deleted from the 1982 season. However, it is possible to fit one – Girling used to do a kit – and the brakes will feel better for it.

10. One noticeable difference between the Plus 4 and Plus 8 is the steering column. This is split on the 8 and wear does occur in the universal joints. If this has occurred the shorter of the two shafts may require replacement; the top bush can also wear, which makes the entire column feel loose. As far as the steering itself is concerned, the Cam Gears box used in pre-1985 cars suffered from excessive play when new and today it is difficult to adjust and recondition. Some owners of pre-1985 Plus 8s have fitted the Gemmer steering box used in 1987-on 4/4s and Plus 4s in place of the Cam Gears box. The Gemmer has the advantage of being relatively easy to install, is lighter in use and has the added advantage of having improved self-centring.

deformation in a side impact. The provision of air bags, in particular, reflected the fact that the Plus 8 was about to return in earnest to the American market, from September 1998.

All of these changes – 21 in all – improved comfort and helped accommodate taller drivers. Helping

achieve this was a rearrangement of the battery and fuel system which made it possible to redesign the back of the car. The result was a precious two extra inches of cockpit space – although admittedly this was taken up by a new hood and its attendant larger sidescreens.

A supplementary 1998 model with a

4.6-litre engine was introduced for the home market, alongside the existing car; the federal-specification Plus 8 continued solely as a 3.9-litre. The enlarged power unit produced 220bhp, and Morgan claimed a top speed of 128mph and a 0-60mph figure of 6 seconds. These figures were confirmed by *Autocar*, the magazine pronouncing

This is the cockpit of a 1999 example. There is now more interior room, thanks to packaging changes introduced during the 1998 season, together with the option of dual airbags. (LAT)

The top of range 4.6-litre V8 was offered in the Plus 8 from 1998; this is a 1999 car. (LAT)

the 4.6 litre V8 to be 'torquier than ever . . . but judging from the ease with which it pulls away from idle in fifth, most of this must be available from tickover'. The only occasion that the engine failed to deliver, it felt, was at the top of the rev range. Above 5000rpm, it wrote, the engine was 'disappointingly flat compared with the harder-hitting TVR versions'.

The testers applauded Morgan for the changes it had made to the cockpit, which had 'done wonders for ease of access and comfort'. Swing open the featherlight doors on their leather retaining straps, and 'you can now ease yourself down the slim gap between the steering wheel and seat cushion without too much trouble'. The new dashboard was deemed a useful improvement too, although the steering wheel obscured much of the speedometer.

But the days of the robust but ageing pushrod V8 were clearly numbered, principally because it was unable to meet increasingly rigorous emission regulations. American homologation for the Plus 8 expired at the end of 2003 and the final cars were built in March 2004. However, in 2003, the last full year of production, Morgan celebrated the 35th anniversary of the Plus 8 launch with a special Anniversary model. A total of

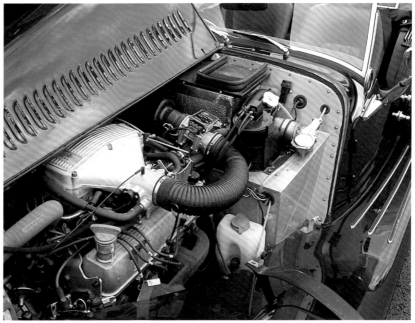

200 were made, evenly split between the European and American markets. These had such goodies as special or metallic paint, overriders and undertrays, leather upholstery and a walnut dashboard.

The Rover V8 has been replaced by the Ford 3-litre V6 which powers the current Mondeo ST220. Despite the engine's smaller capacity, it develops more power, having an output of 217bhp, as opposed to the 190bhp of

the Rover unit. The revised model, which outwardly resembles its predecessor, is both lighter and quicker and is called the Roadster. It was launched at the 2004 British Motor Show and outwardly resembles its illustrious predecessor. Costing £34,992 for the standard car, this made it some £500 cheaper than the 4 litre Plus 8. There was also a lighter version of the Roadster for use on the track which sold for £29,374.

The Aero 8

The first Aero 8 on the road, showing its lines to good effect. Although the traditional Morgan radiator grille is retained, the engine's air intake is located beneath it. (LAT)

Press day at the 2000 Geneva Motor Show was held on 29 February and there Morgan unveiled the Aero 8, its first wholly new model since 'HFS' had launched his Runabout in 1910. Showgoers, reported *Autocar*, were 'bemused' by the newcomer – although, apparently, 'Morgan fans loved it' and 60 orders had been received before the car had been revealed to the public at the Show.

From the very outset here was a model that would be the subject of debate, some of it heated. But there can be little doubting the car's significance in Morgan's history as a company. Apart from a mere 16 body parts, the Aero 8, which inherited its name from a celebrated three-wheeler, was a completely new model with a

purpose-designed chassis and body. It was also the first Morgan to be powered by a BMW engine, and marked a significant shift up-market for the Malvern Link company. Selling at £55,000 in 2004, it costs at the time of writing some £20,000 more than the last Plus 8 – the sort of money that would buy *two* 4/4 four-seaters.

Whilst the body, with its separate wings and running boards, quite intentionally displays some family relationship to its Malvern cousins, the styling has proved to be controversial. This is mainly on account of the front end, in which the traditional Morgan radiator grille is flanked by a pair of headlights that are recessed into the wings in what some see as an unsettlingly cross-eyed fashion. Fortunately there is much more to the

The architects of the Aero 8 project, Charles Morgan (left) and technical director Chris Lawrence. (LAT)

Charles Morgan's styling sketches of the Aero 8 closely resemble the finished product. (LAT)

Aero 8 than its 'retro' body lines. In particular there is a bespoke aluminium chassis which plays host to Morgan's first all-independent suspension system. HFS Morgan's famous sliding pillars have, at long last, been sidelined although they survive on the Plus 8's successor and the four-cylinder cars.

To examine the origins of this immensely significant model, which took some four years and about £3 million of company money to develop, it is first necessary to retrace our steps to 1992. It was then that Charles Morgan, together with newly recruited

Chris Lawrence, who provided Morgan with its celebrated class win at Le Mans in 1962, set down their thoughts for a wholly new car. Their intention was to repeat the impact that the Plus 8 had made on its introduction in 1968 – most notably thanks to its impressively flexible performance, made possible by fitting a large-capacity lightweight engine in an equally light chassis.

The brief was for a target weight of 1000kg (19.7cwt), with power to come from a large unstressed V8 with plenty of torque, and for there to be 50:50 weight distribution and a coupling of high speed with aerodynamic stability. The car also had to be quieter and easier to live with than the Plus 8, and to retain coachbuilt construction despite the introduction of modern aluminium technology. Intended initially for sale only on the home and European markets, American type approval would follow later.

The Morgan/Lawrence parentage provided an essential ingredient in the Aero 8's evolution, namely the contribution made to the design by racing. The first tangible steps in this direction were taken in 1994 when Charles Morgan promoted a racing Plus 8 coupé for the 1995 racing season. It was built around a chassis which was in effect the familiar but all-too-flexible Morgan Z-section frame reinforced with sheet aluminium and

Morgan Aero 8
2001 to date

ENGINE:
V8; aluminium block and aluminium cylinder heads

Bore x stroke	82.7mm x 92mm
Capacity	4398cc
Valve actuation	Twin overhead camshafts, 4 valves per cylinder
Compression ratio	10.0:1
Fuel injection	Bosch, with engine management
Power	286bhp at 5500rpm
Torque	322lb ft at 3700rpm

TRANSMISSION:
Rear-wheel drive; six-speed all-synchromesh gearbox in unit with engine

SUSPENSION:
Front: Independent, single upper link, wishbones, coil springs
Rear: Independent, double wishbones, coil springs

STEERING:
Rack-and-pinion; variable power assistance
Turns lock-to-lock: 2.4

BRAKES:
Anti-lock
Front: Hydraulic; ventilated 330mm disc
Rear: Hydraulic; ventilated 306mm disc

WHEELS/TYRES:
Cast magnesium alloy 9 x 18in
Tyres 225/40 ZR18 Pirelli P6000

BODYWORK:
Coachbuilt construction, aluminium panels on ash frame. Glued and rivetted aluminium hull
Open two-seater

DIMENSIONS:

Length	13ft 6in
Wheelbase	8ft 3in
Track, front and rear	8ft 3in
Width	5ft 9in
Height	3ft 11in

WEIGHT:
22.3cwt

PERFORMANCE:
(Source: *Autocar*)

Max speed	151mph
0–50mph	3.7sec
0–60mph	4.8sec
0–70mph	6.2sec

PRICE INCLUDING TAX WHEN NEW:
£55,500 (March 2004)

NUMBER BUILT:
272 (to January 2004)

Third-generation Morgan

Charles Peter Henry Morgan is as identifiable with the Aero 8 of 2000 in the same way that the Runabout was the product of his grandfather's fertile mind 90 years before. Now Morgan's chairman, having succeeded to the position in 2003 following the death of his father, he is Peter Morgan's only son, although he does have two sisters. Born on 29 July 1951, like his father he went to Oundle, during which time he was given practical engineering instruction from the foreman of a local business. From there, instead of following the Morgan tradition of attending technical college, he went to Sussex University, graduating with an honours degree in the History of Art. He spent a year as a bookseller before joining ITN as a film cameraman, remaining with the organisation until 1985.

Charles Morgan has inherited his father's and grandfather's passions for motor sport, having learnt to drive on his grandmother's F-type three-wheeler. But it is the racing circuit rather than rallies and trials that has captured his interest and in 1978 he won the Production Sports Car title, following this with a class win in the series in 1979.

Before joining Morgan in 1985, his artistic sensibilities were expressed through his designs for the company sales brochures. Once established at Pickersleigh Road as managing director, he was able to work successfully in tandem with his father and although they had their inevitable disagreements the relationship worked, to the credit of both parties.

The Aero 8 is Charles Morgan's creation. His passion for competition is reflected in the race-proven chassis and he was also responsible for its albeit controversial styling. He has also overseen the restructuring of the company's manufacturing facilities, having in 1990–93 taken a three-year part-time course at Coventry Polytechnic for a Diploma in Modern Manufacturing, followed by a Master of Business Administration.

Charles Morgan has three children: the eldest is a son, Xan (born 1985) by his first wife, and he has two daughters, Harriet and Kate, by his second wife Jane. His present wife is Kira, whom he married in New York on Christmas Eve 2003.

Charles Morgan pictured with a Plus 8 in the mid-1990s, when the Aero 8 was under development. (Author's collection)

bonded honeycomb aluminium sheet produced by adhesive specialist CIBA-Geigy. This hybrid frame had been tested by the Motor Industry Research Association and it was found to be approximately twice as stiff as the production chassis.

Even more significantly, this structure was an ideal platform for a completely new type of suspension which bore no relationship to Morgan's time-honoured combination of front sliding pillars and rear leaf springs. Developed by Andy Rouse Engineering, the racer's suspension was all-independent, using double wishbones and coil springs at the front and Sierra-inspired trailing arms and coils at the rear; anti-roll bars and telescopic dampers were fitted all-round. The frame underwent a 10,000-mile road-test programme and as a result the company designed a revised layout in conjunction with suspension specialist Roddy Harvey-Bailey. This entailed Rouse's trailing arms being replaced by a coil-and-wishbone arrangement, and further changes were made to the front suspension before the car, still with Rover V8 power, made its debut at Silverstone in 1995.

There, on a wet track, this blue-painted aluminium-chassis'd coupé shaved six seconds off the previous best Morgan time in the wet, and a full 10 seconds on a dry circuit. Buoyed by this, Charles Morgan undertook a second racing season in 1996, the car's body having undergone aerodynamic refinement by his nephew, Lawrence Price, as part of a graduate project at Imperial College, London.

Together with co-driver Bill Wykeham, Morgan drove what was designated the Plus 8 GTR in that year's BPR Global Endurance Cup series. Despite lavishing considerable sums of money on the project, in the face of his father's opposition, the be-winged GTR failed to make much impact on Cup events. At the opening race of the 1996 series at the Paul Ricard circuit it was placed 50th out of 51 competitors – although its best performance at Brands Hatch was 12th in class. In the

final round of the series it came in last. Despite this, Charles Morgan persevered with the car.

In 1997 came a GT2 racer intended for the FIA GT Championship. Although this closed car was powered by a 400bhp version of the Rover V8, it did not prove to be competitive on account of the lack of aerodynamic refinement of its traditional body, derived from that of the Plus 8. More significantly, the GT2 displayed the practicality of a new aluminium chassis, rather than the previous hybrid arrangement, and this encouraged the company to move forward to the next stage of technical evolution towards the ultimate new road car. A public pointer to Morgan's future thinking, meanwhile, was indicated in that year's sales brochure, which declared that the racer was being used to test 'many components . . . to determine whether they are suitable for production'. And so it has proved.

The GT2's new frame had followed on from CIBA's input to the 1995 racer and had resulted in a basic honeycomb tub. But this concept was not pursued because of the difficulty of attaching components to it. There then followed discussions with Alcan of Germany, who came up with a specially-treated pre-coated aluminium. This was an important refinement because an earlier version of this material had the protection applied by heat with an accompanying risk of distortion. Although created for the motor industry, this pre-coated aluminium had at that time only been used by General Motors, for its EV1 electric car of 1996. Morgan thus became the first European motor manufacturer to adopt the product. It was at this stage that the company received an approach from Jim Randle of Birmingham University's Automotive Engineering Centre; formerly Director, Vehicle and Concepts Engineering, at Jaguar, Randle had enjoyed overall responsibility for the second-generation 'XJ40' Jaguar XJ6.

As a result, work on the design of the chassis was undertaken at Birmingham and Randle and Charles

Ancient: Like all Morgans the Aero 8 has a coachbuilt body. (LAT)

Modern: The bonded aluminium tub endows the Aero 8 with exceptional torsional rigidity. (LAT)

Morgan were responsible for its rear portion which was tailored to accommodate an ash body frame. But in 1997 the two men went their separate ways, and the project was brought in-house, with Chris Lawrence becoming the project's technical director. The definitive chassis, consisting of 32 component parts, emerged built around an aluminium tub that was bonded using a special adhesive by Gurrit Essex and then reinforced with Bollhoff rivets. For the purposes of comparison, the Lotus Elise also uses a bonded aluminium chassis but the material has to be shaped and then separately coated before bonding can take place.

Aluminium extrusions are used for the Aero 8's engine bay, suspension and braking systems. The components are cut by laser, the assembly being

undertaken by Radshape of Birmingham. Morgan's aim has been the universal one amongst car makers of combining maximum strength with minimum weight.

The all-independent suspension is similarly adventurous and is derived from that used on the 1997 GTR racer. At the front are long cantilever upper arms with lower wishbones and inboard coil-spring-and-damper units with racing-specification Eibach springs and Koni dampers. The rear suspension uses long transverse wishbones with cantilever-mounted, fully-floating coil springs and dampers from the same makers. The advantages of this design, says Morgan, is that the suspension remains consistent over the full extent of its travel and therefore does not require the usual anti-roll bars – their absence saving

The finished product, the aluminium dashboard enhanced with 1920s-style engine-turning. (LAT)

There's nothing old-fashioned about the Aero 8's 4398cc BMW four-cam alloy V8 engine. (LAT)

both weight and cost. In order to keep unsprung weight as low as possible the five-spoke wheels are OZ Racing components with competition-style centre-lock hubs and peg drive. They are 18in diameter and 9in wide, and shod with Dunlop Sport SP 9000 tyres which incorporate a foam-filled run-flat capability so that there is no need for a spare wheel which would otherwise take up valuable space and add to the car's weight.

The rack-and-pinion steering, as that of the most recent Plus 8s, is by Jack Knight Developments, but now has variable power assistance; there are 2.4 turns lock-to-lock. The steering column, complete with its stalks, is from the BMW 7-series. As for the brakes, these are ventilated discs all-round with, as customary, the fronts larger than the rears; anti-lock

is standard. And then of course there is the engine.

Choosing a supplier began in 1996 when Charles Morgan established contact with BMW, initially to consider a possible alternative in the face of an anticipated demise of the Plus 8's Rover engine. Fortunately the ex-Buick unit enjoyed a stay of execution but BMW's all-alloy 286bhp V8, which today powers the company's 5-series and 7-series models, proved ideal for the new Morgan's needs.

The BMW V8, embellished with Morgan badges, has a capacity of 4398cc and possesses the now customary twin overhead camshafts per cylinder bank and four valves per cylinder. It features BMW's VANOS variable inlet valve timing, although the Bosch management system is peculiar to Morgan. Drive is conveyed to a limited-slip differential via the six-speed Getrag gearbox fitted to the BMWs. To develop the Morgan installation BMW engineer Gunther Ranzinger was enrolled, while Robert Bosch's Thomas Moessner was responsible for the bespoke electronics.

The first development Aero 8 was built in 1998. By this time the essentials of the styling had been finalised and were intended to combine Morgan's world-famous tradition for coachbuilding its cars with lines that looked forward to the 21st century. It also had to be utterly distinctive. No one could argue with the latter attribute . . .

The body construction does indeed follow the time-honoured practice of an ash frame clad with metal panels. However, the wood, which normally never sees the light of day in the traditional Morgans, is exposed in the cockpit where it surmounts the instrument panel. It is similarly revealed in the top door rails, with a secondary spar running diagonally across the trim. As with all current Morgans, the Aero 8's panels are

made entirely of aluminium. Although some of these are shaped by hand, many of the most complex shapes – the combined front wings which incorporate the headlamps and front apron, for instance – are produced by Superform, down the road in Worcester. The company uses a process called superplastic aluminium forming – this referring to the state of the metal prior to it being preformed. To do this the aluminium has to be heated to 400 degrees centigrade by electrical induction, and then subjected to air pressure being blown over a male mould. The result is a panel that, once cold, is both robust and light.

So much for the essentials of the Aero 8 body construction. But the most controversial aspect of the model is its styling. Charles Morgan has overall responsibility for how Morgan cars look and a sketch he produced in 1998 shows a remarkable similarity to the finished product.

Charles Morgan presided over a 'styling committee' which included colleagues Mark Ashton, Tim Whitworth and Matthew Parkin. The design process was executed in-house using CATIA-CAD software and the finished product, tested in the MIRA wind tunnel, recorded a drag coefficient of 0.39. This figure, the company was able to claim, was a 40 per cent improvement on that of the Plus 8, rooted as its design was in empirical 1930s thinking.

The finished product certainly seems to be loved or hated in approximately equal proportions. When the car was announced at Geneva, Andrew English, motoring correspondent for *The Daily Telegraph*, memorably mused whether Charles Morgan was 'keen to go down in history as the man who gave the world its first strabismic sports car'. And before you reach for your dictionaries, the word means squint-eyed. He was, of course, referring to that front end. English was equally vehement in his denouncing of the rear, describing the

An Aero 8 in the rain. The hood has subsequently been redesigned as the original let in water. Unlike the 4/4 and Plus 8, which still retain traditional sidescreens, the Aero 8 has wind-up windows. (LAT)

panels as looking 'as though they've been cold-chiselled off a 1950s Triumph TR2, which was not exactly a high point in British car design'.

Journalists on *Autocar* were equally divided on the car's appearance after its road test, undertaken in 2001, and they probably fairly reflect the opinions of the Morgan-buying public. Peter Robinson wished 'the clumsy styling wasn't such a parody of Morgan', while Stephen Sutcliffe gave the model a firm thumbs-down as far as its performance was concerned but, perversely admitted that 'from the moment I saw it, I fell head over heels in love with the way it looks'.

So what is it about the Aero 8's lines that generates such sound and fury? First and foremost it is those integrated headlamps that cause all

The Aero 8's distinctive rear. The location is Malvern College, the public school established in 1865 where in 1909 HFS Morgan was able to benefit from the engineering facilities. (LAT)

the bother. For instead of being located at the apex of the wing line and therefore pointing directly ahead, they are positioned along their inner edges. From there they flank the traditional Morgan radiator grille although its role is purely a decorative one because the air actually cools the core via a wire-meshed intake located beneath it.

The lamps are less apparent from the side, where the familiar Morgan sweeping wing line, complete with running boards, has been maintained. The trailing segments of the front wings incorporate louvres to permit hot air to escape from the disc brakes, and these are echoed at the rear end of the bonnet top. Equally traditionally, the windscreen is flat and steeply raked while the door surfaces are flattish; now, though, they incorporate winding windows, a first for Morgan, as is an air-conditioning

system. While the boot lid is similarly profiled, an element of curvature has been introduced.

As might be expected from a company that prides itself in the quality of its handmade products, the cockpit is beautifully trimmed in leather if this is specified as a £2000 optional extra. The dashboard, finished in engine-turned aluminium, is comprehensively instrumented, with the cream-faced speedometer and rev-counter positioned directly in front of the driver and a trio of secondary dials located ahead of the gearlever. Nice touches include the aluminium door tread-plates bearing the Morgan winged badge. As for the hood, when lowered this resides in a space behind the seats.

So much for the new Morgan's lines. But how does the Aero 8 perform on the road? The *Autocar* road test was published in October 2001, some 18 months after the model's announcement. The verdict was mixed. Here was a car that turned the scales at 22.3cwt, could achieve 151mph and sprint to 60mph in a mere 4.8 seconds. Yet the magazine

judged the Aero 8 to be 'no focused sports car but an appealing and comfortable tourer'. This might come as a surprise bearing in mind its race-breed credentials. Having said that, in-gear times were deemed 'stunning', with 50–70mph in top (6th) being covered in 6.3 seconds, a full 1.9 seconds faster than the Porsche 911 Turbo. Less positively, those who were looking for new standards of handling and ride among contemporary sports cars would be in for a disappointment, said the magazine. 'Like the engine, the Morgan's chassis is at its unhappiest when the driver constantly tries to wring speeds out of it', it commented, while all the same praising the Aero 8 for 'a level of ride comfort and body control that will be utterly foreign to current Morgan owners'. In sum, it decided, the Morgan was 'best suited to touring, covering ground at an impressive rate, although it prefers the easy life'.

On the debit side, according to the test, was the steering, which lacked feedback and had insufficient self centring, while raising and lowering the 'terrible' hood proved to be a bit

of a palaver, with the top neither being snug nor keeping the wind and rain out. Morgan swiftly addressed this shortcoming, and there is now a new hood which is more rigid when in position and quieter at high speed. The testers also had misgivings about the Aero 8's brakes, and summed up their feelings thus: 'As a modern interpretation of a motoring tradition . . . it transcends much objective criticism and is a car that gives as much pleasure as frustration'. There were echoes here from the same magazine's verdict on the Aero's Plus 8 ancestor.

By the time that this appraisal had been published, the Aero 8 had just entered production, construction of the first 50 being underway by the autumn of 2001. Morgan intended that output would build up to some 200 cars a year and *Autocar* prefaced its road test by reporting that dealers had taken more than 600 deposits. But company expectations have fallen short of that figure and at the time of writing (January 2004), a total of 272 Aero 8s had been built.

Meanwhile a successful racing

programme (see Chapter Nine) has spawned the limited-edition, race-proven Aero 8 GTN, which broke cover in February 2004. Based on Morgan's GT racer of 2003, just 15 examples, which is the number of engines that BMW has supplied to Morgan, will be built, at £72,500 apiece. Capable of in excess of 165mph, the GTN uses a special, mildly-enlarged 4619cc version of the V8, developing some 330bhp. Further changes from the mainstream Aero 8 include black centre-lock OZ wheels complete with semi-slick Yokohama 048 tyres, a racing exhaust the pipes of which emerge from the rear sills just ahead of the back wheels, and uprated suspension. Inside is a synthesis of carbon-fibre, leather and black trim.

With astounding acceleration, an estimated 0–60mph figure of 4.3 seconds with 100mph arriving in less than 10 seconds, the GTN has few rivals outside the supercar league and it can certainly be guaranteed to raise the Aero 8's profile, as well as Morgan's. Built at Malvern Link but then completed by Morgan's

Modern suspension: a 2001 Aero 8 crossing a bridge at speed. In addition to the usual paint finishes, the car can be ordered in metallics, special solid colours and in two-tone finishes. (Morgan)

subsidiary company, Aero Racing, the GTN is instantly identifiable by its carbon-fibre hardtop and blue and silver livery.

Morgan has also been busy developing a federal version of the mainstream Aero, displaying the model at the 2004 Los Angeles Motor Show ahead of a June launch. In addition to left-hand drive, other changes will be the use of the latest 4.4-litre BMW M62 V8, a wider body, air bags as standard, and a carbon-fibre hardtop as used on the GTN.

With American type approval for the Plus 8 having expired at the end of 2003, this means that there will be a hiatus of approximately six months before Americans begin to take deliveries of new Morgans once again. And it may be that the Aero 8's idiosyncratic lines will chime more with transatlantic tastes than they have with European ones . . .

Maintaining the Morgan *Tradition*

The way in which the Morgan is manufactured has contributed as much to the marque's mystique as the car itself, because of the hand-built nature of the product. Having said that, the process has been considerably refined in recent years – without sacrificing the individuality which is at the core of the Morgan's appeal. Of course until nostalgia became a key factor in the desirability of the cars, the production methods were simply regarded as archaic!

The Pickersleigh Road factory, the first stage of which opened in 1914, actually faces Pickersleigh Avenue. But that thoroughfare was not built until 1920 and so the original address has stuck. The other end of Pickersleigh Road, incidentally, emerges opposite Morgan's original Worcester Road works, which in its time eased communications between the two premises.

The foundation stone for the new factory was laid by HFS Morgan's five-year-old daughter, Sylvia, on 5 March 1919, although he had acquired the two-acre site, with its 240ft south-facing frontage, over five years before, in November 1913. It was located in what was then open country, and there was plenty of room for expansion – although the plot did slope away to the north. The gradient was barely noticeable when the lightweight trikes were being built, but it became more apparent with the arrival of the heavier four-wheelers, when rolling chassis and near-completed cars had to be manhandled from one bay to another.

Built by local contractor Martin Wilesmith, the factory became operational in 1914, following the construction of two bays for painting, upholstering and finishing bodies. The manufacturing area was effectively doubled in 1920 with the completion of a further two bays, allowing chassis construction to be moved from Worcester Road. Two more bays were added in 1926, making a total of six, and a seventh had been completed by 1933. It was not until May 1935 that the machine shop moved into the latter bay from the original premises.

The Morgan factory frontage, completed in 1919, as it appears today: it fronts Pickersleigh Avenue rather than Pickersleigh Road, its original address! (Author)

The Morgan Motor Company was registered on 1 April 1912 when the business was located at its Worcester Road site. The corporate structure changed little until the mid-1960s when it was reorganised following HFS Morgan's death. (Author)

The initials on the foundation stone stand for Sylvia Morgan, who was HFS Morgan's eldest daughter, and just five years old when she performed the ceremony. A silver half-crown is buried beneath it. (Author)

Peter Morgan pictured in the mid-1990s at Pickersleigh Road, from where he so successfully directed Morgan's fortunes for some 40 years. (Author's collection)

These were then sold, and reverted to being a garage. The new proprietors, ED Bowman and WH Acock, were appointed, very appropriately, as Morgan distributors. Although the original factory was demolished in 1984, a garage occupied the site until 2003, when it was redeveloped and a new block of retirement apartments built in its place.

The Pickersleigh Road works is, by contrast, still very much in business. Single-storey throughout and brick-built, with the roof supported on steel ridge trusses, it is modest in proportion and extent. HFS Morgan's cautious approach to manufacturing was in striking contrast to some of his contemporaries, who built massive edifices and then had difficulty in filling the available space.

By 1937, with three-wheeler output dwindling and the 4-4 four-wheeler firmly occupying centre stage, the

A *Plus 8's bonnet receiving final adjustment, viewed through the arc of a wheeling machine.* (LAT)

Pickersleigh Road works consolidated a production process that, to all intents and purposes, was still being followed in 1989 when Sir John Harvey-Jones made his memorable visit. Let's take a closer look at how the space was allocated . . .

Bay One, the southern frontage of which faces the road, features a modest gable which contains a stone plaque bearing the initials 'M.M.' – perhaps for 'Morgan Motors'? Back in 1937, as now, offices occupied about two thirds of this elevation, with the stores immediately behind them. The service department absorbed the remainder of the frontage to the west and also extended back into Bay Two, the balance of which contained the despatch shop.

The chassis-erecting shop took the whole of Bay Three, which also contained the engine store. Next, in Bay Four, was the paint shop, an area which at one end also incorporated the varnishing facility, with trimming at the other end.

The adjoining Bay Five was the sheet-metal shop, while Bay Six was occupied by the body shop and the all-important sawmill – although the wood was stored in a separate building just to the west of the complex. As already mentioned, the machine shop was located in Bay Seven. The total area of the entire factory was 18,000 square feet.

A few changes were apparent after the Second World War, the most significant of which was the arrival of spray-painting, with a booth for this purpose being introduced to Bay Four in 1953. As previously mentioned, before that date all Morgans were hand-painted. Even after spraying had been introduced, in fact, some motor show cars were still brush-finished.

Production in the early 1950s was running at about 5–6 vehicles a week, equivalent to some 150 cars a year. But it was a very different story ten years later, when in 1965 Peter Garnier, sports editor of *Autocar*, visited the Malvern factory. He

reported that Morgan had produced 434 cars in 1964, of which 374 – or 86 per cent – had been exported. In 1965 production was running at about nine cars a week, five of which were destined for the American market, followed by the UK, Holland, Canada, Germany and Sweden.

The factory was then employing 94 people and included many men who had begun their careers when HFS Morgan was still a relatively young man. For instance the foreman trimmer, AB Gulliver, had joined the company in 1915 whilst G Cummings, foreman of the sheet-metal shop, was a relatively newcomer, having arrived in 1925. Small wonder that the assembly process had changed so little.

In 1971 author and Plus 4 owner Gregory Houston Bowden visited the Morgan factory and he set down, probably for the first time in book form, just how Morgans were assembled. The procedure had clearly evolved over the years since the 4-4's introduction, with plenty of toing and froing apparent. He also found that accounts of the procedure varied in detail, depending on to whom he was talking . . .

The build process began in Bay Three, where every Friday seven factory porters delivered nine chassis frames from the stores in Bay One and these were laid out on wooden trestles. Engines had already been brought to the area and they were then fitted with any bespoke items of equipment. The Rover V8 for the Plus 8, for instance, received its bellhousing and the driveshaft and separate gearbox (talking here of early cars) were fitted in this area. Only two or three engines were pre-assembled at a time. Then the process was repeated. Just-in-time assembly, as practised in modern car factories, was already a well-established Morgan procedure!

Next the men went to the nearby racks where they returned with a

The Morgan factory in 1985, with supplies of Fiat twin-cams, destined for the revived Plus 4, in the foreground. (LAT)

number of parts, including the pedals and the handbrake lever, together with the all-important front suspension subframe. The chassis was then drilled and the components fitted. Once this was completed, the frames were manhandled by a number of workmen to another side of the bay. The front brake pipes were then fitted, and the engine installed using a manually-operated overhead hoist.

With the power unit in place, the bulkhead, steering column, dampers, springs, axles and wheels were fitted, from small piles of components that had been placed alongside the frame. With the rolling chassis now complete, these were to be manually pushed into the yard on the eastern side of the building, down a slope into the body shop in Bay Six.

This also contained the wood mill and was where the wooden body frame had by now been constructed from Belgian ash. Here a three-strong team produced about 40 examples of a single body part and then moved on to the next part. Eight men were responsible for assembling the individual parts into wooden sub-assemblies. A particularly demanding part of this work was the rear wheelarches, which were laminated in jigs and then subjected, three at a time, to nine hours in a drying cupboard.

Once the chassis had been fitted with its full ash frame, it was manhandled up the slope to the sheet-metal shop in Bay Five, to be duly clad in either steel or aluminium, hand-formed to fit each individual frame. This was done back to front, so to speak, the first part of the process being to fit the rear panels, the adjacent quarter panels and the doors. With the completion of this part of the cladding, the bulkhead, the front and rear wings, and the radiator cowl,

In 1985 the cars were still being produced in batches; in this instance four-cylinder models are under construction. (LAT)

Cars with bodies-in-white, with a Plus 4 in the foreground and a Plus 8 on the right. (LAT)

Three near the chassis-erecting area. The lights were installed, the wiring loom clipped loosely in place and the cars then moved to the trim shop adjoining the body facility in Bay Six. Trimming came next, with the wiring loom hidden by the interior panels. The department also made the seats, with the exception of those for the Plus 8, which at the time Bowden was writing were supplied by Restall. Trimming completed, windscreens were fitted and the cars returned to the electrical department, where the last of the wiring was undertaken. Then it was back to Bay Six, and the finishing area, which shared the same part of the building as the trim shop. It was here that the badges, bumpers and sidescreens were added.

Completed Morgans were handed over to chief tester Charlie Curtis, who had begun this work in 1927 and was still carrying out the same functions in 1971. Driving bereft of a hood and sidescreens, he undertook a ten-mile run around the country roads of Worcestershire, the route including plenty of gradients and demanding twists and turns. Any mistakes that came to light were rectified at the factory, and then the cars were delivered to the despatch bay in Bay Two, after which they were loaded onto transporters or collected by their new owner. The entire build process had taken some three months.

But modest change was in the air as in September 1972 Peter Morgan was able to purchase a factory which adjoined the works on its eastern side. While he let some of it, he retained about 12,000 square feet of new space. This was an extremely welcome development as the move allowed him to transfer to the new premises the crowded trim shop, and the finishing, final electrical checking and test facilities. He hoped that this expansion, together with resulting improvements to the flow of chassis through the buildings, would help him to increase production to 750 cars a year.

Although working conditions were improved, these new facilities did not in fact make much difference to production totals, mainly because the

these all already sprayed with primer, were fitted. Next came the bonnet, its manufacture being a particularly skilled operation, as it was tailored to its particular chassis. What was now rapidly resembling a complete car was then pushed into the adjoining paint shop in Bay Four. Afterwards colour was applied, usually two coats but sometimes as many as six.

The fledgling Morgans moved next to the electrical shop, located in Bay

A Plus 8, *having received its engine, awaits the fitment of the bodywork.* (LAT)

cars were becoming increasingly complicated and thus took longer to build. This was because of the growing complexity of international motor industry legislation and the demands of the market place which sought higher levels of finish and refinement.

At this time Morgan was experiencing its longest-ever waiting list and in 1976–77 some dealers were having to quote a ten-year hiatus between a customer placing an order and the car's delivery. Fortunately this was reduced over the years and further improvements to the build process followed in 1986 in the wake of Charles Morgan's arrival at Pickersleigh Road.

One of his first initiatives was to improve the quality of the cars, and in came zinc-plated nuts and bolts. Owners could also specify a hot-dip zinc-coated chassis frame and most chose this option. External metal fittings, meanwhile, became either powder-coated or galvanised. More crucially, the ash frame was submerged in a tank of Cuprosol wood

preservative for about half an hour and then left to stand for three days, whereas previously it had received no protection at all.

In addition a new painting facility and spraying process was introduced, the intention, in part, being the elimination of a notorious bottleneck in the production process. The paint used was a two-pack acrylic which in theory offered customers a choice of some 34,000 shades although the standard hues were, and still are, Connaught Green, the favourite, Corsa Red, Indigo Blue, Royal Ivory or plain black. Significantly, instead of the paint being applied to the cars *after* the wings had been fitted, so trapping moisture and thus triggering rust, the wings were now painted separately.

The company was continuing to work in this time-honoured way when on a chilly but bright March day in 1989 Morgan was paid a visit by Sir John Harvey-Jones, formerly chairman of ICI. He had been commissioned by BBC Television to visit six businesses which, it was thought, would benefit

from his management expertise. The resulting *Troubleshooter* programme on Morgan was broadcast on BBC2 on 1 May 1990.

This was at a time when Peter Morgan was attempting to spur the workforce into increasing production, from nine to ten a cars a week, although with patchy results. Between 450 and 500 Morgans were then being built every year and the waiting list had been reduced to between four and five years. At the time of the Harvey-Jones visit, Germany was Morgan's largest export market, followed by Italy and Japan.

'The factory gives the impression of being run by a bunch of enthusiastic amateurs', Sir John wrote in his accompanying book, *Troubleshooter*. The machine shop was 'antique, badly under capitalised and in need of some fresh investment': Harvey-Jones commented that he hadn't seen so many ancient machines since he had

Visiting the Morgan works

The Morgan factory is open to visitors throughout the year. Visiting times are 9.00am to 12.30pm and 1.30pm to 5.00pm Monday to Thursday and 1.30pm to 4pm on Fridays. There is a visitors' car park within the factory and on reporting to Reception you will be issued with a map which sets down a recommended route. The tour, which is free, is unaccompanied but the Morgan workforce is both friendly and well-informed and will readily answer any questions that you may ask. Full details can be found on the company website www.morgan-motor.co.uk.

As will be apparent from this notice, Morgan welcomes visitors – and they come from all over the world. (Author)

Morgan Motor Company Ltd.
← **Visitors Car Park**
All visitors must park and report to Reception
Möchten alle gäste sich beim empfang anmelden
Visiteurs on vous prie de vous rendre à la Réception

been a boy. The layout of the factory was 'historic and apparently had changed much since 1919' [sic]. As a consequence it was 'very badly organised . . . the material flow is chaotic and a ludicrous amount of time is wasted', a failing which he put down in particular to a bottleneck in the sheet-metal shop. He believed that the only answer was to 'change the whole method of manufacturing the car'. He also thought that Morgan should charge more for its products, increase production, and try to reduce the waiting list – which then stood at about 3600 cars.

Peter and Charles Morgan countered that the way in which the Morgan was built by hand was part of its appeal, and that they looked upon the waiting list as something of an insurance policy for when the market experienced a downturn. After the programme the following issue of the by-then amalgamated *Autocar & Motor* carried a letter from Charles Morgan refuting many of the points raised by the presenter.

'The Morgan is a hand-built sports car; the degree of craftsmanship and skill that goes into its construction is what differentiates it from a mass-produced car. Our customers are enthusiasts buying a Morgan, not just a set of wheels,' he wrote.

'To bring radical change to our production methods would undoubtedly increase the numbers we produce, but at what cost? The loss of our integrity, our unique appeal and future, we would say . . . .Sir John's opinions have been noted but his solutions are unworthy of us'.

The company found a doughty champion in the shape of motor-industry consultant Professor Garel Rhys, of the Cardiff Business School, who believed that the main failure of Sir John's approach had been to 'ignore the fact that Morgan had been following a *long-term* survival strategy'. Morgan sold its cars in a price-sensitive sector and only by finding a niche in the market could it operate profitably while paying attention to quality details, he said. 'Any major increase in price would, notwithstanding waiting lists, erode Morgan's customer base, especially as any doubling of production would undermine its exclusivity'.

Although most of the letters to *Autocar & Motor* were in support of Morgan, Sir John also had his champions. One correspondent praised him for his 'eminently sensible suggestions'. It was a great pity, he wrote, that the Morgan family's only response had been 'to defend at all costs their management of an industrial museum'. But the factory, industrial museum or no, received some 30,000 letters from all over the world in defence of its position.

It is only fair to observe, though, that when he penned his riposte to *Troubleshooter*, Charles Morgan stressed that the company was open to change. 'We are adopting new technology', he wrote, 'but only when it enhances our product and only when its adoption makes sound business sense to a small, hand-crafted business'.

Some ten years on, Charles Morgan, reflecting on the impact of the programme, told Morgan writer Brian Laban that 'what's interesting is that when Harvey-Jones came along it was exactly the right time for change, and I give him credit for drumming that message in'.

Changes there have indeed been. Since the broadcast, Morgan's manufacturing process has been altered, investment has dramatically increased, the waiting list been cut, and the company now charges more for its cars. But these changes have been evolutionary rather than revolutionary, and carefully implemented so as not to detract from the unique appeal of a hand-built motor car. They are also a reflection of the fact that in 1990 Charles Morgan had enrolled part-time at the Coventry Polytechnic and was to spend three years learning about engineering management, first for a Diploma in Modern Manufacturing and then for an MBA. A key by-product has been to make quality a watchword although, inevitably, this has meant an increase in prices.

Morgan – the great survivor

Morgan, hoping to build about 650 cars in 2004, up from 496 in 2003, is today one of a mere handful of makes which constitute Britain's indigenous motor industry.

With the exception of MG Rover, which returned to the UK fold by default in 2000 when BMW sold out to a British consortium for £10, these are almost exclusively manufacturers of specialist sports cars.

Diametrically opposed to Morgan in almost every respect, Blackpool-based TVR dates only from 1954. It passed through a succession of owners before being acquired in 1982 by Peter Wheeler. He was not only the proprietor but also styled his highly individual ultra-modern glassfibre-bodied sports cars. In 2003 TVR completed 871 cars, but in 2004 was bought by the Russian Nikolai Smolensky.

Caterham took over production of the Lotus Seven in 1973 and in 2003 a total of 435 Caterhams left its factory in Dartford, Kent.

Then there are the likes of Ginetta (established 1957), Westfield (established 1982) and Noble

(established 1985). Meanwhile AC predates Morgan by six years, having begun production of a tradesman's tri-car in 1904; but in 2003 it moved its manufacturing operations to Malta. Lea-Francis, another British firm with a chequered history, built its first car in 1903 and may well be revived: a new 30/230 sports car is supposedly poised for production. Bristol, finally, has been around since

Morgan is unique as a family-owned business which is still manufacturing its cars using methods rooted in the pre-war years. (LAT)

1946, but produces its costly Grand Tourers in very limited numbers.

Way ahead of the field, however, is London Taxis International, which in 2003 built 2346 examples of a very different type of vehicle at its Coventry works.

The results that became apparent at Morgan in 1997 constitute the biggest change at Pickersleigh Road since the introduction of the 4-4 in 1936. At the heart of the transformation was the elimination of buffer stocks and the reduction of the numbers of cars in particular processes. Not only that, but work did not start on a car until all the components had been assembled, which had not always been the case in the past!

A significant investment in the manufacturing process, to the tune of £350,000, came on stream late in 1996 with the opening of a new paint shop. This was built on the easterly side of the works and used the latest ICI water-based paint technology. Apart from conforming with the Environmental Protection Act, this also removed the spraying process from

Bay Four, so releasing valuable space to become a new assembly shop.

Soon afterwards a spacious reception area was built just to the north of the paint shop to replace the original modest panelled lobby that had sufficed for many years in Bay One of the factory. The new building also holds the spare parts and service departments.

By 1999 Morgan was building 580 cars a year, which compared with the 420 produced in 1989 at the time Harvey-Jones visited. Charles Morgan's long-term aim is to manufacture 1500 Morgans per annum, although production is currently running at about a third of that figure. According to the Society of Motor Manufacturers and Traders, the industry body, in 2003 Morgan built 496 cars.

When the author visited Pickersleigh Road in January 2004 output was running at 12 cars per week although this figure – and the model breakdown – does vary throughout the year. Of this dozen, nine were 'Traditionals', Morgan parlance for the Plus 8 (seven built) and 4/4 (two built), and the balance was made up of three Aeros.

One significant change from past practice is that the chassis are no longer wheeled from one bay to another via the main yard, although they still have to be pushed to the nearby but separate paint shop. Instead, existing apertures between each bay have been opened up and ramps built to service them. This means that much of the operation now proceeds under cover, unaffected by the weather.

One of the most significant

The progress of the cars throughout the works is far more logical, with the rolling chassis, having been assembled in the erecting shop in Bay Three, then passing into the new assembly area in Bay Four, where the cars were previously painted. Here they are united with the bodies. These, as before, begin life in the body shop in Bay Six which also contains the saw mill. Today the ash frames used in all Morgans begin as ready-sawn planks from managed forests in Lincolnshire. Kiln-dried before delivery, the wood takes up much of the wood store, which is a separate building just to the north-west of Bay Six.

The timber is shaped to the appropriate dimensions in the saw mill. Each body consists of 82 parts, of which about two-thirds are wooden members. These are first built up as sub-assemblies, and then assembled into the complete body tub. A simple Japanese-inspired card system has been introduced to inform the wood mill when supplies of a particular part are running low. The ash frames are then moved to Bay Five, the sheet-metal shop, where they are clad.

The laminated wheelarches are clamped in this simple jig, prior to being placed in a curing cupboard. (LAT)

A galvanised-chassis 4/4 in the foreground with Charles Morgan (left) and Autocar editor-in-chief Steve Cropley in the background. (LAT)

differences from past practice is that, instead of nine chassis being laid out on a Friday morning, then being moved only when they are all completed, the frames are now built up individually and moved on when each stage of the operation has been completed.

An ash frame in the process of construction.
(LAT)

Today all the panels are made of aluminium rather than steel or a combination of the two. The petrol tanks are also made in the sheet-metal shop.

Once the chassis and body have been united in the adjoining bay they are pushed across the yard to the paint shop. This is only used for 'Traditionals', the Aero 8 having a facility in its own new building adjoining the trim shop. After a day in the paint shop the cars are moved to the nearby facility where the interior trim, seats (mainly leather these days), and wiring are added, together with the hood.

Finally, the wings, which have already been sprayed, are fitted. In the past the wings were attached earlier, but it was found that they could be damaged during assembly. They are also pre-formed now, with it only being necessary to add the headlamp pods. This is another departure: in the past the wings were made from four panels welded together, which was not only more labour-intensive but also introduced a potential rust problem.

The cars then pass into a final finish and test facility. After road test, any faults that have become apparent are rectified and the completed Morgans are taken up to Bay Two for despatch. Although in the past some owners used to collect their cars from the factory, nowadays most are despatched to dealers by transporter or are sent directly for shipping abroad.

This streamlining of the process means that in 2004 it takes just four weeks to build a car, which compares with the 18 weeks taken some 30 years before. Theoretically, it is now possible to produce a Morgan in just 18 working days. In 2004 approximately half the output is sold on the home market, with Germany and America taking some 15 per cent apiece. The balance is sold throughout the rest of the world.

The famous – or infamous – waiting list is now down to some 18 months. This is thanks largely to the improved

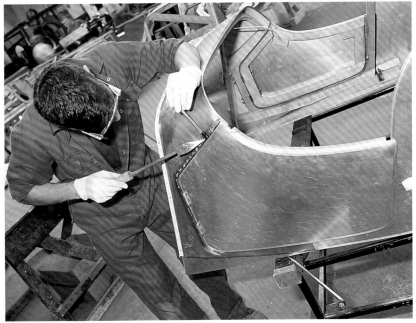

manufacturing process, but Morgan has also adopted a more rigorous approach to the list itself. In the late 1990s this stood at a substantial 6000, the orders being placed without charge or obligation. So the factory wrote to prospective customers to ascertain their commitment to the order and the results of this communication produced a far more realistic figure.

Morgan has a workforce of 150, of

A joint between two body panels being lead-loaded, a skilled exercise. The ash/aluminium construction of the door in the background is readily apparent. (LAT)

which 125 or so are craftsmen. Today they assuredly produce cars in a way which 'HFS', the company's founding father, would, despite recent refinements, have instantly recognised. Long may this very British institution continue to flourish!

Morgan
in Competition

Three-wheelers in a modern context. In 1965 and 1970 the Vintage Sports-Car Club invited The Morgan Three-Wheeler Club to participate in its Oulton Park race meeting. (LAT)

Although the Morgan three-wheeler was created as a so-called Runabout, its impressive performance and handling, coupled with HFS Morgan's abilities as a driver, meant that its competition history began even before it officially entered production. This established a tradition that was maintained by his son Peter and, in recent years, by the

third generation of Morgans in the shape of grandson Charles.

The man himself got off to a flying start by entering a JAP-engined single-seater, complete with tiller steering, in the Motor Cycling Club's first ever London Exeter Trial, held on 26–27 December 1910; he received a gold medal. It was the first of many Morgan triumphs in this event, a tradition that

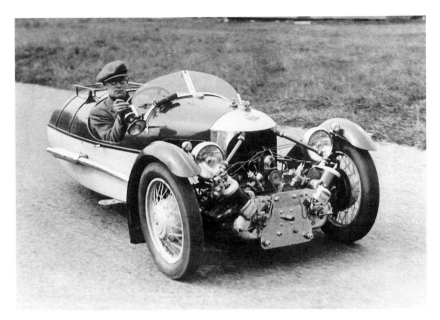

This fearsome Scott-engined trike was built in 1936 by Brooklands habitué John Granville Grenfell. Taking a 1935 barrel-back Super Sports, he removed the Matchless engine and replaced it with two water-cooled Scott motorcycle units, making a V4. It had the reputation for being somewhat nose heavy! (LAT)

Fred Willis, for many years secretary of The Morgan Three-Wheeler Club, in his F-Super at Woodcote during the Motor Cycling Club's fourth Silverstone meeting, held in June 1953. (LAT)

was maintained when in the 1930s the trike made way for the 4-4.

Morgan, once again at the wheel of a single-seater, was at Brooklands on 9 November 1912, where he set a new record for cyclecars by covering 59 miles in an hour. In its issue of 4 December *The Cyclecar* magazine carried on its front cover a photograph of Morgan before making his bid. Standing alongside, in a top hat, was his father, clearly a hands-on chairman. On a broader front, 'HFS' could not have wished for better publicity.

The magazine's editor was W Gordon McMinnies, and on 13 July 1913 he won the Cyclecar Grand Prix at Amiens in an ohv JAP-engined car, at 41.9mph, only to be disqualified on the grounds of the Morgan being a 'sidecar'. He had in fact been the first machine to complete the distance but the authorities declared the winner to be Bourbeau's Bédélia, which came in a little less than three minutes later. As far as 'HFS' was concerned, this was a victory and it spawned the Grand Prix Morgan of the same year.

After the First World War it was not until 1919 that 'HFS' resumed his competitive activities. That year he won gold medals in the London–Edinburgh trial and the Auto Cycle Union's Six Day event. Across the Channel in France, Honel – who

went on to campaign Salmson-built GNs – triumphed in the cyclecar class of the Circuit de l'Eure.

The Cyclecar Grand Prix of 1914 had been cancelled because of the outbreak of war but Edward Ware, at the wheel of a 980cc car built for that event, won the British Motor Cycle Racing Club's three-wheeler race at Brooklands in 1920.

Trials gold medals came thick and fast in the early years of the decade. In 1921 Morgan received no fewer than three in the ACU's Six Days and 'HFS'

won the premier award in the Union's 1922 Stock Trial. The trikes from Malvern Link collected three golds in the Six Days and an impressive eight in the London–Edinburgh of the same year. Then there were victories two years running for Ware in the Junior Car Club's General Efficiency events.

The 1926 International Six Days, meanwhile, saw Goodall, Horton and Carr win the team prize, together with three golds. The following year's London–Edinburgh was a vintage event for the marque. A total of 14

Desmond McCracken's 4-4

One of the cars which helped Morgan to establish the competition credentials of the 4-4 was sold by auctioneers Cheffins of Cambridge in 2001. It also has the distinction of being the first Irish-built 4-4, having been assembled in 1937 by the Gorman Brothers in Dublin, from a factory kit of parts.

Such a procedure was necessary because Ireland had imposed heavy import tariffs on complete cars, and the first batch of three 4-4s was built up at the Gormans' Frankfort Garage in the Upper Rathmines district of the city. Whilst practically all the components were supplied by Malvern Link, the cars incorporated local window glass, paint and batteries.

Registered ZC 1176, this example was owned by Desmond McCracken, then reading law in Dublin, who in 1935 had won a local event at Bray at the wheel of his Frazer Nash. As recorded in this chapter, he won the Leinster Trophy event of July 1937 in the 4-4 and in September ran in the Irish Motor Racing Club's races at Phoenix Park.

But he was unable to repeat his earlier success, being placed fifth in the handicap competition. This followed the loss of a minute due to a loose carburettor float, although he averaged a respectable 70.07mph. Soon afterwards, McCracken came second overall in the Leinster Motor Club's October Trial and won a First Class Award.

He ran a big end in the 1938 Leinster Trophy after just three laps but regained his form in the IMRC's Ballinascomey Hill Climb when he won the handicap section of the over 1100cc class. In October McCracken took ZC 1176 to Britain to form part

of the Morgan team in the MCC's Sporting Trial, held in Derbyshire, but he retired with overheating. Back in Ireland he redeemed himself by winning the IMRC Autumn Trial and in November the Leinster Night Trial.

Unfortunately by this time McCracken's health had begun to falter – he later succumbed to tuberculosis – and he sold the 4-4 to Stanley Woods, the famous Irish motorcyclist, who generously offered McCracken further drives in the car during the 1939 season.

Woods fitted separate exhaust pipes, which emerged just below the passenger's door, and he entered the Morgan in the 1939 Leinster Trophy event, no doubt hoping to repeat McCracken's 1937 triumph. But he also had the misfortune to run a big end, this time on the ninth lap.

Woods had intended to run the car in the 1939 TT race but the event was cancelled because of the impending war. However, Ireland was a neutral country and the IMRC's Phoenix Park races were held on 9 September, six

Desmond McCracken's 4-4, still bearing its Irish registration number, as auctioned by Cheffins in 2001. The car has been bereft of its front wings since McCracken's day. (Cheffins)

days after the outbreak of hostilities. Unfortunately the 4-4's gearlever broke off during the race, but Woods soldiered on to finish fifth.

McCracken took the wheel of his old car again for the Leinster MC's Lincolan Cup Trial, which he won, and also for the IMRC Autumn Cup Trial when the Morgan was judged the best open car. He was again in winning form for the IMRC Trial on Boxing Day 1939, when he received the Premier Award. It was an appropriate note on which to bow out.

By good fortune ZC 1176 had survived in remarkably original condition and following many years off the road was in a loosely-assembled state in 2001 for the auction at Chilford Hall, Linton, Cambridgeshire. There this historic 4-4 was acquired for £26,250 by a Morgan enthusiast from the Channel Islands.

Morgans entered and all finished, collecting 11 golds and three silvers in the process. The marque ended the decade by collecting a further nine golds in 1929.

Racing was more problematic. A

Morgan-Blackburne won the 1923 Three-Wheeler Championship at Brooklands at an average of 86.77mph but between 1924 and 1928 the track authorities banned three-wheeler competitions at the circuit and

Morgan owners instead embarked on a spate of record breaking.

In 1921 Ware's trike had covered a kilometre at 86.04mph, pushing this figure to 92.38mph in 1923. Subsequently, in 1925, Harold Beart's

JAP-engined 1100cc Morgan took the flying kilometre at 103.37mph, which was the first occasion that a three-wheeler had been timed at over 100mph.

In truth by the 1930s the three-wheelers were ceasing to be competitive, although this did not prevent doughty owners campaigning them with some success in trials throughout the decade. But by then the firm's emphasis had switched from three wheels to four.

For three successive years between 1937 and 1939 the company's George Goodall, in a 4-4, won the 10hp class in the RAC Rally. The arrival of the drophead version saw Morgan attain a double triumph in the 1939 event, when 'HFS' also won the closed class. For his part, Goodall went on to win the open 10hp class in that year's Scottish Rally.

The 4-4 also earned its racing spurs, with a surprise win by Robert Campbell in the 1937 Ulster Trophy race held in June at the new Ballyclare circuit. The car in question was owned by the wife of Morgan's Belfast agent, Jack Parish, and when the intended driver was unable to produce his competition driving licence, Campbell, who was the mechanic, stepped in for the handicap event. He drove an exemplary race, and the car ran faultlessly throughout. He was lying fourth three-quarters through the event, but pulled ahead to win in 2 hours 9 minutes 30 seconds, a full two minutes ahead of a pair of supercharged MG K3s. This was a great endorsement of the 4-4, and it marked the first major success for the model in a road race.

Across the border in the Irish Republic a trio of 4-4s was entered in the Leinster Trophy road-race held in July. Campbell was there with Mrs Parish's winning car and the Dublin-based Gorman Brothers, which assembled 4-4s in the Irish republic, had a car driven by Desmond McCracken, who was studying law in the city. The other 4-4 was driven by Freddy Smyth for its owner, a Mr Duigan from Belfast.

Campbell was unable to repeat his

Ulster triumph and withdrew with what were described as 'oiling problems'. Smyth crashed, but McCracken won at 61.95mph, giving Morgan welcome publicity on both sides of the Irish Sea and its second racing victory in two months. The racing history of this particular 4-4, which happily survives, is charted in the accompanying box.

Next up, a car was specially prepared for the 1937 TT race, held for the first time at Donington Park. Lightened, with cycle wings and no running-boards, it had the Coventry Climax engine reduced in capacity to 1122cc so that, being under 1200cc, it would qualify for a special handicap.

Graham Stallard of Worcester at the wheel of his 1949 4/4 at the newly-formed Morgan 4/4 Club's first road rally – which he won. Held between Burton-on-Trent and Banbury on 5 August 1951, the event finished with a driving test. Note that the Morgan in the centre background is shod with whitewall tyres. (LAT)

Second place in the 4/4 Club's inaugural 1951 rally went to Bill Parkes of Pershore, Worcestershire, in his Standard-engined car. (LAT)

Prudence Fawcett and Le Mans

The daughter of a Sheffield solicitor, Prudence Fawcett learnt to drive at the age of 17, having been encouraged by her Bugatti-owning uncle Percy, and she became a Wolseley Hornet owner. Whilst in her twenties she spent some time in the Italian city of Genoa, where she was soon to be seen at the wheel of the

Le Mans 1938 and Prudence Fawcett at the wheel of 4-4 which finished a creditable 13th. There were, in all, 42 entrants and only two British cars completed the race, the other being an HRG. (LAT)

latest 1750 Alfa Romeo. Her only racing experience came after being placed second in a minor event at the wheel of that car.

Back in England, she teamed up with her friends Lance and Constance Prideaux-Brune, who owned the Winter Garden Garages in London, and imported Alfa Romeos. However, the establishment was better known for its Aston Martin agency and indeed Lance Prideaux-Brune had briefly owned the company in 1932, one of its bleaker years, before passing it on to Newcastle shipping

magnate Sir Arthur Sutherland.

A regular attender at Brooklands, Prudence Fawcett began to move in royal circles. In 1937 she was a member of the Duke of Kent's entourage and joined his party to travel by private plane to that year's Le Mans 24-Hours. It was probably as a result of that visit she decided to compete in the race – and thus needed a suitable car. Winter Garden Garages having lost its Aston Martin agency and become a Morgan outlet, a 4-4 became the natural choice.

Fawcett was far from being the first British women to drive in the classic 24-hour event. Not least, in 1935 racing driver George Eyston had fielded his three-strong ladies MG team, 'The Dancing Daughters', all of whom completed the race, finishing in 24th, 25th and 26th positions. However, Prudence Fawcett was the best-placed British woman driver at the event in the inter-war years, while her participation marked Morgan's first appearance at the Sarthe circuit.

Her success, in 1938, with Geoff White as co-driver, came in a year when there were relatively few British entries, and so her 13th-placed 4-4 was only the second British car home, three cars behind an HRG in tenth position. Prudence Fawcett never raced again but retained a passion for sports cars until her death in 1990.

Other ministrations included a balanced crankshaft and flywheel, an external four-branch exhaust manifold, magneto ignition, and a Solex carburettor; the result was an output in excess of 50bhp. Despite these careful preparations, the car, driven by Henry Laird and RMV Sutton, survived only until the 84th lap, when the nearside stub axle broke. This racing experience was transferred to the production 4-4s which were accordingly modified from January 1938 onwards.

The major and wholly unexpected

competition success of 1938 was a 13th placing at Le Mans, which was also the first occasion that a Morgan had been entered there. The entrant was a lady, no less, Miss Prudence Fawcett (see box), who was friends with Constance and Lance Prideaux-Brune, who ran the Winter Garden Garages in London and in 1937 had acquired a Morgan agency. Its workshop was placed in the capable hands of CM 'Dick' Anthony, who also had Le Mans experience. Previously the garage had a strong commitment to Aston Martin,

and the Prideaux-Brunes had entered Astons in the 1933 and 1934 events. But with Aston Martin all but having ceased production in 1937, 'HFS' acceded to Prudence Fawcett's request for a suitable 4-4 and supplied – on loan – one based on the 1937 TT car, with final preparation by 'Dick' Anthony at Winter Garden Garages. The co-driver would be sales manager, Geoff White.

So that the car would be eligible for the 1100cc class, the 63mm-bore 1122cc Coventry Climax engine was linered back to 62.3mm to give a capacity of 1098cc while the inlet-over-exhaust unit was tuned with advanced cam timing, smoothed-out inlet ports, and special hairline valve seats. The crankshaft was balanced, a special exhaust manifold fitted and the compression ratio raised to 8:1. The net result was over 50bhp at 5000rpm, which compared with 48bhp for the regular competition engine; the standard unit, by contrast, gave 34bhp. On 17in pressed-steel wheels, top speed was said to be a little under 100mph.

To the delight of Morgan and the Prideaux-Brunes, the Fawcett/White duo not only completed the race, but were placed a respectable 13th at an average speed of 57.2mph. They would have done even better, had it not been for a misfire that occurred on the Sunday afternoon, by which time the 4-4 was fifth in the 1100cc class behind two Simcas, an MG and the eighth-placed Singer. However, if the original bore had been retained they would have been third in the 1500cc class. Such is the lottery of motor racing . . .

Rather closer to home, across the Irish Sea Robert Campbell was unable to repeat his success in the Ulster Trophy event, coming in second at the wheel of Mrs Parish's 4-4, having averaged 51.96mph. Less successful was the 1938 TT: the factory entered the former Le Mans car, but it suffered from leaking radiator hoses and although Laird completed the race, he had to content himself with seventh place.

In 1939 Morgan sought to build on the success of its 1938 Le Mans achievement, re-entering the same car in that year's event. This time, though, Prudence Fawcett did not drive, as she had become engaged to an airman and had agreed to give up motor racing if he abandoned flying. So her place was taken by 'Dick' Anthony, sharing the driving with White. Although the participation of Winter Garden Garages was all too apparent, the factory took over the 4-4's preparation. Outwardly the car differed from the previous year, having revised bodywork which lacked doors

and had the spare wheels recessed into the tail rather than being proud of it. With the previous year's class placing no doubt in mind, the engine was re-bored to 62.5mm, which took it to 1104cc and into the up-to-1500cc class. Twin SU carburettors replaced the original single Solex.

The Morgan once again finished but it was slightly down on the previous year, coming in 15th – albeit at a higher average of 64.5mph. But the change to the engine's capacity was justified by a second-in-class behind the Clark-Chambers HRG.

The 4-4's Coventry Climax engine made way for the 1.1-litre Standard unit in 1939. But Morgans did not feature significantly in post-war competitive events until the arrival for the 1951 season of the 2088cc Vanguard-engined Plus 4 and more particularly after the TR2 engine had become an option in late 1954. This transformed the model into the perfect club racer.

There were echoes of the immediate pre-war years when a Morgan factory team, headed by Peter Morgan, took the team prize in the 1951 RAC Rally. Class victories in the

This green 1952 Plus 4 was owned by Basil de Mattos of Laystall Engineering and, although his business ministered to the engine, it still reportedly produced the standard 68bhp! He is seen here ascending Beggar's Roost. (LAT)

Lisbon and Evian-Mont Blanc followed, and these triumphs were repeated in the Portuguese and British events. In the same year Jimmy Ray won the London Rally, and repeated this success in 1953.

A Morgan was entered for the 1952 Le Mans race but unfortunately the Lawrie/Isherwood Plus 4 dropped a valve on the third lap. It would be another ten years before the make ran again at the Sarthe circuit – although then the results would be much more satisfactory.

The 1953 MCC Rally, meanwhile, saw Morgan put up an impressive showing when Roy Clarkson took second place, the ladies prize was won by the Misses Neil, and there were class wins and also a team award for the marque. The following year saw Ray victorious in the Scottish Rally while Les Yarranton took a second in the MCC National. In 1955 there was a

A Plus 4 *pictured during a rally organised by the* Glasgow Herald *in 1959.* (LAT)

driving his Plus 4, memorably registered TOK 258, to 19 victories in 23 BRDC Freddie Dixon Trophy events. These successes were not wasted on Peter Morgan, who recruited Lawrence to represent the factory in International GT Racing. That same year the Morgan team won the National Six Hour Relay Race, and Peter Morgan took a sixth place in the RAC Rally.

Lawrence retired in the 1960 TT but Richard Shepherd-Barron was placed second in class in the 1961 Spa GP. It was in that year that Chris Lawrence entered his trusty TOK 258 for Le Mans, only to have his entry turned down on the grounds that the car appeared 'too old-fashioned'. There were echoes here of Morgan's disqualification in the Cyclecar Grand Prix back in 1913 but Peter Morgan has subsequently acknowledged that the Plus 4 was 'rather scruffy'. Lawrence was however of the opinion that undue pressure had been applied by the Triumph team. It was fielding a trio of special TRX cars, powered by an experimental twin-cam engine and he believed did not wish to risk being trounced by an older car using one of its pushrod TR units. In the event Triumph won the team prize, after which its competition department was closed down, for the time being at least.

There would be no such mistakes in 1962. The Super Sports was entered and prepared by the factory and was, in Peter Morgan's words, 'immaculate'. It was run in the GT class and was therefore fitted with a glassfibre hardtop. There was also a standby car, although only one vehicle was used in the race proper.

Morgan's chairman had also taken the precaution of briefing dealer Jacques Savoye, who had first entered Le Mans in a Singer in 1935 and had competed in five further post-war events. Peter Morgan also mentioned the entry in a few other influential ears. But for whatever reason, there

class victory in the Scottish and in 1956 a third place in the RAC Rally, while Peter Morgan won his class in an

example of the newly-introduced 4/4, a result repeated in the 1958 event by Les Yarranton.

The year 1959 was destined to be one of some significance in Morgan's competition activities, Chris Lawrence

Chris Lawrence's TOK 258

This is the most famous racing Morgan of all, the Plus 4 in which Chris Lawrence was placed 13th and won the 2-litre GT class at the 1962 Le Mans race.

Dating from 1956, the TR2-engined, Birmingham-registered Morgan was acquired by Lawrence in 1958, from London sports-car dealers Performance Cars. He got off to a flying start in 1959 when he won the Freddie Dixon Trophy, having taken the chequered flag in 19 out of 23 races.

In 1960 the car was rebodied, the original shell being replaced by the latest Morgan coachwork, instantly identifiable by its sloping rear deck housing one spare wheel rather than the previous twin wheels. In 1962 its performance was much improved by the engine modifications (see pages 68–69) that were to form the basis of the Morgan Super Sports.

By 1964 Lawrence was becoming closely involved with his SLR programme (see page 148) so he sold 'TOK' to Adrian Dence, who followed in his predecessor's wheeltracks by winning the Freddie Dixon and Motor Sport Trophies.

Later the car passed to the Stapleton brothers, and was rebuilt following an accident. Subsequently Chris Lawrence bought back his old car and restored it to its 1962 Le Mans state. This rejuvenation was completed in time for 'TOK' to participate in Morgan's 60th anniversary meeting at Prescott in 1970.

Lawrence subsequently ran the car in the 1973 Charles Spreckley series of races for thoroughbred sports cars. He won a round at Brands Hatch and gained three second places. Some of the driving was shared with Robin Gray, who scored a single victory; the following year Gray undertook all the driving and achieved two outright victories.

In 1960 Lawrence built a new 'TOK', carrying the registration number over from his old car. It is pictured here in 1974 when being run in the Charles Spreckley series for thoroughbred sports cars. (LAT)

TOK 258, Chris Lawrence's 1956 Plus 4, photographed in December 1960. In that year he forged an association with Morgan, so paving the way for the Super Sports version of the Plus 4. (LAT)

Graham Bryant has been a regular competitor in his 1977 Plus 8 in recent years and is currently running in the Morgan Motor Company's Challenge Series. (LAT)

was no repeat of 1961 and the Plus 4, driven by Chris Lawrence and Richard Shepherd-Barron, was accepted.

At the end of the first lap, the Plus 4 was lying 43rd. But Lawrence and Shepherd-Barron drove an excellent race, and by the 12th hour they had moved up to 22nd position and

thereafter continued improving their placing to reach 12th position in the 19th hour. However, in the 21st hour they ceded a place to the Porsche of Buchet and Schiller and continued in 13th place until the end, echoing Prudence Fawcett's 1938 achievement. They had covered 2255.13 miles at an

average of 93.96mph, to win the 2-litre class. This was destined to be Morgan's best Le Mans showing ever and is a great credit to Chris Lawrence and to the preparation undertaken by the factory.

As far as the company was concerned, this Le Mans class victory

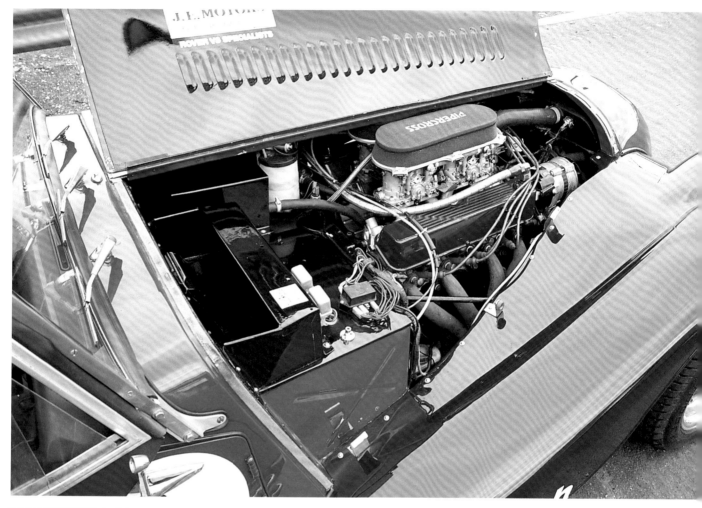

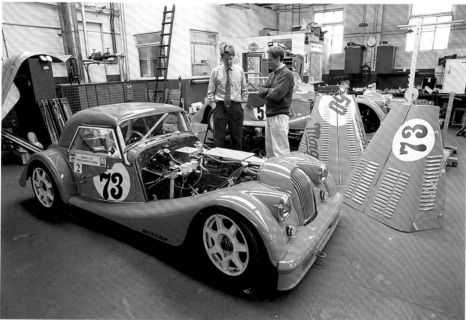

The 4.6-litre engine of Graham Bryant's Plus 8, which competes in Class A for modified Plus 8s in Morgan's Challenge Series events. (LAT)

Charles Morgan (left) shows Mark Hughes, then of Classic and Sports Car, the 5-litre Plus 8 he campaigned in the 1994 BRDC GT Championship. (LAT)

The SLR Morgan

In the wake of his Le Mans success, Chris Lawrence decided to team up with John Sprinzel. The latter had secured the British Rally Championship in 1960, initially in a somewhat unlikely Austin A35, although he subsequently graduated to an Austin-Healey Sprite. A direct result of this association was the creation of Sprinzel Lawrence Tuning.

While the Plus 4's competition record had been impressive, Lawrence was all too aware of the limitations of the model's archaic bodywork. However, Group 4 GT racing permitted body modifications, providing that they did not reduce the car's overall weight by more than 15 per cent.

The result, in 1963, was the SLR Morgan, the initials standing for 'Sprinzel Lawrence Racing'. The car retained the Plus 4 chassis, suitably lightened, but had a new aerodynamically-refined GT body: a joint styling effort by Lawrence and Sprinzel, it drew on visual elements from the Chevrolet Corvette at the front and the Jaguar E-type coupé at the rear. Being designed for racing, there were no headlights, the windows were Plexiglas, and there was a single centrally-located windscreen wiper.

The aluminium shell was built by Williams and Pritchard and initially

the SLR was powered by a TR4 engine fitted with a special Lawrence-developed crossflow cylinder head with staggered 90-degree valves. Interestingly, Morgan shared the costs of the engine with Lawrence, which was the only occasion it had invested in an engine, as opposed to helping with chassis and body development.

Unfortunately the head did not prove to be a success. The design required 10mm sparking plugs, which continually oiled up, and the lubrication of the rockers proved to be less than satisfactory. The cylinder head was therefore dropped in 1964

Nice lines! Tony Howard's SLR Morgan exiting from the Russell Chicane at Snetterton during a round of the Morgan Motor Company's Challenge race at Snetterton on 26 April 1998. (Roger Tatton)

and the three subsequent cars used engines that were more closely related to the usual Lawrencetune units.

Just the four SLRs were built, three on Plus 4 frames and a fourth on a Triumph TR4 chassis; the Triumph was raced by Sid Hurrell in 1963, by which time it was owned by Neil Dangerfield, one of John Sprinzel's drivers.

could not have been better timed. Not only was it a world-famous event, but it was also one that was held in Europe, at a time when Peter Morgan was beginning to turn to the continent as the hitherto buoyant American export market started to falter in the early 1960s.

Later in 1962 Lawrence achieved an eighth place in the TT but he could do no better than a 27th place in the Nürburgring 1000kms. This result underlined the fact that although the cars displayed remarkable reliability, the Plus 4 had its chassis firmly rooted in the 1930s, a suspension system of 1910 vintage, and no aerodynamics to speak of; in the face of such

parentage, it had been a remarkably successful sports-racing car but by the mid-1960s it was beginning to be overhauled by the more modern opposition.

Morgan's competitive fortunes received a significant fillip with the 1968 arrival of the Plus 8. Since then the model has been a versatile performer in many motorsport arenas, successful contenders varying from mildly-tuned roadgoing cars to extensively modified racers which bear only a passing outward resemblance to the production cars.

Drivers worth singling out include Robin Gray, whose Plus 8 won the 1974 Modsports series; he also took

second place in Thoroughbred events at the wheel of TOK 258, the famous racing Plus 4 which had given Chris Lawrence his celebrated class win at Le Mans in 1962.

Meanwhile in 1975 Chris Alford, at the wheel of a Ford-engined 4/4, won the British Production Sports Car Championship. There had, in all, been 17 rounds and Alford, driving for John Britten's 'All-British Racing Team', won his class in every race he entered.

HFS Morgan's grandson, Charles Morgan, maintained the marque's competition profile by winning the 1978 Production Sports Car title outright. He clinched the award with successive wins over a

In 2002 Morgan launched its commemorative Le Mans 62 model in celebration of Chris Lawrence's 2-litre class win in the 24-hour race 40 years previously. The series was limited to 80 cars, evenly distributed between the 4/4 and Plus 8; the latter version is illustrated. (Morgan)

Le Mans, 2002: The DeWalt RSS Aero 8 was driven in the event by Richard Stanton, Richard Hay and Steven Hyde; it succumbed to engine failure after 17½ hours. (Morgan)

weekend at the end of the racing season, with a victory at Silverstone on the Saturday and Cadwell Park on the Sunday. He drove the first production Plus 8, prepared by Libra Motive. The following year Morgan achieved a class victory in the same championship and in 1981 and 1982 Rob Wells of Libra Motive and Steve Cole, variously driving the

same car, won the British Production Sports Car Championship.

With Morgan's backing, Wells subsequently produced a fearsome racer, which bore the memorable MMC 3 numberplate – the Plus 8 prototype, it will be recalled, was MMC 11 – with a single-piece glassfibre body, complete with massive aerofoil, cloaking a spaceframe chassis

powered by a 300bhp V8 engine. He went on to win the 1981 British Modsports Championship in this car. In the following year he was similarly victorious in the Prodsports Championship and he was also a member of a three-man team which drove a 3.9-litre Plus 8 in the 1987 Birkett Six-Hour Race at Snetterton. Not only did they put up the fastest

An Aero 8 GT at the Bugatti circuit in 2003 in the opening round of the European Le Mans Series race. Driven by Neil Cunningham and Adam Sharpe, it was placed seventh in class. (Morgan)

The prototype Aero 8 GTN which ran in the British GT Championship races in 2003, when cars were placed second and third overall. (Morgan)

lap but they also beat three Porsche teams in the process!

The unstoppable Wells, at the wheel of a 4/4-based Plus 8 road car, registered ROB 8R, added further feathers to his cap when in 1989 he became the first winner of the Peter Collins Tray, having won the factory-supported Morgan Challenge. This had begun life in 1985 as the Morgan national championship, Mary Lindsay having been the first victor at the wheel of her Plus 8.

In complete contrast, just to prove that a 1961 Plus 4 could show its mettle an example driven by Bill Wykeham and Ludovic Lindsay was run successfully in the 1990 Classic Carrera Panamericana road race. This seven-day 2000-mile event saw the Morgan move into pole position in its class by the second day and remain there until the finish, taking overall fifth place in an event won by a C-type Jaguar.

Charles Morgan signalled that he had not lost his appetite for the competitive fray when at the end of the 1994 season of the International GT Championship he unveiled details of

A GTN *driven by Neil Cunningham leads the field to win round three of the 2003 British GT Championship at Knockhill, the first occasion on which a Morgan had triumphed in a round of the series.* (Morgan)

Morgan by night. A GTN, driven by Keith Ahlers, Cunningham and Sharpe, pictured during the Bathurst 24-hour race in Australia in the 2003 GT Championship. The car succumbed to engine trouble after six hours. (Morgan)

his advanced Plus 8. As recounted in Chapter Seven, this formed the starting point for the Aero 8 project. Although the car and its successors were important in that context, it has to be said that they were less successful from a competitive standpoint.

Morgan returned to Le Mans in 2001 with the Aero 8 but it was forced to withdraw on the 16th hour. In 2003 the factory's entry was refused, echoing the 1961 rebuff.

In the meantime the company had established Aero Racing to develop the model for competition. The result was the sports-racing Aero 8 GT, which was the first racing Morgan to have been conceived, built and homologated by the factory. Powered by a 4.4-litre, 500bhp version of the M62 BMW V8, drive was courtesy of a six-speed sequential gearbox. The chassis was strengthened and an FIA-approved rollcage fitted, and external modifications included a front splitter, a carbon-fibre hardtop and an aerodynamically-refined rear wing.

This state-of-the-art racer got off to a flying start and in 2003, its first

Driven by Ahlers/Cunningham/Sharpe at Sebring 2004, the Aero 8 was placed 11th in class and finished 20th overall out of 48 starters. (Morgan)

Showing the flag. The Aero 8 flanked by classic Morgans prior to the Sebring 12-hour race in Florida in 2004. (Morgan)

season, Aero 8 GTs finished second and third in the British GT Cup Class Championship.

The car was duly approved for participation at Le Mans and in 2002, to commemorate that celebrated success of 40 years before, Morgan produced a limited-edition road car.

The Le Mans 62, of which 80 were built, was available in 4/4, and Plus 8 guises. Finished in what the company called Morgan Racing Green, with a black leather interior, the cars were fitted with a lined glassfibre hardtop. In addition there were polished stainless-steel wire wheels with two-eared spinners, white-faced instruments, drilled racing-style clutch and brake pedals, and an organ-type accelerator. Morgan says that it could have sold many more than the 80 cars it produced, an indication, if one were needed, that competition remains at the heart of the marque's appeal.

Engines

Since the first Runabouts of 1911 Morgans have been powered by a seemingly infinite variety of engines. These have ranged from air-cooled and water-cooled motorcycle V-twins to in-line 'fours', two V8s and a V6, but have never included a straight-six. Even if transplanted from a mass produced saloon, they have invariably endowed the lighter Morgan sports car with accelerative qualities and top speeds not envisaged by their designers.

Valves have been side and overhead, or a combination of the two, with actuation by tappets, pushrods or overhead camshafts. And over the past 90 or so years the engines have variously been of British, American, Italian and even Swiss manufacture.

Such a range reflects the fact that HFS Morgan never made the mistake of producing his own engines. Instead, crucially, he relied on mainstream car makers, or suppliers of proprietary units, to shoulder design, development and manufacturing costs. Although on occasions the impending demise of a particular engine has presented the company with a short-term problem, it has repeatedly risen to the challenge and found an alternative. The perpetuation of HFS Morgan's policy is one of the principal reasons why Morgan has survived into the 21st century.

Having said that, when faced with an engine shortage in the years immediately after the Second World War, 'HFS' did toy with the idea of producing a bespoke Morgan unit. It was then that he commissioned a

An overhead-valve water-cooled 1096cc JAP engine fitted in a 1933 Super Sports. (LAT)

conventional four-cylinder 67mm x 77mm 1093cc overhead-valve unit from Harry Hatch, whom he had known since his earliest days in the motor industry. Up until 1913 Hatch had been JAP's chief designer and he had subsequently been responsible for Blackburne's KM series of V-twins

which had successfully powered some Morgan three-wheelers of the 1920s.

The factory received the plans of Hatch's design in October 1946. He charged Morgan £250 for his work

The 990cc water-cooled sidevalve Matchless unit that replaced the JAP from 1934 onwards. (LAT)

and there would have been a further consultancy payment incurred for the engine's development, plus a royalty of 5 shillings (25p) per engine when it entered production. Perhaps these figures were sufficient to put 'HFS' off the idea, and the engine was never built.

Ford

The first car engine to be used by Morgan was the Ford sidevalve unit which appeared in the F-type three-wheeler of 1934. In fact Ford has supplied Morgan for longer than any other manufacturer, with only a three-year break in 1952–1955 between the cessation of three-wheeler production and the revival of the 4/4. Not only that, but with the demise in 2004 of the Plus 8, all Morgans, the Aero 8 excepted, are currently Ford-powered.

The first Ford unit to be fitted in a Morgan, engine number Y38054, left Malvern Link on 25 April 1934, in an F-type destined for Birmingham. The four-cylinder sidevalver drove the single rear wheel by chain, via a rear-mounted Morgan three-speed gearbox. The 933cc engine had been designed in America to power a very different type of car, Ford's 8hp Model Y saloon, which had entered production at Dagenham in August 1932.

Soon afterwards, in November 1932, as Sam Roberts recounts in *Ford Model Y* (Veloce, 2001), Sir Percival Perry, the chairman of Ford's British subsidiary, informed the company's Detroit headquarters that it was to supply 'about 300' engines per annum to Morgan. 'This vehicle is a little 3-wheeler made by an old-established firm of coachbuilders, who have been using a bought engine . . . ', Perry wrote, later stating that 'although the quantity is not big, we should like to have the added volume'. This is a reflection of the fact that Ford-England's finances were then in a parlous state as it strove to absorb the

massive overheads incurred by its recently-completed Dagenham plant. Amusingly, it is apparent from the text of this letter that he confused Morgan with the Leighton Buzzard coachbuilder of the same name which had gone out of business in the late 1920s . . .

The Model Y was the first Ford to be designed for an overseas market and although Henry Ford himself had overall responsibility for the car's mechanicals, the detail engineering was undertaken by chief engine designer Lawrence Sheldrick. His cast-iron power unit had a bore and stroke of 92.5mm x 56.6mm and it developed 23.4bhp at 4000rpm. Rated at 7.9 RAC horsepower, it was therefore an 8hp for taxation purposes (see page 13).

The engine of the Model T of 1908 had pioneered the concept of a

combined block and crankcase, rather than a separate aluminium crankcase and cast-iron block, and the new small Ford unit was no exception to this by then well-established rule. As with its illustrious forebear, it lacked adjustable tappets, the ends of the valve stems having to be ground to obtain the correct clearance. However, the lubrication system broke with past Ford practice in that rather than utilising a 'spit-and-hope' splash system, it featured a conventional pressurised pump-fed arangement. The crankshaft ran in three bearings, although it had started its pre-production life with a more flexible two-bearing crank.

The 8hp Ford unit continued to be available in Morgan's F4 four-seater three-wheeler until after the Second World War, and in 1934 it was joined by a supplementary 10hp version. With a 63.5mm bore to give an 1172cc capacity, the bigger engine developed 30bhp at 4000rpm. Initially used in Dagenham's Model C 'Ten' of October 1934, it appeared at the Motor Cycle Show of the following month under the bonnet of Morgan's F2 two-seater. It would continue to be offered until the end of three-wheeler production, the last example (chassis F1301), by then designated the F Super, being delivered in July 1952.

When the '1172' was used by Ford in its popular 16cwt Prefect saloon of 1938–1953, top speed was 65mph, a rather alarming velocity given the old-fashioned transverse-leaf suspension of these 'perpendicular' Fords. Morgan's two-seater F-Super, a positive lightweight by comparison, was on the other hand capable of over 70mph with the 10hp engine in standard tune.

With the 1952 demise of the three-wheelers, Morgan ceased to use Ford engines, but then shortages of Standard's TR units for the Plus 4 caused Peter Morgan to reactivate the 4/4 line. Ford agreed to supply him with the latest version of the 1172cc engine used in the 100E saloon of 1953, for £66 per unit, a substantial saving of £53 over the big Standard

'four'. Unlike its predecessor, the 100E engine was delivered complete with its three-speed gearbox. Further savings on ancillaries, to the tune of £16–£17 per engine, permitted Morgan to offer the 4/4 Series II at £217 less than the Plus 4.

The only similarities between the 100E sidevalve engine and the earlier 10hp unit used in the three-wheelers were its cubic capacity and its unchanged bore and stroke. Everything else was different, it having a completely new block casting and a crankshaft with larger bearings than enjoyed by its predecessor. It also sported such refinements as adjustable tappets and a water pump. Possessing a 7:1 compression ratio, as opposed to 6:1, it developed a dizzy 36bhp, some 6bhp more than the old unit had managed. It remained in production until 1962.

When the Series III Morgan arrived in October 1960, under the bonnet was the latest Ford engine with overhead valves and oversquare dimensions. Used to power the wholly new 105E Anglia saloon of 1959, it marked a significant landmark in the history of Ford's subsidiary: rather than being designed in America, it was the work of the company's British engineers. The first of a line that was

to be known as the 'Kent' engine, it was so named because Alan Worters, the executive engineer for power units, lived in that county. Initially conceived to have 997cc and 1340cc capacities, the early 'Kent' engines were respectively to power the 4/4 Series III, produced between November 1960 and October 1961, and the Series IV of October 1961 to March 1963.

Being a Ford engine, cost played a significant role in the design but an equally important influence was that the disappearance of the horsepower tax in 1947 meant that British manufacturers were no longer constrained by the need to keep the bore as small as possible. So this was an oversquare engine, in that the dimensions of the bore were greater than the stroke. The attraction was lower piston speed and consequent improvements in piston-ring and cylinder life.

For price considerations, both engines shared a 80.96mm bore. Although varying bore sizes had been considered, keeping the same bore and changing crankshafts and connecting rods proved to be a cheaper alternative – a solution typical of the lateral way in which Ford looked at cost-conscious design issues. In the same vein Ford had already pioneered the use of cast-iron crankshafts, which were cheaper than forgings and required less machining, and the 105E engine accordingly featured a hollow three-bearing crank.

For the same financial reasons both engines shared cylinder heads and valves. The smaller unit developed 39bhp at 5000rpm, endowing the 14.75cwt two-door Anglia saloon with a top speed of about 75mph, which was some 3mph slower than when it was used under the 4/4's bonnet. As well as the 105E's engine, the 4/4 also inherited its gearbox which was Ford's first four-speeder for its passenger cars.

The trusty 1172cc Ford engine that powered the Series II 4/4 from its introduction in 1955 until 1960. It is rather lost in the engine compartment, the dimensions of which are essentially those of the Plus 4. (LAT)

Ford's 'Kent' family of engines was used in the 4/4 from 1968 until 1982. (LAT)

The 1340cc version of the 'Kent' engine, with a 65.07mm stroke and an output of 54bhp at 4900rpm, was destined for Ford's Consul Classic 109E saloon, positioned in the market above the Anglia and unveiled in May 1961. Alas the Classic proved to be one of Ford's flops, not least as at 18.75cwt it was much heavier than planned, and with the 1.3-litre was embarrassingly underpowered. Therefore a 1½-litre version of the 'Kent' engine was speedily developed – although it was soon recognised that the three-bearing crankshaft would have to be replaced for refinement reasons by a five-bearing item. Again the 80mm bore was retained but the 72.7mm stroke meant the block was slighter taller. With a capacity of 1496cc, the new unit developed 59bhp at 4600rpm, and was fitted to the Classic and its Capri coupé derivative in August 1962; both models, however, were soon overshadowed by the runaway success of the lively lightweight Cortina, announced in 1200cc form the following month and in 1500 Super guise in January 1963. All this meant that the 1340cc Series IV 4/4 was short-lived indeed, as in February 1963 the 1496cc unit was

standardised, to create the 4/4 Series V – as current until March 1968.

From April 1963 Ford also produced a GT version of the Cortina, and from 1964 the GT engine powered Morgan's Competition 4/4. With larger inlet valves, a Cosworth-developed high-lift camshaft, a 9:1 rather than 8.3:1 compression ratio, and single DCD 16/18 twin-choke Weber carburettor, it developed 78bhp.

For 1968 the Mark II Cortina used an enlarged 80.97mm x 77.62mm 1597cc engine (2737E) which featured a crossflow cylinder head with bowl-in-piston Heron-head combustion chambers. Employed in the Morgan 4/4 1600, introduced in February 1968, the new unit again had a GT version (2737GT), which now developed 95bhp, and this engine was used in the 4/4 Competition model before being standardised across the 4/4 range in May 1971. This 4/4 variant, which had a top speed in excess of 100mph, enjoyed an 11-year production run and survived until March 1982. Its demise marked the end of the 'Kent'-engined Morgan, because Ford had designed a new power unit for its 'Erika' project, which emerged in 1980 as the front-wheel-drive Escort.

The new engine was designed jointly at the company's Research and

Development facility at Dunton, Essex, and at Merkenich, Germany. Ford had to decide whether to opt for twin overhead camshafts in the manner of Alfa Romeo, Lotus, Toyota and Fiat, or whether to adopt single-cam units as used by Audi, BMW and Mercedes-Benz. The consensus was that providing large enough valves were used the cost and complication of twin overhead camshafts could be avoided. The resulting CVH engine – short for for 'Compound Valve-angle Hemispherical combustion chamber' – therefore used a centrally-positioned belt-driven single overhead camshaft which operated the two valves per cylinder via hydraulic tappets. Tappet adjustment thus became a thing of the past. The CVH unit was produced at Ford's new engine factory, opened at Bridgend, South Wales, in 1978.

Having a cast-iron block with an aluminium cylinder head, and a five-bearing crank, the new engine was made over the years in a range of capacities, but was launched in 1117cc, 1296cc and 1597cc forms. The 1597cc unit used in the Morgan 4/4 1600 of March 1982 to November 1991 had a stroke of 79.52mm, a 9.5:1 compression ratio and a single Weber 32/34 DFT twin-choke carburettor. Producing 96bhp at 6000rpm, it gave the 4/4 a top speed of about 103mph, some 3mph faster than the equivalently-engined Escort could manage.

When in January 1986 Ford introduced a facelifted Escort, it came with an improved range of lean-burn engines. The 1.6-litre version, fitted to the 4/4 in 1987, had a redesigned cylinder head, with what Ford described as high-swirl lean burn. There was also a change in carburettor to a 28/32 TLDM twin-choke. An at-a-glance way of identifying this engine is that the pancake-style air-filter cover is black rather than being grey-painted.

Ford announced a new Escort range in August 1990 and included was a 1.6EFi catalyst engine, with electronic fuel injection using Weber solenoid-type sequential injectors. Management was by Ford's EEC IV engine computer which monitored rpm, exhaust-gas temperature and the oxygen content of the catalysts, together with engine load readings from inlet-manifold pressure and throttle position. From gathering such information it made the necessary adjustments to fuelling

In March 1982 Ford's CVH replaced the 'Kent' engine in the 4/4; it was to remain under its bonnet until 1993, when the Zeta unit took over. (LAT)

and ignition. 'Smart' chips retained data when the engine was turned off. This unit was fitted to the 4/4 in November 1991 but it only lasted until 1992, when it was replaced by a version of Ford's new Zeta twin-cam.

The Zeta replaced the CVH for the 1992 season in the larger-capacity Escorts, Orions and Fiestas but it was not fitted in what was redesignated the 4/4 1800 until March 1993. The engine didn't arrive a moment too soon, as delays in Morgan receiving its engines had meant that no 4/4s had been built for much of 2002 and early 2003.

Ford had begun work on the Zeta in 1987. As previously, it was an Anglo-German development and followed its predecessor's configuration of an alloy cylinder head and a cast-iron block. However, the most obvious difference was the use of twin overhead camshafts actuating four valves per cylinder. With a bore and stroke of 80.6mm x 88mm, it was undersquare, unusually for Ford, and had a capacity of 1796cc. Fuel injection was a sequential multipoint system, whilst engine management used a 16-bit EEC IV computer with 56kB memory and a three-way catalytic-converter exhaust system was fitted. The new engine was available in two states of tune and

Morgan used the more powerful variant, as found in the Fiesta RS1800 and the Escort XR3i.

With a claimed 128bhp on tap, prospects looked good, but in reality this figure proved to be over-optimistic when checked by Morgan on its own dynamometer and then at Ford's Bridgend factory. This was particularly relevant in the all-important German market, where customers could return cars which did not conform to a manufacturer's figures. So Morgan reduced its claim to 121bhp and 119lb ft of torque. In any event January 1997 saw power output reduced as a result of more robust emissions legislation, the revised figures being 114bhp at 5750rpm and 118lb ft of torque at 4500rpm. Currently Morgan uses the 1.8 litre alloy Zetec twin cam, as fitted on the Ford Focus.

When production of the Morgan Plus 8 ceased in March 2004 its Roadster replacement was powered by the Ford 3-litre Duratec V6 used in the Mondeo ST 220. Introduced in May 2002, this was the fastest model of the line, with a claimed top speed of 151mph and a 0–62mph figure of 6.8 seconds. The all-alloy US-produced engine, with twin overhead camshafts actuating four valves per cylinder, was developed in conjunction with Porsche and originally appeared in 170bhp 2.5-litre form in the 1994 Mondeo. The ST220 version, bored out to 2967cc, produces 217bhp at 6150rpm in the form used in the Morgan, and delivers its maximum torque of 207lb ft at 4900rpm.

Coventry Climax

Between March 1936 and September 1939 a total of 791 examples of the 4-4 were powered by a 1.1-litre Coventry Climax engine; a further four were completed after the war, making a grand total of 795 Climax-engined 4-4s. But as was the fashion of the day, Morgan did not always acknowledge the source of the engine.

Coventry Climax Engines was a company established in Coventry in 1903 by former Daimler 'improver'

The overhead-inlet/side-exhaust Coventry Climax engine that powered the 4-4 from its introduction in 1936 until 1939. This example is fitted in a 1939 Le Mans Replica, and is therefore non-standard. (LAT)

H Pelham Lee, who had studied electrical and mechanical engineering, and a Dane named Stroyer. After briefly producing the Lee-Stroyer car, the latter departed and Lee renamed his business Coventry Simplex.

One of his first contracts was a vertical-twin engine for the friction-drive GWK of 1910, a great rival in trials events of Morgan's three-wheelers. In 1917 the name of Lee's company was changed to Coventry Climax and during the 1920s it supplied sidevalve engines to such manufacturers as AJS, Clyno and Crouch, and an example powered Morgan's prototype F-type of 1929.

The power unit used in the 4-4, designated the OC type, was the smallest member of a family of three monobloc overhead-inlet/side-exhaust ('IoE') units – the others being the

1496cc D type and the 1476cc six-cylinder J type. In 1932 the 'OC' was adopted by Triumph for its Super Nine, in 1018cc (60 x 90mm) guise. It then powered Triumph's Southern Cross of 1933, by which time it had been enlarged to the more familiar 63mm x 90mm capacity of 1122cc. It was in this form that the engine was used by Morgan.

Outwardly the cylinder head of the Climax 'four' was dominated by polished rocker covers for its overhead inlet valves. The sidedraught Solex carburettor was mounted directly above the exhaust manifold on the nearside, with all electrics located on the offside of the engine. The unit had a compression ratio of 6.8:1, and developed 34bhp at 4500rpm and had an RAC horsepower rating of 9.8hp.

Initially produced at Coventry Climax's Friars Road premises, from 1933 it was also built under licence by Triumph, in both four-cylinder and six-cylinder forms. Triumph found that the engines had a propensity to

overheat and to suffer from burnt-out exhaust valves. As a result it ceased to fit the Climaxes in 1937, the engines being replaced by a range of Triumph's own overhead-valve units, designed under technical director Donald Healey.

In November 1937 Morgan noted that it was contracted to receive a further 250 engines priced at £29 each with the figure thereafter rising appreciably to £36 apiece. Presumably at least in part as a result of this price hike, the Climax engine was replaced from June 1939 by the Standard Special unit, which had the virtue of being considerably cheaper.

However, when in 1947 Peter Morgan was looking for an eventual replacement for the Standard unit, he approached Coventry Climax, only to find that it was fully occupied manufacturing fire pumps and forklift trucks. The company did introduce a new range of competition engines in 1954, but by that time Morgan was using Standard's new wet-liner 'four' in the Plus 4.

Standard

The 1267cc Standard overhead-valve unit used by the 4-4 from March 1939 until February 1951 was unique in that it was specially designed for Morgan. In consequence it was never fitted to any other car.

For 1936 Standard had introduced its 'Flying' saloon range, so named because of its distinctive fastback styling. Initially available in 12hp, 16hp and 20hp guises, the cars were powered by sidevalve engines with a common 106mm stroke. In 1937 the 'Flying' family was expanded downwards, and one of the new models, the 'Ten', had a 1267cc engine with dimensions of 63.5mm x 100mm. In this form it developed 33bhp at 4000rpm.

The capacity of this unit was ideal for the 4-4 but Morgan felt that a more powerful overhead-valve configuration would be preferable. As it happened, since 1936 Standard had been supplying ohv versions of its bigger engines to SS, the design of the pushrod cylinder heads having been commissioned by SS from tuning specialist Harry Weslake.

Following this SS precedent, Standard managing director John Black sanctioned the creation of an ohv version of the 10hp engine, the work being overseen by technical director Edward (Ted) Grinham. With an unchanged bore and stroke, the somewhat tall pushrod unit with its long 100mm stroke developed 39bhp at 4200rpm, a significant improvement on the sidevalve version.

Although discussions between Black and Morgan were well advanced by November 1937, it took over a year for them to reach fruition. Once agreement was reached, the Morgan name was cast on the engine's rocker cover, although the power unit was accorded the Standard Special name by Malvern.

Looking at the engine in more detail, it featured a combined inlet and exhaust manifold on the offside and used a single downdraught Solex carburettor. Despite these outward differences to the Climax unit, the switch in engines was achieved with the minimum of underbonnet modification, a process aided by the 4-4 gearbox conveniently remaining separate.

As a simpler design based on a mass-produced unit, the new engine was an appreciable £11 cheaper than its predecessor, Standard charging Morgan some £25 per engine against the £36 latterly asked for the Coventry Climax F-head. On a broader canvas, it also marked the beginning of an association between Morgan and Standard that was destined to endure until 1969.

The first 4-4 to use the Standard power unit was HFS Morgan's Avon-built drophead coupé, registered in January 1939 – the engine did not become publicly available until June of that year.

Standard reintroduced its 'Flying' series after the war, but only in 8hp, 12hp and 14hp forms. This meant that the 10hp 1267cc overhead-valve engine used in the 4/4 was even more bespoke – although a version of the sidevalve 'Ten' was latterly revived for the Triumph Mayflower. More to the point, it was all-change in June 1948 when all Standard's pre-war cars were discontinued in favour of a single model, the all-new Vanguard powered by an ohv 2-litre four-cylinder engine.

This, in essence, was the engine destined to power the Plus 4 between June 1951 and January 1969, and for which Morgan initially paid Standard £119 per unit. Ted Grinham's design was a no-nonsense concept of great durability which from 1947 also saw service in the Ferguson TE-20 lightweight tractor that Standard built for many years.

The short-stroke, high-revving cast-iron 'four' was fitted with nickel-chrome iron wet liners, inspired by the similar unit in Citroën's legendary and influential Traction Avant model. As unveiled in July 1947 it had a capacity of 1849cc, with internal dimensions of 80m x 92mm, and developed 65bhp at 4500rpm via a downdraught Solex carburettor. With the demise of the horsepower tax at the end of 1947, the bore was increased to 85mm, which brought capacity up to the more familiar 2088cc. In this form it developed 68bhp at 4200rpm and

Standard's wet-liner Vanguard engine used in the Plus 4 from its introduction in 1950 until supplanted by the TR2 engine in December 1953. It remained an option until 1958 and was an obligatory fitment in the drophead coupé. (LAT)

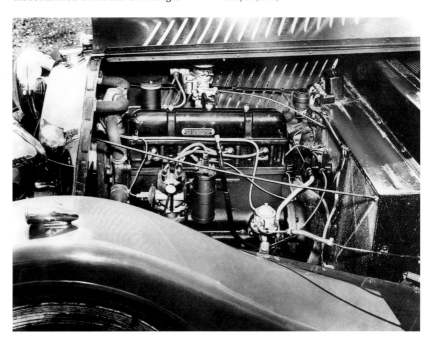

propelled the bulbous 21cwt four-door Vanguard saloon to 78mph.

When the engine was used in Triumph's TR2 sports car of 1953, with twin 1½in SUs replacing the single Solex, output was boosted to 90bhp at 4800rpm – this despite the capacity having been reduced to 1991cc by employing 83mm liners, so that the TR would qualify for the 2-litre class in competition. In this form the 16.5cwt Triumph was capable of 102mph. The Plus 4, by contrast, which tipped the scales at 16.07cwt, was slightly slower, one assumes on account of its aerodynamics, or rather the lack of them.

For the TR3 of 1956 power was boosted to 100bhp at 5000rpm: although the Triumph's top speed remained about the same, the Morgan became a 100mph car. Engine capacity was constant until the arrival of the TR4, which witnessed the first increase, taking the engine back through the 2-litre ceiling; at 2138cc, it developed 100bhp at 4600rpm. But weight was up, and the TR's top speed remained about the same. With the arrival of the independent-rear TR4A of 1965–67, engine output, on twin-Stromberg 175CD carbs, was boosted to 104bhp at 4700rpm and performance began to nudge the 110mph mark. This signalled the end of the Vanguard-derived 'four': Triumph's TR5 used a stroked version of the Triumph 2000 in-line 'six'.

Rover

Morgan used Rover's aluminium V8 for longer than any other power unit – a total of 36 years by the time that production of the Plus 8 ceased in March 2004. This is an impressive record for an engine that began life as a General Motors paper project back in 1950.

The principal reason for using aluminium, as the respected automotive authority Karl Ludvigsen wrote in 1960, was 'because it makes far better overall performance possible at only a *slight* increase in manufacturing cost.' By 1952 GM had

built roadgoing prototypes, but work on the V8 did not begin in earnest until 1957. The first engine ran in mid-1958 and the concept was then dispatched to Buick to turn a raw idea into a production reality.

Initially there were thoughts about making the bores as well as the block from aluminium, but while encouraging results were achieved, excessive scuffing by the piston rings from a cold start ruled out this innovation. Wishing to avoid 'wet' cylinder liners on the grounds of potential leaks, and the fact that they did not contribute to the structural strength of the block, the Buick team under Joe Turlay opted for thin-section cast-iron liners. Yet despite this departure, as Ludvigsen pointed out, this remarkable V8 ended up weighing almost exactly the same as a typical imported-car engine, the 1.6-litre Volvo 'four', which had less than half its displacement.

At 215cu in (3.5 litres), the new GM engine had a small capacity by American standards, and had been conceived to power a trio of GM's so-called compacts, produced in response to European imports such as – in particular – the Volkswagen Beetle. American Motors had quickly come up with its Rambler and this had been followed in 1959 by the Chevrolet Corvair, Ford Falcon and Plymouth Valiant. It was now the turn of GM's Buick, Oldsmobile and Pontiac marques to produce their compacts, and the Buick Special, Oldsmobile F-85 and Pontiac Tempest were duly introduced in the autumn of 1960 for the following season, complete with the new V8.

The Buick Special four-door saloon, which sold for $2384 in its cheapest form, used the basic 155bhp version of the V8 with a two-barrel Rochester carburettor, endowing the 24.1cwt car with a comfortable 80mph top speed. However, the more expensive 100mph Skylark, which followed in the spring of 1961, used a 185bhp tune with a four-barrel Rochester.

The new V8, the first mass-produced aluminium engine in American motoring history, was well received,

particularly by the press, and – largely on account of its engine – the Buick Special won the 1962 *Car and Driver* 'Car of the Year' award. The Oldsmobile version would later form the basis of Jack Brabham's Repco-Brabham Formula 1 car enhanced with single overhead camshaft heads. In 1966 it gave him the World Drivers' Championship, an accolade which was repeated in 1967 by team-mate Denny Hume.

Yet despite the many plaudits, when the 1964 Buick range was introduced the aluminium engine had been dropped, replaced by a 300cu in V8 with a cast-iron block. The principal reason was that the aluminium V8 was simply too expensive for a low-priced car; but equally it was the case that thin-wall iron casting techniques had improved to such an extent that the difference in weight between an aluminium and a cast-iron engine had become insufficient to justify the extra cost of using aluminium. Recognition of this had already spawned a supplementary 198cu in (3.2-litre) cast-iron V6 derivative, the first instance of a frontline American manufacturer adopting this now widely-used configuration.

In 1962, meanwhile, Rover had acquired a new managing director in the shape of William Martin-Hurst, who had joined the company in 1960 to succeed Maurice Wilks, who became chairman. John Barber, later deputy chairman of British Leyland, had a high regard for Rover in general and Martin-Hurst in particular, and described him to the author as 'a visionary sort of chap'. In the US in 1963 Martin-Hurst literally stumbled over the recently-discontinued engine and this led to his company taking a licence to manufacture it.

Martin-Hurst was on a trip to General Motors and it is now a part of British motoring legend that while visiting Carl Keikhaefer of Mercury Marine at his workshop at Fond du Lac in Wisconsin, he was shown the aluminium V8 that the corporation had just taken out of production. At this time Rover was developing a six-cylinder version of the 2000. But

Morgan's longest-lived power unit was Rover's V8: introduced in the Plus 8 in 1968, it survived until 2004. Initially produced in 3.5-litre guise, it was progressively enlarged, being finally offered in 4.6-litre form. (LAT)

Martin-Hurst recognised that the compact lightweight V8 was only 12lb heavier and half an inch longer than Rover's own 'four', and would probably fit under the 2000's commodious bonnet. The available space was particularly generous because there had been thoughts about offering the saloon with gas-turbine power.

Although faced with strong opposition from Solihull, Martin-Hurst persisted, and the engine, with only a modest amount of persuasion, was made to fit in the 2000. In January 1965 General Motors granted Rover a licence to manufacture the unit. But Rover needed to effect a number of modifications to gear it to British production and these were overseen by the engine's original designer, Joe Turlay, whom the company was able to bring over for the purpose and who was briefly domiciled in Solihull.

Although the original intention had been to use the V8 in the 2000, in October 1967 it made its UK debut under the bonnet of Rover's slow-selling 3-Litre saloon, which was thereby transformed into the Rostyle-wheeled 3.5-Litre – internally designated P5B, with the 'B' standing for 'Buick'. Six months later, in April 1968, the engine appeared in the 2000 shell, in a supplementary 115mph model called the 3500, or P6B in Rover's internal parlance.

The principal difference between the American and British versions of the 90-degree 3528cc V8 was that in its original form the alloy block was a gravity casting. Rover, however, opted for sand casting and, at the same time, increased the size of the main bearing diaphragms to allow for a larger-diameter crankshaft in the event of a future increase in cubic capacity.

The Rover-Buick engine was a conventional and robust unit. The two-plane crankshaft ran in five main bearings and the connecting rods differed little from their American counterparts. The crank drove the centrally-located single camshaft by a front-located chain and thereafter actuated the valve gear by stubby small-diameter pushrods. But because alloy engines are noisier than their cast-iron equivalents, hydraulic tappets were used. These were the only American components employed by Rover, being supplied by the Diesel Equipment Company of Grand Rapids. An interesting detail is that while General Motors used to machine the combustion chambers, Rover's die castings were left untouched.

With oversquare dimensions of 88.9mm x 71.12mm, a compression ratio of 10.5:1 was relatively high for the day. In this form, ouput was 160bhp, but the figure progressively dropped over the years, on account of the effects of increasingly stringent

Tight fit! On the fuel injected Plus 8s, a small section of the bonnet hinge had to be cut away so that the plenum chamber would clear it. (LAT)

emissions regulations and because of the adoption of different standards of measurement. With the use of new international DIN standards, the quoted figure slipped to 151bhp, and to 143bhp in 1973.

Fortunately the arrival in June 1976 of the Rover SD1 saw the V8's output increased to 155bhp, and the Plus 8 was to benefit from this revised engine from the 1977 season. BL later decided to produce a high-performance fuel-injected version of the SD1, the 190bhp Vitesse arriving for the 1983 model year. In October 1983 Morgan announced that the injected engine would be available as an option in the Plus 8 from mid-1984. Standardised in 1987, it continued to be fitted until June 1990 when it was replaced by the enlarged 3.9-litre version that had been announced in October 1989 for the Range Rover.

This represented the first capacity increase since the unit had been introduced 22 years before, the 3946cc displacement being achieved by over-boring from 88.9mm to 94mm. This resulted in an output of 185bhp at 4750rpm. Maximum torque was

improved further, from 220lb ft at 4000rpm to 235lb ft at a much lower 2600rpm, with 90 per cent of this available between 1500rpm and 4500rpm. This unit continued to be fitted until the Plus 8 ceased production.

Meanwhile, a supplementary 4.6-litre engine arrived for the significantly revised Plus 8 launched for the 1998 season. This enlarged V8 had first appeared three years before in Land Rover's new Range Rover of 1994. This time the stroke had been increased by 11mm, from 71mm to 82mm, which required a new crankshaft, larger-diameter main and big-end bearings, and in turn a reinforced block. The 4555cc unit produced 220bhp at 5000rpm, with torque up to 260lb ft at 2600rpm.

In the Range Rover it was used with a four-speed automatic transmission, and because Rover was unable to supply the revised unit with a manual gearbox, Morgan's engines were specially assembled by Powertrain Projects Engineering of Hinckley, using the 3.9-litre block but the internal components of the later engine. This permitted Morgan to retain the all-important manual gearbox. The cylinder heads were equally to '3 9' specification, as were the Lucas 14 CUX injectors. As with the 3.9-litre

engine, the 4.6-litre unit continued to be available on the Plus 8 until it ceased production.

In the 37 years since Rover had begun its manufacture in 1967, some 909,000 examples of the V8 had been produced. William Martin-Hurst's chance encounter in that Wisconsin boat house had certainly paid dividends.

So much for the V8, with its now-distant American parentage. By contrast, the 2-litre twin-overhead-camshaft M16 Rover engine which powered 357 Plus 4s from 1989 until 1992 has a wholly British pedigree. Its origins are rooted in the 1.8-litre BMC B-Series unit that, amongst many other applications, once powered the MGB. From this was extrapolated a single-overhead-cam update known as the O-Series. This was created for the MG, of which 80 per cent were sold in America, and was conceived above all to restore the Federal-specification MGB's performance while complying with forthcoming US emissions legislation; ironically, the engine's protracted development meant it was never fitted to a production 'B'.

Featuring an alloy cylinder head, and with the camshaft driven by a toothed rubber belt, the O-Series was launched in 1978 in the front-wheel-drive Princess 2, in two capacities,

1695cc and 1993cc. Both shared a 84.45mm bore, with the larger engine having a 89m stroke. The 2-litre version, which developed 93bhp at 4900rpm, subsequently evolved into the dohc 16-valve M16 of 1986, which powered Rover's new fwd 820 executive saloon. A lean-burn unit, its new alloy cylinder head borrowed its configuration from Rover's as yet unseen smaller K-Series engine, which did not appear until 1989. Enhanced with Lucas fuel injection and a 10:1 compression ratio, the M16 developed 138bhp at 6000rpm and maximum torque was 131lb ft at 4500rpm. In the Rover the engine was mounted transversely, and Morgan required a north-south positioning, but the M16 was successfully mated to the Plus 8's SD1-derived gearbox.

In 1992 the Plus 4 inherited the revised T16 which appeared in Rover's facelifted 800 saloon, announced in November 1991. This was essentially an M16 upated with technology pioneered on the K-series twin-cam and featured an internal breathing system in which gases were circulated via channels within the cylinder block and head rather than by a network of external pipes. The arrangement was intended to minimise the number of critical pipe joints, and thereby leaks, while also making the engine look more presentable. Further refinements included an oblong-tract inlet system to improve flexibility at low and medium revs. All engine functions were controlled by a Modular Engine Magagement System (MEMS) and a Lucas L hot-wire injection with digital ignition control was fitted.

In the interests of refinement, the crankshaft had eight balance weights instead of the four previously used. Ancillaries were also improved. A three-way closed-loop exhaust catalyst was fitted and in consequence output was slightly down, at 134bhp, although torque remained the same.

Fiat

The first twin-overhead-camshaft Morgan was the 4/4 1600 TC sold between December 1981 and November 1985 and powered by a 1600cc Fiat engine similar to that used in the 131 Supermirafiori. The 131, which arrived for the 1975 model year, originally used pushrod units derived from the base engine found in the car's 124 predecessor. However in 1978 the Supermirafiori arrived in Britain, powered by a 1585cc twin-cam engine.

Also available in 1995cc form in the Supermirafiori Sport, this engine had started life in Fiat's 124 Sport of 1966 and was also used in the 132 saloon. What *Autocar* described as 'a superb . . . delightfully neat little unit' used a cast-iron block and an aluminium cylinder head. The drive to the twin overhead camshafts was significant because it used the now universally popular neoprene belt, which was something of a novelty in 1966.

The 1585cc version used in the Morgan had an 84mm bore and a 71.5mm stroke, and developed 96bhp at 6000rpm. Just 96 Fiat-engined 4/4s were produced, as the 4/4 1600 TC.

The Plus 4 was Fiat-powered from its revival in 1985 until 1987 – when supplies ceased, following Fiat's wholesale switch to front-wheel drive. (LAT)

The model was briefly sold alongside the Ford-powered cars on the basis that its emissions made it eligible for certain foreign markets, in particular the all-important German one.

When in 1985 Morgan revived the Plus 4, it used a 2-litre version of the same engine, in the injected form, with Digiplex ignition control, used in the Argenta saloon – although some nine cars had a single Weber DCOE twin-choke carburettor. The 84 x 90mm 1995cc unit, which developed 122bhp at 5300rpm (or 113bhp at 5600rpm in single-Weber form), also came with a five-speed Abarth gearbox, as had the 4/4. But the engine was discontinued in June 1987, when Morgan was faced with an impending shortage of gearboxes, Fiat having by this stage gone over wholesale to transverse-engine front-wheel drive.

BMW

The 4398cc V8 which powers the Aero 8 is the same unit as used in BMW's 5-series and 7-series cars, although it has been modified for Morgan's special requirements. Unlike the Ford Zeta engine which powers the 4/4 and which is a modified version of a transversely-located unit, the M62 B44 V8 used in the Morgan was designed for north-south mounting. And whilst the BMW 5 and 7-series saloons sold on the British market are solely equipped with a five-speed automatic transmission, the Aero 8 employs the six-speed manual Getrag gearbox that is an option in mainland Europe.

The engine began life in 1992 and was BMW's first V8 since the unrelated unit used in later versions of the 1951–63 'Baroque Angel' saloons and the 503 and 507 models. The all-new V8, available initially in 3-litre and 4-litre forms, is an all-alloy unit with twin overhead camshafts, four valves per cylinder, and hydraulic tappets. Both are long-stroke designs, adopted for better low-speed torque and emissions. The shape of the combustion chambers draws heavily on BMW's well-established 16-valve four-cylinder unit.

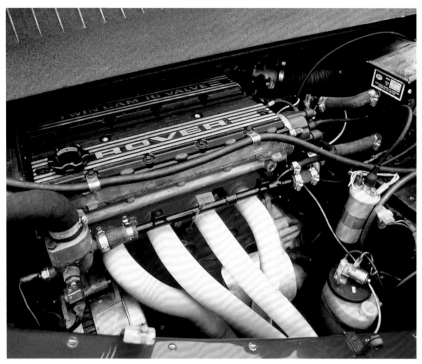

The larger-capacity 3982cc engine, the predecessor of the current 4.4-litre, has a bore of 80mm and a stroke of 84mm, and develops 286bhp at 5800rpm and 295lb ft of torque at 4500rpm, this on a 10:1 compression ratio. A new-generation DME 3.3 engine management system provides fully electronic ignition and cylinder-selective knock sensors. The electronically-controlled fuel injection incorporates hot-film air-mass meters to measure the amount of air demanded by each cylinder.

These engines have proved to be a great success, and by the time of the 1996 announcement of revised 3.4-litre and 4.4-litre versions some 190,000 had been built. This made it Europe's best-selling V8: BMW claimed that it was outselling Mercedes-Benz's S420 and S500 lines by four to one.

The 4398cc unit is essentially the engine used in the Aero 8, and the new capacity has been achieved by increasing the bore to 82.7mm and the stroke to 92mm. Maximum power remains the same at 286bhp, although this is now developed at 5500rpm. Torque is up to 322lb ft at 3700rpm. This allows higher gearing, which

There was a hiatus in Plus 4 production following the demise of the Fiat unit; the model was revived in October 1988 when Rover's M16 twin-cam became available. In 1992 came this engine's T16 derivative, and the Plus 4 survived until manufacture of the T16 ceased in 2000. (LAT)

results in an 8–10 per cent improvement in fuel consumption. BMW also claims a world first in that the cooling-system thermostat is electronically geared.

The aim of BMW engineers was to add refinement to the V8s by reducing friction. To these ends the duplex chain that drives the camshafts is replaced by a single-roller chain, the valvegear is lighter and more compact and the timing overlaps are reduced by 30 per cent to improve engine stability at idling. A new engine management system inherited from the unit's V12 stablemate is intended to produce instantaneous starting. However, the Aero 8 uses a unique Bosch package.

BMW claims a top speed for its 36cwt 740i saloon of 155mph, with a 0–60mph figure of 6.9 seconds. The comparable figures for the Aero 8 are 22.3cwt, 151mph and 4.8 seconds.

Joining the Club

Morgan owners are well advised to join one of the two clubs which cater for their specific needs, whether they are owners of three-wheelers or four-wheelers.

A club for trikes, the Morgan Three-Wheeler Club, had existed in the 1920s and in 1927 was renamed the Cyclecar Club – although most of its members were Morgan drivers. It was revived in 1934 as The Three-Wheeler Club, again covering all makes of trike. But as popularity of the breed declined, by 1937 Morgan was Britain's only manufacturer of three-wheelers. Membership fell away and the Club was effectively finished off by the outbreak in 1939 of the Second World War.

However, in May 1944 a letter to *Motor Cycling* magazine prompted a revival, resulting in the first meeting, in February 1945, of The Morgan Three-Wheeler Club, some three months before the ending of the war in Europe. A gathering was held at the Morgan factory in September 1945, attended by over 50 members. From the start the aim was to maintain the three-wheeler's sporting tradition, and race meetings are still held throughout the year.

Connections with the factory were established early on, with HFS Morgan becoming the Club's first president, a position filled on his death by Peter Morgan; at the time of writing, Charles Morgan is president-elect. Today about 2500 three-wheelers survive worldwide and the majority of these are owned by some 750 members, many having two, three or even four examples. A monthly magazine, *The Bulletin*, is published and the club offers advice on the all-important question of spares. Details can be obtained from E Eyes, 280 Commonwealth Way, Abbey Wood, London SE20 0LD.

Owners of four-wheeled models can join the Morgan Sports Car Club, an organisation that began life in 1951 as the Morgan 4/4 Club but which changed its name in 1971 to embrace all four-wheeled Morgans. Today its worldwide membership stands at some 4500 people. Founded by a group of enthusiasts in the Derby area, it currently embraces centres across the UK, including London, the Midlands, Yorkshire, and the South Coast.

As with the Three-Wheeler Club, the presidential role has been occupied by three generations of the Morgan family.

Competition has always played an important part in MSCC activities. this takes the form of race meetings, hill climbs and sprints although there are less demanding but enjoyable treasure hunts and runs held through scenic parts of the country. These activities are not confined to the UK and an international rally has been a popluar feature on the club calendar for many years. There is a concours d'elegance and the social side is not ignored because the annual dinner dance has long been well supported. The Club magazine, of which more below, is also a good source of used Morgans. There's certainly no shortage of those!

The MSCC publishes *Miscellany*, a monthly magazine, and is also a source of spares for the earlier cars. The Register section has its own committee which monitors parts availability and, as will have been apparent from this book, is a valuable source for the supply of original and newly-manufactured spare parts. The Register can also help with technical and historical information. Full details of the club can be obtained from Mrs Anne Salisbury, 7 Woodland Grove, Gornal Wood, Dudley, West Midlands DY3 2XB.

Bibliography

Books

Morgans to 1997 A Collector's Guide, (Motor Racing Publications, 1997), Roger Bell

Morgan First and Last of the Real Sports Cars (Galleon, 1974), Gregory Houston Bowden

Morgan First and Last of the Real Sports Cars (Virgin 2000), Brian Laban

Morgan Sports Cars The Early Years (Sheffield Academic Press, 1997), JD Alderson and Chris Chapman

Morgan Sweeps the Board (Gentry Books, 1978), JD Alderson and DM Rushton

Original Morgan (Bay View Books, 1992), John Worrall and Liz Turner

The Four-Wheeled Morgan Volume 1: The Flat-Radiator Models (Motor Racing Publications, 1977), Ken Hill

The Four-Wheeled Morgan Volume 2: The Cowled-Radiator Models (Motor Racing Publications, 1980), Ken Hill

The Morgan – 75 Years on the Road, (Blandford, Press, 1984), Ken Hill

Three-Wheelers (Bluestream Books, 1997), Chris Rees

The Three Wheeler – Story of the Morgan (Morgan Three-Wheeler Club, 1970), Brian Watts

Magazines

The Autocar (now *Autocar*); *Autocar & Motor*; *Autosport*; *Classic and Sports Car*; *The Light Car*; *The Motor* (later *Motor*); *The Motor Cycle*; *Motor Cycling*

Index

AC 135
    Cobra 31
Acock, WH 129
Ahlers, Keith 151–152
AJS 158
Alcan 123
Alfa Romeo 142, 157
    1750 142
Alford, Chris 148
All-British Racing Team 148
American Motors Rambler 162
Amiens 18, 139
Anthony, CM 'Dick' 142–143
Ashton, Mark 125
Aston Martin 35–36, 142
    DB4 87
Audi 157
Austin 23
    A35 148
    Seven 23, 33
Austin-Healey 65
    Sprite 80, 148
Austin-Morris 99
Austin, Sir Herbert 23
Australian GT Championship 151
Auto Cycle Union
    Six-Day event 139
    Stock Trial 139

Ballyclare 141
Bampton caravan 28
Barber, John 162
Bathurst 24-hour race 151
BBC TV 133
Beart, Harold 140
Bédélia 139
Beirne, Bernard 31
    Dragonfly 31
Bentley 119
Benz 9
Benz, Karl 9
Berris, Vic 96
Beverley Motors 60
Birmingham Post Rally 55
Birmingham University 123
Birkett Six-Hour Race 149
Black, John, Captain (later Sir) 10,
    47, 51, 61, 74–75
BMW 124, 135, 157, 165–166
    503 166
    507 166
    5-series 124, 165–166
    7-series 124, 165–166
Bodies and coachwork
    Adam & Robinson 60
    Avon Bodies 44, 47, 160
    Coach Bodies 58
    Mulliner 23
    Ranalah 38
    Superform 124–125
    Tickford 44
    Touring 60
    Vanden Plas 35–36, 38
Booth, Chris 17, 23, 28
    Morgan museum 17, 28, 36
Bosch 124
Bostock, Tony 82
Bourbeau 139
Bowden, Gregory Houston 130,
    132
Bowler, Michael 102–103

Bowman, ED 129
Boyd-Harvey, JJ 36, 38
BPR Global Endurance Cup 122
BRA CX3 Super Sports 31
Brabham, Jack 162
Braking systems 52, 71
    Bowden 33, 41
    Girling 33, 41, 55–56, 63, 85,
        102, 111
    Lockheed 38, 85, 116
Brands Hatch 122, 145
Bray 140
BRDC
    Freddie Dixon Trophy 144–145
    GT Championship 147
Bristol 135
British GT Championship 150–151
British Leyland Motor Corpn
    (BLMC) 98–99, 162–163
British Motor Corpn (BMC) 65, 98
    Mini 65
    Mini-Cooper 65
British Motor Cycle Racing Club
    139
British Motor Show 119
British Production Sports Car
    Championship 148–149
Britten, John 148
British Rally Championship 148
Brooklands 17, 22–23, 36,
    139–140, 142
Bryant, Graham 146–147
BSA Ten 16
Buchet, 146
Buckland B3 30
Buckland, Dick 30
Bugatti 20, 31, 142
Bugatti circuit 150
Buick 161–162
    Skylark 162
    Special 162
Buying Hints
    4-4 & 4/4 48–49
    Plus 4 72
    Plus 4 Plus 90
    Plus 8 118
Bysouth, John 33

Cadwell Park 149
Calver, Jeffrey 31
Campbell, Robert 141, 143
Carburettors
    Carburettors Ltd 41
    Holley 97
    Rochester 100, 162
    Solex 55, 76, 143, 158, 160–161
    Stromberg 64, 91, 111, 113, 161
    SU 61, 63–64, 68, 97, 100–101,
        106, 111, 113, 143, 160
    Weber 65–66, 68, 157–158, 165
Cardiff Business School 134
Carr, 139
Caterham 135
Central Garages (Barnstaple) 40
Chambers, 143
Cheffins of Cambridge 140
Chelsea College of Automobile
    Engineering 55
Chevrolet
    Corvair 162
    Corvette 148

CIBA 123
Circuit de l'Eure 20, 139
Citroën
    Traction Avant 160
    2CV 30–31
Clark, 143
Clarkson, Roy 60, 143
Classic Car Panels 31
    Tripacer 31
Classic Carrera Panamericana 150
Clayson, EM 55
Clyno 158
Cole, Steve 149
Cooper 96
Coventry Climax 158–159
Coventry Polytechnic 122, 134
Coventry Simplex 158
Coventry Victor 16
Cripps, Sir Stafford 51
Critchley-Daimler 10
Cropley, Steve 136
Crouch 158
CRS 87
Cummings, G 130
Curtis, Charlie 132
Crystal Palace Engineering College
    9
Cycle & Motor Cycle &
    Manufacturers Traders Union
    13
Cyclecar Club 164
Cyclecar GP 139, 144

Daimler 158
Daimler, Gottlieb 9
Dangerfield, Neil 148
Darmont 20–22
    Aéroluxe 20
    Spécial 20
Darmont, Robert 20
Darracq 11
Dashboards 40, 42, 47, 57, 62,
    64–65, 68–69, 71, 78, 80–83,
    91, 101, 107–108, 114–115,
    119, 124
de Mattos, Basil 143
de Yarburgh-Bateson, R. 43
Dean, William 9
Decauville 10, 12
Dence, Adrian 145
DeWalt RSS 149
Dick, Alick 74
Diesel Equipment Co. 162
Divey, Tony 30
Donington Park 141
DRF 30
Driving experience
    Darmont Morgan 22
    Plus 4 Plus 90
    Plus 4 cowled-rad 69
    Plus 4 Rover M16 71
    Plus 4 Super Sports 70
    Plus 8 116
    4/4 1600 84
Duigan, Mr 141
D'Yrsan 20–21
    BS 21
    DS 21

Earls Court Motorfair (see also
    London Motor Show) 83

EB Plastics 87, 90
EB (Staffs) Ltd 87
    Debonair 87
Edwards, John 87, 90
Electrics and lighting 58–60, 82,
    89, 98, 101, 107, 113–114
    Cibie 111
    Digiplex 165
    Lucas 58–59
Engines
    Anzani 23, 28
    Austin A40 53
    Blackburne 20–21, 23–25, 140,
        154
    BMC
        B-Series 164
        O-Series 164
            BMW 70, 120, 124, 127
            M62 127, 151, 166
    Buick V8 96–97, 100, 124, 161
    Burney 24
    Cosworth 157
    Coventry Climax 13, 32, 34–35,
        37–40, 47–48, 141–143,
        158–160
    De Dion Bouton 11
    Dorman 36
    Fiat 53, 66, 68–73, 77, 83–85,
        131, 163, 165
    Ford 30, 32–33, 35, 41, 69, 75,
        82, 85, 95, 96, 119, 148,
        154–158, 165
        CVH 77, 83–85, 157–158
        Duratec 158
        'Kent' 30, 77–81, 83–85,
            156–157
        Zeta 84–85, 157–158, 166
        Zetec 77
        100E 75, 79, 89, 154
        105E 75
        109E 75
        116E 77
        118E 80
    General Motors V8 95, 98,
        161–162
    Honda CX 31
    Hotchkiss 16
    Hudson 96
    JAP 12–13, 15–26, 28–29, 31–33,
        138–140, 153–154
    Lawrencetune 66, 69
    Lotus 95
    MAG 16, 19, 22, 28
    Matchless 26–27, 33, 139, 154
    Mini 31
    Moto Guzzi 30
    Peugeot 11–12
    Reliant Robin 31
    Renault 30
    Rover 70–71, 73, 84, 161–164
        K-Series 164
        M16 53, 71–73, 163, 165
        SD1 118
        T16 53, 72–73, 164–165
        V8 96, 99–100, 103–104, 110,
            115–119, 122, 124, 130, 166
        Vitesse 111, 118
        2000 162
    Ruby 20–21
    Saab 70
    Scott 139

Standard 48–50, 52–53, 72, 74, 96, 141, 143, 159–161
  Eight 41
  Special 13, 37, 55, 159–160
  Ten 47
  Vanguard 52–53, 57, 62, 69, 72, 143, 160–161
  Triumph TR 47, 55, 57, 63, 72, 75, 96, 99, 144, 155, 159, 161
  TR2 51, 62, 69, 74, 143, 145, 160
  TR3/3A 51, 62, 64, 69, 161
  TR4/4A 53, 64, 69, 90–91, 148, 161
  TR5 69, 161
  Volvo 162
English, Andrew 125
Environmental Protection Act 135
ERF Ltd 90
European Le Mans Series 150
Exhaust systems 106
  Derrington 69
  Offenhauser 97
  Tube Investments 73
Eyston, George 142

Falstaff Antiques 28
Fawcett, Percy 142
Fawcett, Prudence 47, 142–143, 146
Ferguson TE-20 tractor 160
Ferrari 212 Inter 60
FIA GT Championship 122
Fiat 157, 165
  Argenta 70, 165
  124 165
  124 Sport 165
  131 Supermirafiori 83, 165
  132 165
Fink, Bill 99, 105, 110
Ford 75, 154–158
  Bridgend factory 157–158
  Dunton Research & Development facility 157
  Merkenich 157
Ford models
  Capri 157
  Consul Classic 79–80, 156–157
  Cortina 78, 80, 85, 90, 157
  Cortina GT 80, 157
  Erika project 157
  Escort 83, 157–158
  Escort XR3 85, 158
  Falcon 162
  Fiesta 82, 158
  Fiesta RS1800 158
  Model A 28
  Model C 'Ten' 155
  Model T 13, 155
  Model Y 32, 154
  Mondeo 158
  Mondeo ST220 119, 158
  Orion 158
  Popular 87
  Prefect 155
  100E 75
  105E Anglia 78, 156
Ford, Henry 154
Fotheringham-Parker, Philip 60
Frazer Nash 140
French GP 18
Fryer, James 24
Fuel injection 113, 115, 118
  Lucas 163–164

Garnier, Peter 66, 130
Gearboxes and transmissions
  Abarth 72, 165

Borg & Beck 38, 97
British Leyland 110
BTR 85, 116
Burman Douglas 41, 49
close-ratio 61
Ford 75
  Cortina/Corsair 84–85
  Escort 30
  Sierra/Capri 84–85
  100E 155
Getrag 166
Hardy Spicer 38
Meadows 35, 38, 46, 49
Moss 35, 38, 46, 49, 69–70, 97, 106–107, 116, 118
Reliant 30
Renault 31
Rover 73, 107, 116, 118, 164
Salisbury 85, 102, 116
Wooller 80
General Motors 53, 162
  EV1 123
Geneva Motor Show 120
Ginetta 135
Glasgow Herald rally 144
Gomm, Maurice 60
Goodall, George 24, 34–35, 47, 64, 139, 141
Gordon-Keeble 96
Gorman Brothers 140–141
Gray, Robin 145, 148
Great Western Railway 9, 11
Grenfell, John Granville, 139
Grinham, Edward (Ted) 159–160
Group 4 GT racing 148
Gulliver, AB 130
GWK 158

Hales, Alfie 24
Hallett, Ken 31
Harper, Bob 106
Harper, Stuart 22
Harvey-Bailey, Roddy 122
Harvey-Jones, Sir John 55, 110, 130, 133–135
Hastings, Harold 89
Hatch, Harry 154
Hawkes, Douglas 23
Hay, Richard 149
Healey, Donald 159
Heathfield Slingshot 31
Hereford Automobile Club 9
Hill, Ken 39
Hill, WA 43
Hillman Aero Minx 35
Honel, 139
Horton, Ron 25, 139
Houel, Paul 20
Howard, Tony 148
HRG 142–143
Hughes, Mark 147
Hume, Denny 162
Hurrell, Sid 148
Hyde, Steven 149

ICI 133, 135
Imperial College, London 122
Inland Revenue 26
International Cyclecar Race 17
International GT Racing 144, 150
International Six Days event 139
Irish Motor Racing Club 140
  Autumn Trial 140
  Ballinascomey Hill Climb 140
  Leinster Night Trial 140
Isherwood, 143
Isis Motors 105, 110

ITN 122

J Smith & Co. 12
Jack Brabham Ltd 68
Jaguar 51, 65, 123
  C-type 150
  E-type 103, 148
  XJ6
  XJ-12 110
  XK150 87
JBF Boxer 31
JMB (Jones, Mason & Barrow) 16
  Mustang 16
John Ziemba Restorations 31
  JZR 31
Jowett Jupiter 66

Keeping, J 43
Keikhaefer, Carl 162
Kent, Duke of 142
King, Spen 95
Knockhill 151

Laban, Brian 134
Laird, Henry 142
Lamborghini 119
Lanchester 9
Lawrence, Chris 65, 68, 121, 123, 144–146, 148–149
Lawrie, 143
Laystall Engineering 143
Le Mans 24-hour race 47, 66, 68, 121, 142–146, 148–149, 151–152
Lea-Francis 135
  30/230 135
Lecanut 20
Lee, H Pelham 158
Lee-Stoyer 158
Leinster Motor Club 140
  Lincoln Cup Trial 140
  October Trial 140
Leinster Trophy road-race 140–141
Lewens, John & Bridget 33
Leyland 95, 98
Libra Motive 149
Lindsay, Ludovic 150
Lindsay, Mary 150
Little Star, The 11
LMB-Debonair 87
Lomax 30–31
  Lambda 30–31
London Motor Show 23, 41–42, 44, 49, 57–58, 61, 68, 75, 78, 80, 89, 92, 94, 97, 99, 106, 110
London Rally 143
London Taxis International 135
London-Edinburgh Trial 139
London-Edinburgh Trial 139
Los Angeles Motor Show 127
Lotus 87, 157
  Elan 103
  Elite 87, 89, 123
  Seven 135
Ludvigsen, Karl 161

Malvern College 11, 126
Marlborough College 9
Marriott, Arthur 9
Martin, Harry 17
Martin-Hurst, William 162–163
McCracken, Desmond 140–141
McMinnies, Gordon 18, 139
Mercedes-Benz 157
  S420 166
  S500 166
Mercury Marine 162

MG 51, 64, 86–87, 142–143
  J3 41
  K3 38, 141
  MGA 64, 69
  MGB 65, 164
  MGC 103
  Midget 41, 43, 80
  T-type 44, 64
  TA 36, 43
  TC 45
MG Rover 135
Michelotti 95
Midland Automobile Club 55
Minerva 9
MIRA 103, 125
Modsport series 148
Moessner, Thomas 124
Monte Carlo Rally 60
Morgan, Charles 55, 64, 85, 121–122, 133, 136, 147, 164
  competition driving 122, 138, 150
  education 122, 125
Morgan, Dorothy 19
Morgan, Florence 9
Morgan, Harriet 122
Morgan, Rev. Prebendary Henry 9, 17, 35
Morgan, Henry Frederick Stanley 8–9, 12, 48, 55, 64, 87, 122, 129, 164
  competition driving….. 122, 138, 139, 141
  education 9
  homes 11, 18, 23, 26, 34
  patents 10
Morgan, Hilda Ruth (née Day) 18, 122
Morgan, Jane 89, 106
  Morgan, Kate 122
Morgan, Kira 122
Morgan, Peter 18, 41, 50, 53, 55, 64, 66, 122, 129, 164
  competition driving 55, 89, 122, 138, 143–144, 148
  education 55
  homes 55
Morgan, Sylvia 128–129
Morgan, Xan 122
Morgan Motor Co. 9, 17, 46, 55, 61, 66, 129, 135
  Challenge Series 146–148, 150
  factory team 143
  mascots and badges 24, 34, 57, 63, 83
Morgan factories
  Pickersleigh Road 25, 33–34, 41, 46, 55, 128–130, 134–135
  Worcester Road 11–12, 55, 128–129
Morgan models
  Aero 19, 23–25, 28–29, 31
  Aero 8 10–11, 34, 120–127, 135, 137, 150–152, 165–166
  GT 150–151
  GTN 127, 150–151
  GTR 122–123
  GT2 122–123, 127
  De Luxe 18–19, 22, 24, 26
  Eagle 8, 11–12
  F Super Sports 33, 139, 155
  F-type 29–32, 35, 122, 154, 158
  F2 33, 155
  F4 28, 33, 155
  Family 19, 22–28, 32
  Family Aero 24
  Family Sports 27, 29

Grand Prix 19, 22, 28, 139
Plus 4 46, 49–73, 87, 96, 116,
    131–132, 143, 145, 148, 150,
    155, 159, 161, 164
    Competition 69
    Flat Rad 49, 56, 60
    Super Sports 65–66, 68–70,
    144–146
Plus 4 Plus 55, 86–93
Plus 8 38, 46, 49, 55, 69, 73, 80,
    94–120, 129–130, 132, 135,
    146–150, 158, 161, 164, 166
    Le Mans 62 149, 152
    Roadster 119
    Sports Lightweight 106, 110
Runabout 10–17, 37, 120, 138,
    153
Sporting 19
Sports 26
Standard 19, 22, 25, 28
Standard Popular 22
Super Aero 27, 29
Super Sports 29–30, 32–33, 153
Super Sports Aero 23, 25, 28
4-4 & 4/4 8, 10, 13, 20, 33–51,
    54, 64, 69, 80–81, 110, 120,
    129, 135–136, 139–143, 148,
    158–159–160, 166
    Le Mans Replica 39–40, 44,
    69, 159
    Le Mans 62 149, 152
    Runabout 85
    Series II 74–85, 155–156
    Competition Model 76, 157
    Series III 75, 78–79
    Series IV 75, 79–80, 157
    Series V 77–78, 81
    Competition 80
    TT Replica 47
    1600 77, 81
    1600 EFI 77
    1600 TC 77, 165
    1800 77, 158
Morgan (Aero Racing) 127, 151
Morgan Sports Car Club (MSCC)
    48–49, 164
Morgan Three-Wheeler Club
    138–139, 164
Morgan 4/4 Club 141, 164
Morris
    Bullnose Oxford 13, 17
    Flatnose van 28
Morris, William 17
Motor Cycle Show 17, 29, 33, 155
Motor Cycling Club (MCC) 89, 139
    London to Exeter Trial 34, 36,
    138
    National Rally 60, 143
    Sporting Trial 140

National Six Hour Relay Race 144
Neale, CE 144
Neil, Mrs 143
Noble 135
Noble, Dudley 50
Nürburgring 148

Oldsmobile 97, 162
Oulton Park 138
Oundle school 55, 122
Owen, Maurice 96, 99–100, 102

Page, Val 22
Parish, Jack 141
Parish, Mrs 141, 143
Parkes, Bill 141

Parkin, Matthew 125
Paul Ricard circuit 122
Performance Cars 145
Perry, Sir Percival 154
Peter Collins Tray 150
Phoenix Park 140
Pontiac 162
    Tempest 162
Porsche 119, 146, 149, 158
    911 Turbo 116, 126
Powertrain Projects Engineering
    163
Prescott 145
Prestwich, John 13
Price, Lawrence 122
Prideaux-Brune, Lance &
    Constance 142–143
Prodsports Championship 149

RAC horsepower rating 13, 32, 53,
    75, 96, 155–156, 158
RAC Rally 141, 143–144
Racing Car Show 87
Radshape 123
Railton 96
Raleigh Safety Seven 16
Randle, Jim 123
Ranzinger, Gunther 124
Ray, Jimmy 143
Reliant Regal 16
Repco-Brabham F1 162
Repton school 11–12
Rhys, Prof Garel 134
Road Fund Licence 13, 33, 36, 96
Roberts, Sam 154
Robinson, Charlie 60
Robinson, Peter 125
Rolls-Royce 119
    Silver Ghost 23
Rootes 50, 65, 86
    Alpine (Sunbeam) 65
Rouse, Andy 122
Rover 50, 72, 95–96, 100, 110,
    161–164
    Land Rover 81, 100, 112
    P5B 162
    Range Rover 73, 110, 115, 116,
    118, 163
    Range Rover Vogue SE 112
    SD1 100, 110–111, 163–164
    3-Litre saloon 162
    800 164
    820 164
    2000 95, 106
    2000TC 96
    3500 (P6B) 104, 162
Rubery Owen 32

St Peter and St Paul church, Stoke
    Lacy 8–9, 33, 55
Salmson 139
Sandford 20–21
    Sport 20
    Super Sport 20
    Tourisme 20
Sandford, Malcolm Stuart 20–21
Santler Rushabout 16
Savoye, Jacques 91, 144
Schiller, 146
Scottish Rally 141, 143–144
Seats 27, 61, 75–76, 78, 82, 117
    Connolly leather 44
    Restall 102, 132
Sebring 12-hour race 152
Sharpe, Adam 150–152
Sheldrick, Lawrence 155

Shepherd-Barron, Richard 144, 146
Siddeley 11
Silverstone 33, 122, 139
Simca 143
Singer 41, 143–144
Siran, Raymond 21
Sizaire-Naudin 10
Skip 31
Slay, Reginald 36
Smolensky, Nickolai 135
Snetterton 148–149
Society of Motor Manufacturers &
    Traders 135
Spa GP 144
Spare parts 46, 48, 72, 118, 164
Sparrowe, Jeff 40
Specifications
    Aero 8 121
    Plus 4 51, 53
    Plus 4 Plus 87
    Plus 4 Super Sports 53
    Plus 8 95, 97
    4/4 35, 77
    4/4 Series II/III/IV 75
    4/4 Series V 77
    4/4 1600 77
    4/4 1800 77
Spreckley, Charles 145
Sprinzel, John 148
Sprinzel Lawrence Racing (SLR)
    145, 148
Sprinzel Lawrence Tuning 148
Squire 35–36, 38
Squire, Adrian 35–36
SS 51, 159
Stallard, Graham 141
Standard 10, 47, 51, 159–161
    Vanguard 51, 55, 94, 160
Standard-Triumph 46, 94, 99
Stanley, Popplewell & Co. 10
Stanton, Richard 149
Stapleton brothers 145
Steering 61, 72
    AC Delco 97
    Bluemels wheels 41
    BMW 124
    Cam Gears 49, 55, 70, 96, 111,
    118
    Gemmer 71, 73, 116, 118
    Jack Knight 111, 116, 124
    rack-and-pinion 111
Stephens 10
Stephenson-Peach, William 11
Superchargers 41
    Arnott 41
    SS 41
Suspension 52, 122
    Armstrong 69, 80, 102
    Eibach springs 123
    Gabriel 112
    Koni dampers 123
    Morgan independent front 10,
    12, 37, 49, 52, 56, 72
    Multiplex Hartford 38
    Newton Bennett 38, 49
    Spax dampers 70
Sussex University 122, 125
Sutcliffe, Stephen 125
Sutton, RMV 142

Thornley, John 87
Three-Wheeler Championship 140
Three-Wheeler Club 164
Tourist Trophy (TT) races 47,
    140–141, 143, 148
Toyota 157

TR Register 72
Trico 31
Triking 30–31
Triumph 47, 86, 99, 144
    Mayflower 160
    Southern Cross 158
    Spitfire 80
    Stag 99
    Super Nine 158
    TRX 144
    TR2 61, 94, 125, 160
    TR3 62, 94, 161
    TR4 94, 148, 161
    TR5 69, 95, 103, 161
    TR7 110
    2000 95
Troubleshooter TV programme/book
    133–134
Trussler, Paul 46
Turlay, Joe 161–162
Turnbull, George 99
TVR 119, 135
Tyres 34, 78
    Avon 70
    Dunlop 44, 56, 124
    Yokohama 127

'Ubique' 25
UDT-Laystall 96
Ulster Trophy race 141, 143
US Department of Transport 110

Vintage Sports-Car Club 138
Volkswagen 32, 51
    Beetle 82, 162

Ware, Edward Bradford 22, 139,
    140
Webster, Harry 99
Wells, Rob 149
Wells, SS 60
Weslake, Harry 159
Westerham Motors 68
Westfield 135
Whall, Nigel 30
Wheeler, Peter 135
Wheels 56, 63, 66, 68, 70, 73,
    78–80, 85, 105, 117
    alloy 97, 100, 107–110
    Cobra 70
    Dunlop 29, 82
    Easiclean 44
    Lemmerz Rostyle 82, 162
    Millrace 108–110
    OZ Racing 123, 127
    twin spares 59, 62
White, Geoff 142–143
Whitworth, Tim 125
Wilesmith, Martin 128
Wilks, Maurice 162
Wilks, Peter 95
Williams, Tom Lawrence 16
Williams & Pritchard 148
Willis, Fred 139
Winter Garden Garages
    142–143
Wolseley 11
    Hornet 142
Wood-Jeffreys 97
Woods, Stanley 140
Worrall, John 66
Wykeham, Bill 122

Yarranton, Les 143–144

Ziemba, John 31